DO-IT-YOURSELF

Upgrading & Fixing Computers

FOR DUMMIES®

DO-IT-YOURSELF

Upgrading & Fixing Computers

FOR

DUMMIES®

by Andy Rathbone

WILEY

Wiley Publishing, Inc.

...ling & Fixing Computers Do-It-Yourself For Dummies®

...ed by

...ublishing, Inc.

111 River Street

Hoboken, NJ 07030-5774

www.wiley.com

Copyright © 2010 by Wiley Publishing, Inc., Indianapolis, Indiana

Published by Wiley Publishing, Inc., Indianapolis, Indiana

Published simultaneously in Canada

No part of this publication may be reproduced, stored in a retrieval system or transmitted in any form or by any means, electronic, mechanical, photocopying, recording, scanning or otherwise, except as permitted under Sections 107 or 108 of the 1976 United States Copyright Act, without either the prior written permission of the Publisher, or authorization through payment of the appropriate per-copy fee to the Copyright Clearance Center, 222 Rosewood Drive, Danvers, MA 01923, (978) 750-8400, fax (978) 646-8600. Requests to the Publisher for permission should be addressed to the Permissions Department, John Wiley & Sons, Inc., 111 River Street, Hoboken, NJ 07030, (201) 748-6011, fax (201) 748-6008, or online at http://www.wiley.com/go/permissions.

Trademarks: Wiley, the Wiley Publishing logo, For Dummies, the Dummies Man logo, A Reference for the Rest of Us!, The Dummies Way, Dummies Daily, The Fun and Easy Way, Dummies.com, Making Everything Easier, and related trade dress are trademarks or registered trademarks of John Wiley & Sons, Inc. and/or its affiliates in the United States and other countries, and may not be used without written permission. All other trademarks are the property of their respective owners. Wiley Publishing, Inc., is not associated with any product or vendor mentioned in this book.

LIMIT OF LIABILITY/DISCLAIMER OF WARRANTY: THE PUBLISHER AND THE AUTHOR MAKE NO REPRESENTATIONS OR WARRANTIES WITH RESPECT TO THE ACCURACY OR COMPLETENESS OF THE CONTENTS OF THIS WORK AND SPECIFICALLY DISCLAIM ALL WARRANTIES, INCLUDING WITHOUT LIMITATION WARRANTIES OF FITNESS FOR A PARTICULAR PURPOSE. NO WARRANTY MAY BE CREATED OR EXTENDED BY SALES OR PROMOTIONAL MATERIALS. THE ADVICE AND STRATEGIES CONTAINED HEREIN MAY NOT BE SUITABLE FOR EVERY SITUATION. THIS WORK IS SOLD WITH THE UNDERSTANDING THAT THE PUBLISHER IS NOT ENGAGED IN RENDERING LEGAL, ACCOUNTING, OR OTHER PROFESSIONAL SERVICES. IF PROFESSIONAL ASSISTANCE IS REQUIRED, THE SERVICES OF A COMPETENT PROFESSIONAL PERSON SHOULD BE SOUGHT. NEITHER THE PUBLISHER NOR THE AUTHOR SHALL BE LIABLE FOR DAMAGES ARISING HEREFROM. THE FACT THAT AN ORGANIZATION OR WEBSITE IS REFERRED TO IN THIS WORK AS A CITATION AND/OR A POTENTIAL SOURCE OF FURTHER INFORMATION DOES NOT MEAN THAT THE AUTHOR OR THE PUBLISHER ENDORSES THE INFORMATION THE ORGANIZATION OR WEBSITE MAY PROVIDE OR RECOMMENDATIONS IT MAY MAKE. FURTHER, READERS SHOULD BE AWARE THAT INTERNET WEBSITES LISTED IN THIS WORK MAY HAVE CHANGED OR DISAPPEARED BETWEEN WHEN THIS WORK WAS WRITTEN AND WHEN IT IS READ.

For general information on our other products and services, please contact our Customer Care Department within the U.S. at 877-762-2974, outside the U.S. at 317-572-3993, or fax 317-572-4002.

For technical support, please visit www.wiley.com/techsupport.

Wiley also publishes its books in a variety of electronic formats. Some content that appears in print may not be available in electronic books.

Library of Congress Control Number: 2010933461

ISBN: 978-0-470-55743-3

Manufactured in the United States of America

10 9 8 7 6 5 4 3 2 1

WILEY

About the Author

Andy Rathbone started geeking around with computers in 1985 when he bought a boxy CP/M Kaypro 2X with lime-green letters. Like other budding nerds, he soon began playing with null-modem adapters, dialing up computer bulletin boards, and working part-time at RadioShack.

In 1992, Andy and *DOS For Dummies* author/legend Dan Gookin teamed up to write *PCs For Dummies*. Andy subsequently wrote the award-winning *Windows For Dummies* series, *TiVo For Dummies*, and many other *For Dummies* books.

Today, he has more than 15 million copies of his books in print, which have been translated into more than 30 languages.

Andy lives with his wife, Tina, and their two cats in Southern California. Feel free to drop by his Web site at www.andyrathbone.com, or follow him on Twitter at www.twitter.com/andyrathbone.

Dedication

To that sense of satisfaction felt when you fix it yourself.

Author's Acknowledgments

Thanks to Rebecca Huehls, Heidi Unger, Matt Wagner, and Steve Hayes.

Publisher's Acknowledgments

We're proud of this book; please send us your comments at http://dummies.custhelp.com. For other comments, please contact our Customer Care Department within the U.S. at 877-762-2974, outside the U.S. at 317-572-3993, or fax 317-572-4002.

Some of the people who helped bring this book to market include the following:

Acquisitions and Editorial

Project Editor: Rebecca Huehls

Executive Editor: Steve Hayes

Copy Editor: Heidi Unger

Technical Editor: Kit Malone

Editorial Manager: Leah Cameron

Editorial Assistant: Amanda Graham

Sr. Editorial Assistant: Cherie Case

Cartoons: Rich Tennant (www.the5thwave.com)

Composition Services

Project Coordinator: Sheree Montgomery

Layout and Graphics: Christin Swinford, Ronald G. Terry, Timothy Detrick

Proofreaders: Rebecca Denoncour, Betty Kish

Indexer: Christine Karpeles

Special Help: Annie Sullivan

Publishing and Editorial for Technology Dummies

Richard Swadley, Vice President and Executive Group Publisher

Andy Cummings, Vice President and Publisher

Mary Bednarek, Executive Acquisitions Director

Mary C. Corder, Editorial Director

Publishing for Consumer Dummies

Diane Graves Steele, Vice President and Publisher

Composition Services

Debbie Stailey, Director of Composition Services

Contents at a Glance

Table of Contents

Introduction

You're no dummy; we both know that. But something about computers often makes you feel like a dummy. And that's perfectly understandable. Unlike today's kids, you probably didn't grow up with a computer in your kindergarten class, car, or in your back pocket. With this book, you'll no longer feel uncomfortable when you're faced with a computer that refuses to work the way it should.

This book doesn't help you replace your computer's motherboard or build a PC from scratch using custom-selected parts. Plenty of more advanced titles out there can help you with those chores.

No, this book helps you with the types of upgrade and repair tasks that you're most likely to encounter today: Upgrading an older PC to run Windows 7, for instance, and making sure that everything works correctly. Adding a larger hard drive. Upgrading that video card to satisfy the needs of Windows 7 or a new computer game. Making sure your PC's firewall is turned on and working correctly. Turning on the security option for your wireless network. And saving money by replacing your PC's broken parts rather than replacing the entire computer.

Simply put, this book discusses the most common upgrading and repair problems facing computer users today. It explains how to choose the right part to purchase, where to buy it, how to install it, and how to make sure that your computer knows how to put it to work.

About This Book

Welcome to *Upgrading and Fixing Computers Do-It-Yourself For Dummies*. Aimed at people who want to upgrade to Windows 7 or prepare their computers for the latest technology, this book walks you through several tasks:

- ✔ Step-by-step tasks walk you through installation and repair chores, with a photo or illustration at almost every step.

- ✔ A new emphasis on how to find and choose the right part for your computer.

- ✔ An updated visual appendix that explains how to recognize *all* the ports on your computer and add any ports you may need.

- ✔ A network installation guide in Chapter 15 helps you configure a network with both wired and wireless devices.

- ✔ Chapter 18 provides details on installing or upgrading to Windows 7 — even onto a newly upgraded hard drive.

- ✔ Computer parts need *drivers* — special software that helps Windows understand how to talk with them. Without a proper driver, Windows 7 can't talk to some parts of your computer. Chapter 17 explains when you need new drivers, where to find them, and how to install them successfully.

    ✔ Windows 7's Home Premium, Business, and Ultimate editions let you record TV shows onto your PC for later viewing or burning to DVD. The catch? Your PC needs a *TV tuner,* a device I explain how to buy and install in Chapter 11.

    ✔ Now that Windows can record TV shows, a DVD burner comes in particularly handy for saving your movies. I explain how to buy and install both DVD and Blu-ray drives in Chapter 7. (As a bonus, you can back up your files onto blank DVDs for safekeeping.)

Plus, this edition continues to include the information that hundreds of thousands of people have relied on for 17 years: information about upgrading and fixing video cards, hard drives, CD/DVD drives, memory chips, monitors, modems, printers, scanners, hard drives, and other popular computer parts.

Where to Start

Jump in anywhere. Each chapter is a self-contained nugget of information, keeping you from flipping back and forth between different sections.

Chapters start by introducing each new upgrade and offering tips on buying the right computer parts. A step-by-step installation guide follows, complete with screen shots, illustrations, and/or photographs to keep you on track.

Read These Parts

If you're lucky (and your computer is fairly healthy), you don't need to read very much of this book; just skim the step-by-step instructions. But when something weird happens, this book helps you figure out what went wrong, whether it's repairable, or whether you must replace it.

Along the way, you find helpful comments and warnings to help you out.

You find tips like this scattered throughout the book. Take a look at them first. In fact, some of these tips may spare you from having to read more than a paragraph of a computer book — a worthy feat indeed!

Don't Read These Parts

Unfortunately, I did stick a wee bit o' technobabble in this book. After all, you sometimes need to decipher the language on a computer part's box. Luckily for you, however, I have neatly cordoned off all the technical drivel.

Any particularly odious technical details are isolated and posted with this icon so that you can avoid them easily. If a computer nerd drops by to help with your particular problem, just hand him or her this book. With these icons, the computer nerd knows exactly which sections to examine.

How This Book Is Organized

This book has six major parts. Each part is divided into several chapters. And each chapter covers a major topic, which is divided into specific sections.

The point? Well, this book's indexer sorted all the information with an extra-fine-tooth flea comb, making it easy for you to find the exact section you want when you need it. Plus, everything's cross-referenced. If you need more information about a subject, you can figure out exactly which chapter to read.

Here are the parts and what they contain.

Part I: Getting Ready to Upgrade

Start with these two chapters, as they explain the simple tools you need to complete most upgrades and repairs. The chapters explain common mistakes to avoid, as well as techniques to make repairs quickly and safely.

Plus, the chapters make sure you've cast Windows 7's built-in safety nets: special programs that can make your computer *repair itself.*

Part II: Making Your Computer Work Better

Microsoft's latest version of Windows, 7, now lives on millions of the world's PCs. This part of the book explains how to make sure your PC's ready when you choose to upgrade. It explains how to find out whether your current PC can run Windows 7, what parts need to be replaced, and how to add Windows 7 essentials, like better graphics, more memory, a larger power supply, and a DVD drive: Windows 7 requires one.

By the way, upgrading your PC for the graphics-intensive Windows 7 also makes it a prime PC for playing the latest computer games.

Part III: Teaching an Old Computer New Tricks

Flip here quickly for the fun stuff. Rather than focusing on the boring, necessary repairs and upgrades, this part of the book explains the luxuries. You can transform your PC into a home theater, for example, by upgrading its sound and speakers and adding a TV tuner. Another chapter explains how to transform your camcorder footage into an edited movie, stored on an easily viewed DVD.

Bought a new computer? Then I explain how to put your old computer to work as a backup machine, dutifully copying all of your files each night. Or, combined with a scanner, it turns into a fax machine. Or you can recycle some of its parts, placing them in your new computer. Or, if it's *really* ready to pass on for an income tax deduction, I explain how to wipe it clean of your data, but still keep it useable for the charity.

Part IV: Communications

Computers don't like to be alone, and the Internet brings everybody and their computers closer than ever before. This part of the book shows how to connect to the Internet with a dialup or broadband modem. You also find out how to create a small home or small office network, enabling all your computers to share the same Internet connection and files.

If you're worried about hackers breaking into your computer, head to this part to make sure Windows 7's security measures work as they should.

Part V: Introducing Parts to Windows

If anybody's a dummy here, it's your computer. Even after you've stuck a new part in its craw, your computer often doesn't realize that the part is there. If Windows refuses to deal politely with the newly installed device, check out the chapter on finding and installing the right *driver* to make Windows behave. Turn to this section also when you're ready to upgrade to Windows 7 or install it onto a brand-new hard drive.

Part VI: The Part of Tens

Some information just drifts away when it's buried deep within a chapter or even within a long paragraph. That's why these tidbits are stacked up in lists of ten (give or take a few items). Here, you find the cheap fixes you should try first, and ways to put the Web to work when your computer leaves you stumped.

Icons Used in This Book

This book's most exceptional paragraphs are marked by icons — little eye-catching pictures in the margins:

This icon warns of some ugly technical information lying by the side of the road. Feel free to drive right by. The information is probably just a more complex discussion of something already explained in the chapter.

Pounce on this icon whenever you see it. Chances are that it marks a helpful paragraph worthy of a stick-on note or highlighter.

If you've forgotten what you were supposed to remember, keep an eye toward the margins for this icon.

Better be careful when you're about to do stuff marked by this icon. In fact, it warns you about dangerous activities you *shouldn't* be doing, like squirting WD-40 into your floppy drive.

This icon flags areas of special importance to laptop or netbook owners.

Auto mechanics can find the most helpful sections in their manuals by just looking for the greasiest pages. So by all means, draw your own icons next to the stuff you find particularly helpful. Scrawl in some of your own observations as well.

Where to Go from Here

If you're clamoring for more basic information on Windows, check out one of my *Windows For Dummies* books, published by Wiley Publishing. They come in several flavors, including Windows 7, Vista, XP, and earlier.

Also, be sure to check my Web site at www.andyrathbone.com. It contains a complete and updated list of all the Internet sites mentioned in this book, collected for your point 'n' click convenience. Any corrections, heaven forbid, appear there, as well. Feel free to drop me a line if any part of this book leaves you scratching your head.

Ready to go? Then grab this book and a screwdriver. Your computer is ready whenever you are. Good luck.

Part I
Getting Ready to Upgrade

The 5th Wave   By Rich Tennant

"We should cast a circle, invoke the elements, and direct the energy. If that doesn't work, we'll read the manual."

In this part . . .

This part of the book lays out all the tools you need to upgrade or repair your computer. Spoiler: It's a screwdriver.

But more than that, this part of the book helps you become familiar with your computer, identifying its parts both inside and out. You discover how to reveal manufacturer names and model numbers — essential information when tracking down replacements.

You figure out how to find out exactly what's inside your PC — how much memory it has, for example, and which weak links need to be replaced first.

Finally, I walk you through making sure your computer's System Restore and Windows Update features work correctly. That helps keep Windows running smoothly on its own, keeping that screwdriver out of your hands for as long as possible.

Chapter 1

Start Here First

You picked up this book for any of several reasons. You may be eyeing Windows 7, Microsoft's newest version of Windows, and want to upgrade your computer to meet Windows 7's needs. Perhaps one of your computer's parts died, and you're looking for a replacement. Or maybe your computer simply needs some fine-tuning. Either way, start with this chapter.

This chapter starts with the easy stuff by letting you know when it's time to upgrade, and when it's time to simply throw in the towel and buy a new computer.

You discover how to find out what version of Windows lives on your computer, as well as how to identify the CPU and amount of memory hiding inside your computer's case.

This chapter also explains how to identify every part inside your computer's case, so you can see if your computer meets those fine-print system requirements listed on the side of many software boxes.

To keep your work as light as possible, this chapter explains where Windows 7 has the power to repair itself — *if* those powers are turned on and running correctly, that is. You find complete instructions on making sure the self-healing abilities of Windows Update and System Restore are up and running.

Remember, anytime you're not sure what plugs in where, check out this book's Appendix. It's a visual directory of all your computer's connectors and the gadgets that will fit into them.

Determining When to Upgrade

Your computer usually tells you when it wants an upgrade. Some warning signals are subtle, others more obvious. At worst, they can be downright annoying.

In any case, keep track of the following when you're deciding whether it's time to open the wallet and grab the toolbox:

- **When your operating system demands it:** The latest version of Windows, Windows 7, is easily Microsoft's best operating system in years. If you've caught the "latest and the greatest" fever, it's easy to find out if your computer is up to snuff; Microsoft lists Windows 7's system requirements at `http://windows.microsoft.com/systemrequirements`, and I dissect them in Chapter 18.

- **When you keep waiting for your computer to catch up:** You press a button and wait. And wait. When you're constantly working faster than your computer, give your computer a boost with some extra memory and a faster video card.

- **When you can't afford a new computer:** When a new computer's out of your price range, upgrade your computer one part at a time. Add that memory now, for example, then add a new hard drive with that holiday bonus. Time each purchase to match the lowest prices. When you finally buy your new computer, save costs by salvaging your monitor, as well as new parts you've added to your old computer.

- **When you want a new part in a hurry:** Computer repair shops aren't nearly as slow as most repair shops. Still, do you *really* want to wait four days for some kid to install that new video card — especially when you have a nagging suspicion that you could do it yourself in less than 15 minutes?

- **When there's no room for new software:** When your hard drive constantly spits up Disk Full messages, you have three options:

    - Uninstall programs you no longer use and copy unneeded files to CDs or DVDs. (This takes a lot of time.)

    - Better yet, replace your computer's hard drive with a larger and faster one, a task covered in Chapter 6. (Windows 7 makes this easier than ever.)

    - Buy a removable drive to serve as a parking garage for files and programs, also covered in Chapter 6. Most external drives plug into your computer's USB port, a chore as simple as plugging in a thumb drive.

- **When you're afraid to open the case:** Fear of opening your computer's case is no longer an excuse to put off upgrades. Many new computer parts now live on the *outside* of the computer. You find external DVD drives and burners, hard drives, memory card readers, sound boxes, and much more. None of these devices require popping open the case to install them.

Determining When You Shouldn't Upgrade

Sometimes, you shouldn't upgrade your own computer. Keep your hands off during any of the following circumstances:

- ✔ **When a computer part breaks while under warranty:** If your new computer is under warranty, let the manufacturer fix it. In fact, trying to fix or replace a part sometimes voids the warranty on the rest of your computer. Some manufacturers void the warranty if you simply open your computer's case. Read the warranty's fine print before grabbing a screwdriver.

   Keep track of your warranty expiration date; it's usually listed on your sales receipt. Lost it? Some manufacturers (Gateway, Dell, and a few others) provide access to your warranty information through their Web sites, as described in Chapter 21.

- ✔ **On a Friday:** Don't try to install a new computer part on a Friday afternoon. When you discover that the widget needs a *left* bracket, too, many shops will be closed, leaving you with a table full of detached parts until Monday morning.

- ✔ **When you're working on a deadline:** Just like kitchen remodeling, computer upgrading sometimes takes twice as long as you'd originally planned. Most parts install in a few minutes, but always allow yourself a little leeway.

- ✔ **If your computer is *old*:** Not all computers can be upgraded. If you bought your computer before 2004, you're probably pouring money into a sinking ship. Check out your Windows Experience Index in Windows 7, described in Chapter 18, and see how well your computer's CPU rates. (Old CPUs are expensive to upgrade, making a new computer a better deal.) Or, if you're running Windows XP, download Windows Upgrade Advisor, also in Chapter 18, to see if your computer's still powerful enough for Windows 7.

   Before upgrading a computer, check these numbers: Add the cost of needed parts (more memory, a bigger hard drive, a faster video card and/or monitor, a DVD burner, and updated software, including Windows 7) and compare it with the cost of a new computer. Chances are, a new computer costs less. Plus, it already comes with Windows 7, and its parts will all be compatible.

Upgrade Do's and Don'ts

Over the years, as hungry computer repair technicians swapped tales of occupational stress, they gradually created a list known as The Upgrade Do's and Don'ts. The following tips have all been salvaged from lunchroom discussions across the nation and placed here for quick retrieval.

Do upgrade one thing at a time

Even if you've just returned from the computer store with more memory, a wireless network card, a new hard drive, and a new monitor, don't try to install them all at once. Install one part and make sure that it works before going on to the next part. If you can stand it, wait a day to make sure no problems turn up.

If you install more than one part at the same time and your computer doesn't work when you turn it on, you may have trouble figuring out which particular part is gagging your computer.

Do make a restore point before every upgrade

The Windows System Restore feature does a great job of reinstating your computer's settings that made it run smooth and clean. However, System Restore works only if your computer has a restore point for it to return to.

If you're installing anything that involves software, drivers, or setup programs, head to the section, "Making sure System Restore is working," later in this chapter. That section describes how to make your own restore points to supplement the ones Windows automatically creates. So, make a restore point that describes what you're about to do: Before installing that wireless network adapter, for instance, make a restore point with the name, "Before installing the new wireless network adapter."

Then, if the wireless network adapter bulldozes your finely tuned network settings, System Restore can return to those peaceful days when your network buzzed happily, giving you time to troubleshoot the problem.

Do watch out for static electricity

Static electricity can destroy computer parts. That's why many computer parts, especially things on circuit cards, come packaged in weird, silvery bags that reflect light like the visor on an astronaut's helmet. That high-tech plastic stuff absorbs any stray static before it zaps the part inside.

To make sure that you don't zap a computer part with static electricity, you should discharge yourself — no matter how gross that sounds — before starting to work on your computer. Touch a piece of bare metal, like the edge of a metal desk or chair, to ground yourself. You also must ground yourself each time you move your feet, especially when standing on carpet, wearing slippers, or after moving the cat back out of the way.

If you're living in a particularly static-prone environment, pick up a wrist-grounding strap at the computer store. (They usually sell them near the packages of memory.)

Do hang on to your old boxes, manuals, warranties, and receipts

When you need to pack up your computer for a move, nothing works better than its old box and packaging material. I keep mine on the top shelf in the garage, just in case I move. Don't bother hanging on to the smaller boxes, though, like the ones that come with a video card or mouse.

Hang on to *all* your old manuals, even if you don't understand a word they say. Sometimes a new part starts arguing with an older part, and the manuals often have hints on which switch to flip to break up the fight. At the least, they list the part's model number, an important fact when troubleshooting.

Just push some dust mice aside under the bed and slide all the manuals under there.

Don't force parts together

Everything in your computer is designed to fit into place smoothly and without too much of a fight. If something doesn't fit right, stop, scratch your head, and try again using a slightly different tactic.

When trying to plug a cable into the back of your computer, for example, look closely at the end of the cord and then scrutinize the plug where it's supposed to fit. See how the pins are lined up a certain way? See how the plug's shape differs on one side? Turn the plug until it lines up with its socket and push slowly but firmly. Sometimes it helps if you jiggle it back and forth slightly. Ask your spouse to tickle you gently.

Things that plug directly into things *inside* your computer seem to need the most force. Things that plug onto the *outside,* by contrast, slip on pretty easily. They also slip off pretty easily, so some of the cables have little thumb screws to hold everything in place firmly.

Don't bend cards

Many of your computer's internal organs are mounted on fiberglass boards. That's the reason there's a warning coming up right now.

Don't bend these boards, no matter how tempting. Bending the board can break the circuits subtly enough to damage the card. Worse yet, the cracks can be too small to see, so you may not know what went wrong.

If you hear little crackling sounds while you're doing something with a board — plugging it into a socket or plugging something into it — you're pushing the wrong way. Stop, regroup, and try again. Check out Chapter 9 and make sure you're pushing the right type of card into the right slot.

How to fish out dropped screws

When a screw falls into the inner reaches of your computer, it usually lands in a spot inaccessible to human fingers. The following should call it back home:

✔ Is it in plain sight? Try grabbing it with some long tweezers. If that doesn't work, wrap some tape, sticky-side out, around the end of a pencil or chopstick. With a few deft pokes, you may be able to snag it. A magnetized screwdriver can come in handy here, as well.

✔ If you don't see the runaway screw, gently tilt the computer to one side and then the other. Hopefully, the screw will roll out in plain sight. If you can hear it roll, you can often discover where it's hiding.

✔ Still can't find it? Pick up the computer's case with both hands, gently turn it upside down, and tilt it from side to side. The screw should fall out.

✔ If you still can't find the screw and it's not making any noise, check the floor beneath the computer. Sometimes screws hide in the carpet, where only bare feet can find them.

Don't power up your computer until you can account for every screw, or you'll find yourself with even worse problems: a shorted-out motherboard. (Give your computer a final shake before putting the case back on. Any lost screws will announce their presence with a telltale rattle.)

Don't rush yourself

Give yourself plenty of time to install a new part. If you rush yourself or get nervous, you're much more likely to break something, which can cause even more nervousness.

Start early in the week, or even on a Sunday, so you'll know the stores will be open the next day if something goes wrong.

Don't open up monitors or power supplies

You can't repair anything inside monitors or power supplies. Also, the power supply stores up voltage, even when it's not plugged in.

Don't ever try to open your power supply or monitor! They can store electricity inside that may really zap you.

Do Your Prep Work

Before beginning to upgrade, make sure you've fastened your seat belt by carrying out all the steps in the following sections.

Turn on Windows Update

Bored youngsters work late nights probing Windows to locate programming problems. When they discover a new flaw, they write a *virus* or *worm* (a small, malicious program meant to do damage, such as erasing important files) to take advantage of it. These kids release the virus, and it begins damaging people's computers as it spreads worldwide.

When alerted to a new *security exploit,* as they're called, Microsoft programmers scratch their heads and wonder what's wrong with today's youth. Then they release a special piece of software to fix the problem. To grab that special software, called a *patch* or *update,* your computer needs *Windows Update.*

Microsoft's free Windows Update program automatically downloads patches that plug the latest holes found in Windows' defenses. Windows Update works only if it's turned on, however. Follow these steps to make sure Windows Update is turned on and working to protect your computer.

1. **Click the Start button and choose Control Panel. Then choose System and Security, as shown in Figure 1-1.**

   The System and Security window appears. If you see a sea of icons rather than what's shown in Figure 1-1, click the Windows Update icon, and click Change Settings from the window's left pane.

   Still using Windows XP? Then click the Start button, click Control Panel, and click Security Center.

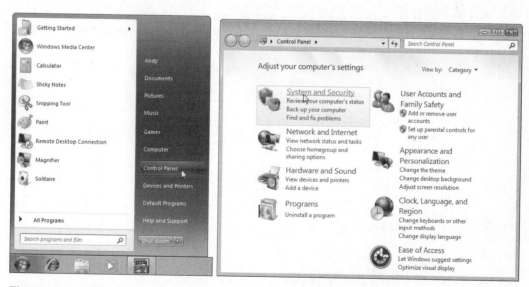

Figure 1-1: After you open the Control Panel, choose System and Security.

2. **In the Windows Update section, click Turn Automatic Updating On or Off, as shown in Figure 1-2.**

   The Windows Update Settings window appears. (Here, Windows XP users should click "Turn on Automatic Updates" if the updates are turned off.)

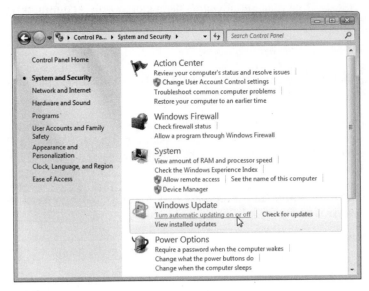

Figure 1-2: Click in the Windows Update section to find settings for turning on Automatic Updates.

3. **In the Important Updates section, shown in Figure 1-3, choose Install Updates Automatically, and click the OK button to save your settings.**

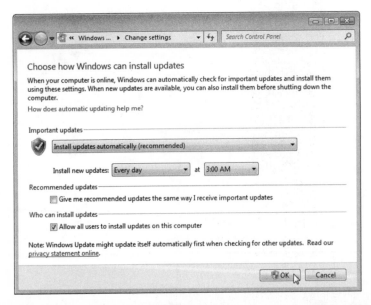

Figure 1-3: When the Install Updates Automatically option is selected, Windows Update can automatically update your computer.

The downloaded updates normally install every day at 3 a.m. If you normally turn off your computer at night, change the installation time to the afternoon by clicking the 3:00 AM drop-down and choosing a different time.

Windows Update organizes patches into two categories. *Always* install the ones in the Important Updates category, as they contain patches for security problems. You needn't install updates from the Recommended Updates categories unless you think they will correct problems you're currently experiencing with your computer.

Making sure System Restore is working

System Restore, built into Windows 7, Windows Vista, and Windows XP, often works miracles for problematic computers. If your computer suddenly stops working correctly, System Restore often enables you to bring your computer back to a time when everything worked fine.

When it's working correctly, System Restore automatically creates restore points that save important settings when Windows is up and running smoothly. The more restore points you have available, the more options you have for finding a time when your computer was running strong and lean.

You can also create your own restore point, a useful tool before installing a new part or software, by following these same steps.

To make sure System Restore's running — or to fix it if it's not working correctly — follow these steps:

1. **Click the Start button, right-click Computer, and choose Properties, as shown in Figure 1-4.**

   The System window appears.

Figure 1-4: Check in with Sytem Restore via your computer's Properties option.

2. **From the System window's left pane, click System Protection, as shown in Figure 1-5.**

   The System Properties window appears, opened to the System Protection tab.

3. **Select the drive called System, if necessary (it's usually already highlighted, as shown in Figure 1-6), and click the Configure button. Or, to create a restore point, click the Create button.**

4. **Choose the setting called "Restore System Settings and Previous Versions of Files," as shown in Figure 1-7. If necessary, slide the Max Usage bar to the right until it shows around 5%. Then click the OK button to save your changes.**

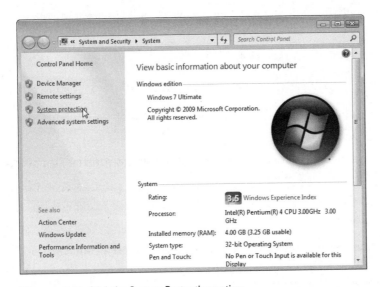

Figure 1-5: Click the System Protection option.

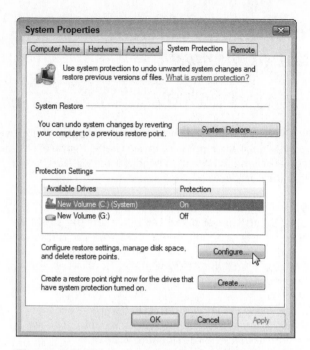

Figure 1-6: Click the Configure button to find System Restore setup options; click the Create button to create a restore point.

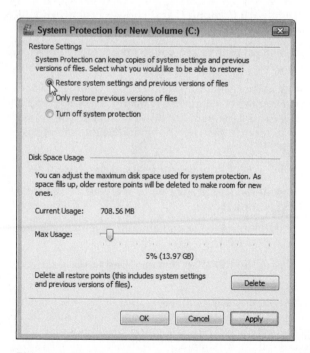

Figure 1-7: You set options for System Restore in this dialog box.

Identifying your Windows version, CPU, and amount of memory

Computers come in a wide variety of makes and models pieced together with parts made by a variety of manufacturers. So how do you know who made what part?

Luckily, Windows takes pity on its users and tells you exactly what parts lurk inside your computer — you don't even need to remove its case. The first step is finding out your Windows version, your computer's central processing unit (CPU), and its amount of random access memory (RAM).

And why should you care, you might ask, shifting impatiently in your chair? Because when you buy computer software or parts, the box's fine print lists the system requirements, followed by lots of details about what your computer must have to use the software or part. If your computer doesn't meet those detailed requirements, the software or part won't work very well — if at all — on your computer.

To add insult to injury, many stores won't let you return software — even if it doesn't work on your computer. Some stores even refuse to accept *unopened* software. Check your store's return policy before opening your wallet.

Follow these steps to locate your version of Windows, your computer's type of CPU, and its amount of memory.

1. **Click the Start button, right-click Computer, and choose Properties. (Refer to Figure 1-4.)**

2. **In the Windows Edition section, look to see your version of Windows, as shown in Figure 1-8.**

   In the System section, look at the System Type line to see whether you're running the *32-bit* or *64-bit* version of Windows. Thinking about upgrading your memory? You need a *64-bit* version of Windows to access 4GB or more of memory. (I explain the difference between 32-bit and 64-bit versions of Windows in Chapter 18.)

   Using Windows XP? Your version of Windows appears in the System section.

3. **In the System section, look at the Processor line to see your computer's type of CPU, and its speed in gigahertz (GHz).**

   Windows XP users will find their processor and amount of memory listed in the Computer area.

4. **In the System section, look at the Installed Memory line to see your amount of memory.**

   This particular computer contains 4GB of memory. But because it's running a 32-bit version of Windows, only 3.25GB of that memory can be used; the rest of the memory in this computer is wasted. The moral? Don't upgrade a 32-bit version of Windows to more than 4GB of memory.

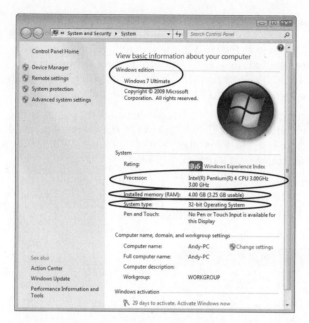

Figure 1-8: Find out what edition of Windows your computer runs, as well as other computer properties you need to know before upgrading.

Identifying parts inside your computer

The big three — Windows version, CPU, and RAM — usually have the most influence on which software and new parts your computer can handle. But sometimes you need more detailed information — especially about your type of video card, for instance, or perhaps your DVD drive's make and model.

Windows burps up this type of information when you prod further, as described below.

1. **Click the Start menu, right-click the Computer icon, and choose Properties. (Refer to Figure 1-4.)**

   Choosing Properties unleashes the System Properties dialog box.

2. **Click the words Device Manager in the task pane along the window's left. (Refer to Figure 1-8.)**

   The Device Manager dialog box jumps to the screen, displaying your computer's parts. When first opened, the Device Manager lists the parts found in a typical computer: the display adapter, for example, monitor, keyboard, and disk drives. The next step shows how to reveal the exact brand and model of those parts living in your computer.

   In Windows XP, fetch the Device Manager by clicking the Hardware tab, and clicking the Device Manager button.

3. **To see the make and model of a specific part, click the little triangle to the left of its name.**

For example, to see what type of video card sits inside your computer, click the tiny icon next to Display Adapters — the Windows term for a computer's video circuitry. As you can see in Figure 1-9, the name of your video card's model and manufacturer appear, invaluable information when the part stops working. Armed with that information, for example, you can search for updated *drivers* — translators between Windows and the part.

To see even *more* information about that part, double-click its name, and a window appears. Click that window's Driver tab to see the manufacturer, date, and version number of the currently installed driver — essential information when you're troubleshooting a part's driver.

When a particular part stops working, look for its make and model in the Device Manager. Then head to the manufacturer's Web site and download that part's latest driver, a chore covered in Chapter 17.

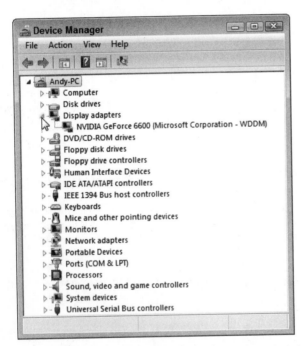

Figure 1-9: The Device Manager can tell you all the details you need to know about the parts in your computer.

Chapter 2

Assembling Your Tools

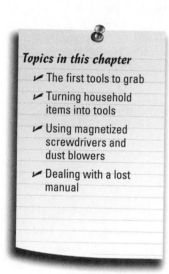
When you're at the computer shop, be sure to pick up a computer toolkit, if you don't already own one. The toolkits include most of the tools mentioned in this chapter and a snazzy, zip-up case to keep them in. Most kits cost less than $20 and include the right sized screwdriver, some handy tweezers, and the right-sized nut driver. If you don't want to spend money, you can probably salvage most of this chapter's handy items from a garage, junk drawer, kitchen, or laundry room.

But no matter whether you buy a toolkit or assemble your own, make sure that you keep it within reach when you're ready to open your computer's case.

This chapter tells you about these and other tools to put on your Computer Repair Shop wish list.

The First Tools to Grab

You'll find these essential tools in nearly every household, but if you don't, they're at your neighborhood hardware store. After you collect them, keep them together, and leave them within an arm's length of your computer. You'll constantly be reaching for them.

> ✓ **Phillips screwdrivers:** Phillips screwdrivers have a little square cross on their tip, not a flat blade. The pointed tip fits directly into the crossed lines on the screw's top. Regular screwdrivers don't work.
>
> The Phillips screwdriver doesn't need to be a tiny thing, as most computer screws have fairly deep holes. Sometimes an overeager computer nerd overtightens the screws that hold your computer's case together. In that case, a nut driver does a better job of removing it.

TIP

> Just tighten screws enough so they won't come out by themselves. Don't overtighten them. In fact, overtightening the screws that hold in a hard drive can damage the drive.

✔ **Nut drivers:** By far, my favorite tool, the nut driver looks like a common screwdriver but with a socket wrench on the end. It's useful because most computer screws not only work with a Phillips screwdriver, but also a ¼-inch socket wrench. Notice how the Phillips screw in the margin also has six sides along its top?

When you want to insert a screw and you push its six-sided head into the six-edged nut driver, the screw usually stays put. From there, you can often guide the end of the screw to its target deep inside your computer, push it into the hole, and start turning. The socket end grips the screw the entire time, so the screw doesn't fall out. You can't do that with a Phillips screwdriver — even the ones with magnetized tips don't always grip as well as a nut driver.

A nut driver works well when unscrewing things, too. Again, the screw stays lodged inside the socket better than it would with a screwdriver, enabling you to lift it out of the computer's case without dropping it.

Almost all the screws lurking inside your computer — including the frequently accessed screws holding in the extension cards — work well with a quarter-inch nut driver.

Turning Household Items into Tools

Don't put these tools on your shopping list. No, you'll find them in nearly every house, and just about every office. After you've collected them, keep them with your other tools near your computer.

✔ **Paper clips:** They don't look like much, but you'd be surprised what they can do when they're partially straightened. Then they come in handy for several things:

  • *Making a stuck disc drive spit out its tray.* Look for a tiny hole on the front of most disc drives — a hole much smaller than the headphone jack. If the disc gets stuck, try pushing the end of your bent paper clip into the hole. The hole serves as an Emergency Eject System that pushes out the tray, letting you retrieve your disc.

  • *Prying jumpers off pins.* Although needle-nose pliers work better for this, a paper clip is often handier, and it doesn't damage the pins. (You'll come across unruly jumpers when installing older hard drives and disc drives.)

  • *Flipping DIP switches.* DIP is short for dual inline package. These little rows of switches appear on some motherboards and hard drives. How do you flip those tiny things, shown in Figure 2-1? Grab the paper clip.

✔ **Empty egg cartons:** An egg carton works great for holding screws from a computer's recently removed part. Drop screws from different parts into different depressions. Forgetful people label each depression with a pen so that they remember which screw attaches which part.

✔ **A small flashlight:** Most of the stuff inside your computer's case is jammed pretty tightly together. When everything's dark inside, a flashlight helps you locate the right part, find a tiny printed model number, or locate missing screws.

Small key chain flashlights work well to illuminate your computer's crevices, as do the flashlights that are no bigger than a fountain pen.

Look for freebie key chain flashlights the next time you stay at a fancy hotel or visit a trade show. Flashlights are handy tools to add to your computer repair arsenal.

✓ **Pad of paper and a pen:** These come in handy for writing down part numbers, which you may need to look up later on Google.

Figure 2-1: Use a straightened paper clip to flip tiny switches.

Magnetized Screwdrivers and Dust Blowers

The following items aren't crucial, but oh, they certainly are handy at the right times. If you spot one while shopping, think about buying it for an upcoming repair. They're both found at stores selling office supplies and computer parts.

✓ **A magnetized screwdriver:** The magnet makes it easier to grab a fallen screw you've just spotted with the flashlight. Just touch the screw with the end of the screwdriver; when the screw sticks, gently lift it out with the screwdriver.

Computers no longer use floppy disks for storing information, so magnetized screwdrivers no longer pose any risk to your computer or your information.

✓ **Compressed air canisters:** Commonly found at stores selling office supplies and computer parts, compressed air canisters let you blow all the gross things out of the inside of your computer. They'll shoot the cat hairs out of a keyboard, as well. Pranksters can also squirt coworkers in the back of the head when they're not looking. Remember to recycle the can!

To avoid making a mess, take the computer *outside* before you blow the dust out of it. If you blow out the dust indoors, your computer's fan will eventually suck the particles back inside.

Don't blow with your own breath on your computer's innards to remove dust. Although you're blowing air, you're also blowing moisture, which can be even worse for your computer than dust.

Every few months, vacuum off the dust balls that clog the air vent on the back of your computer. The cooler you can keep your computer, the longer it lasts.

Monitoring Your Computer's Power Draw

Everybody wants to cut down on their electricity bill. And going "green" — not using parts that suck more energy than needed — helps lower the monthly utility bill, as well. To see exactly how much power your computer consumes, you need a special tool: an electric usage monitor.

I bought a P3 International P4400 Kill A Watt electric usage monitor for less than 20 bucks on Amazon (www.amazon.com), and it's fascinating to use. Simply plug the Kill A Watt monitor into a wall outlet, then plug your computer (or anything else) into the Kill A Watt's outlet.

When you turn on your computer, the Kill A Watt's readout says exactly how much power is being consumed. Do this before and after installing a part to see what's changed.

This lets you know how much (or how little) your computer upgrade adds to your energy bill. Plus, by knowing exactly how many watts your computer draws, you'll know whether your computer's power supply is powerful enough to handle it, a subject covered in Chapter 10.

Dealing with a Lost Manual

You *did* save all your computer's documentation, didn't you? Those manuals and papers come in handy when you're upgrading your computer. The documents describe the parts and model numbers of your computer's innards — essential information when trying to replace them. Keep the manuals in a safe place, preferably inside a large Ziploc freezer baggie.

But if you've lost the manual, it's not too late. Head to your computer manufacturer's Web site to see its vital statistics. Did you buy a Dell or Gateway computer? Find the computer's serial number on the sticker affixed to your computer's case, then head to www.dell.com or www.gateway.com for a list of your computer's parts and drivers. (You can sometimes find out whether your computer is still under warranty, too.)

Almost all computer manufacturers now offer their manuals for download as PDF files, readable with Adobe's Reader software (which is available for free at http://get.adobe.com/reader).

A working knowledge of the Internet helps you keep your computer running smoothly, no doubt about it. The Internet contains information posted by millions of computer users, and some of them have gone through the same problems you have. When you can't figure out an annoying error message, head for Google (www.google.com). Type the exact wording of the error message in quotes, and you'll find dozens of posts from people with the same problem. In many cases, you'll also find a post from somebody with a solution.

I describe how to diagnose and fix your computer through the Internet in Chapter 21.

The Internet does you no good after you've installed a part and your computer stops working. Do your research *before* you start your fix-it job, or keep another computer handy for online research while upgrading.

Part II
Making Your Computer Work Better

The 5th Wave   By Rich Tennant

"I bought a software program that should help
us monitor and control our spending habits, and
while I was there, I picked up a few new games,
a couple of screensavers, four new mousepads,
this nifty pullout keyboard cradle..."

In this part . . .

This part holds the meat of the book and explains how to perform surgery. You'll open your computer and remove its internal organs, swapping them out for faster, more powerful replacements.

It's all here, whether you're upgrading your monitor, keyboard, mice, printer, scanner, memory, hard drive, DVD drive, sound, video, power supply, or battery.

When you're done, your computer will be ready to run Windows 7, play games, record TV shows, and edit movies.

Grab your scalpel, er, screwdriver, and turn the page.

Chapter 3

Keyboards, Mice, Game Controllers, and Monitors

This chapter deals with the common folk of computing: your keyboard, mouse, monitor, and game controller. Your hands or eyes are on them constantly, but you rarely notice that they're there.

In fact, you notice their existence only when something's wrong: a key no longer works, the mouse pointer jumps haphazardly, the monitor displays odd stripes, or the game controller's cable rips apart.

When that happens, turn to this chapter to choose your replacement, install it, and begin to happily ignore it, once again.

Updating Your Keyboard

Keyboards contain more than 100 moving parts, popping up and down hundreds of times during the day.

Keyboards don't die very often, but when they start to go, the problem is easy enough to diagnose. A few keys start to stickkkk or stop working altogether. And when almost any type of liquid hits a keyboard, every key stops working at the same time.

This section helps you choose a replacement keyboard. It describes the types of keyboards in today's market and explains which works best in different situations. The "Installing a Keyboard" task near the end of the chapter shows how to replace a keyboard that's no longer a trusted friend.

Buying a keyboard that's compatible with your computer

All keyboards — even wireless ones — come with either of two connectors: USB (Universal Serial Bus) or PS/2. Since most computers come with both of those ports, either type of keyboard will work. So, which type is best, USB (shown in Figure 3-1) or PS/2 (shown in Figure 3-2)?

Figure 3-1: A USB plug, found on most of today's keyboards and mice.

Figure 3-2: A PS/2 plug, found on some older or less-expensive keyboards and mice.

Actually, both types work equally well. Some USB keyboards even come with a PS/2 adapter, a little gadget that lets you plug a USB keyboard into a PS/2 port. So, if your computer has a spare USB port, pick up a USB keyboard. No USB ports to spare? Go with PS/2.

One caveat: Unlike USB keyboards, PS/2 keyboards aren't "hot swappable," meaning you can't unplug them and plug them back in while your computer is running. Also, PS/2 keyboards are inexpensive and basic; fancier, more expensive keyboards require a USB port.

Unlike desktop computers, laptops and netbooks *don't* include PS/2 ports. If you want a full-size keyboard to supplement your tiny laptop or netbook, buy a USB keyboard.

Deciding what features are worth your money

After you've chosen between a USB or PS/2 keyboard, examine your budget. The cheapest keyboards cost as little as $10; if you pack on some special features, they could reach $100.

Why the huge price range? Because today's keyboards come in a wide variety of flavors: wireless, ergonomic, backlit, and mouse/keyboard "all-in-one" units. Keyboards have never been more complicated.

To help you choose your new keyboard, here's an explanation of the terms found on keyboard boxes and in Web stores:

- ✔ **Standard 101 key:** Make sure your keyboard has *at least* 101 keys. That magic number guarantees the standard typewriter layout, a separate numeric keypad along the right, and a row of function keys (F1, F2, and so on) along the top. It even includes a few keys added by Microsoft, most importantly, the *Windows key.* Shown in the margin (with the newer version on top), the Windows key offers quick access to Windows 7 commands, as described in Table 3-1.

- ✔ **Gaming/multimedia/multifunction keyboard:** Some companies insist that 101 keys aren't enough. So they add even more keys along the keyboard's top or sides. Often devoted to single jobs, these specialized keys can increase or decrease the volume, skip to the next song, or open a favorite program. Keyboards designed for gamers offer programmable keys: One key press lets you open a map to find quick exit routes in World of Warcraft, for example.

  Those specialized keys won't work as soon as you plug in your keyboard. No, those keys require special *drivers,* included on the keyboard's bundled software. It's an inconvenience, making specialized keyboards a little more troublesome to install.

- ✔ **Ergonomic keyboards:** Ergonomic keyboards, like the one shown in Figure 3-3, resemble a thick boomerang and spark a love/hate relationship. Some folks say the shape helps them spend hours on the keyboard; others find it awkward and gimmicky. Most computer stores offer display models, so definitely try before you buy.

Table 3-1	Windows 7's Windows Key Shortcuts
To Do This	*Press This*
Display Windows Help	Windows key+F1
Display the Start menu	Windows key
Cycle through open windows	Windows key+Tab
Pin window to monitor's left edge	Windows key+left arrow
Pin window to monitor's right edge	Windows key+right arrow
Display Windows Explorer	Windows key+E
Find files	Windows key+F
Minimize or restore all windows	Windows key+D
View System window	Windows key+Pause/Break
Lock PC	Windows key+L

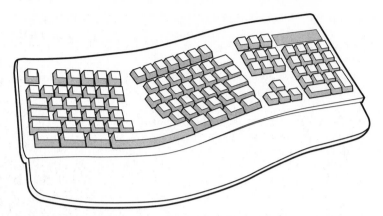

Figure 3-3: Some folks love the shape of ergonomic keyboards; others hate them.

✔ **Wireless:** Wireless keyboards bear no cables, making for tidy desktops. They all come in two parts: The keyboard and a receiving unit, which usually plugs into your computer's USB port. (Since most wireless keyboards plug into a USB port, make sure your computer has an unused USB port, described in the previous section.) Batteries last from three to eight months, depending on how much time you spend typing.

✔ **Touchpad/trackpad:** Found on many netbooks and laptops, these rectangular pads let you move the mouse pointer by sliding your finger across their surfaces; a tap on a corner mimics a click of a mouse button. If you love your laptop's touchpad, buy a keyboard that includes a touchpad. (Trivia: Windows refers to a newly plugged-in touchpad as a "Human Interface Device.")

✔ **Media Center keyboard, mouse, and/or remote:** All but the least expensive versions of Windows 7 include Windows Media Center software for automatically recording and playing back TV shows. To keep you rested firmly on the couch across from the TV, several companies offer special remote controls and wireless keyboards for channel changing and living room Web surfing.

A few of these new Media Center keyboards, remotes, and mice use Bluetooth, the same wireless technology that links cellphones with headsets. Because older computers didn't include built-in Bluetooth, some Media Center keyboards include a tiny Bluetooth receiver that pushes into your computer's USB port.

Before buying a new keyboard at the store, remove the keyboard from the box and try it out. Only by trying the keyboard can you see if it "feels" right beneath your fingers.

Making Way for a New Mouse

Mice all tackle the same computing chore. When you nudge your mouse, a little arrow called a mouse pointer moves on your computer's screen. By pointing the arrow at buttons on the screen and pushing buttons on the mouse, you "push" the buttons on the screen.

For years, all mice looked like a beige bar of soap with two buttons and a long tail. Now, mice come in dozens of shapes, sizes, colors, and button arrangements. (Wireless mice even do away with the tethering tail.)

Fixing a wireless mouse that's acting strangely

If your wireless mouse is acting funny, try replacing the batteries. Some batteries fit in the mouse's receiving unit as well as the mouse itself. Better yet, look for rechargeable batteries, or consider a rechargeable wireless mouse that can occasionally plug into your USB port to grab an energy fix.

An *infrared* wireless mouse needs a clean line of sight between itself and its *receiving unit,* the thing that plugs into your computer. But because that clean line of sight is probably the only clean spot on your desk, that's the first place you may tend to set down books and junk mail. Move away your books and junk mail, and the mouse calms down.

An *RF* (radio frequency) wireless mouse uses radio signals. These mice don't need to point in any particular direction. (Except for the battery drawer, unfortunately. These little critters feast on batteries.)

Weird Tales Department: One woman wrote to me that she kept seeing *two* mouse pointers on the screen. The problem? Her ailing wireless mouse was sending a ghost image, similar to the one you see on a TV screen with a bad signal.

Buying a mouse that's compatible with your computer

Like keyboards, mice come with one of two connectors: USB (Universal Serial Bus) or PS/2. Since most desktop computers come with both of those ports, both types of mouse are compatible. So, which type is best, USB or PS/2, as shown earlier in Figures 3-1 and 3-2?

The answer depends on your needs. PS/2 mice cost less, and often come with an adapter that also lets the mice work in USB ports, if needed. Or, if you're short on USB ports, a PS/2 mouse lets you save those versatile USB ports for other gadgets.

If you choose USB, however, you'll find a better selection of wireless mice. Plus, USB mice are hot swappable, meaning you can unplug them and plug them back in while your computer is running. PS/2 mice must remain plugged in at all times.

Laptops and netbooks rarely include PS/2 ports. If you want a mouse to replace your laptop's erratic trackpad, buy a USB mouse.

Deciding what features are worth your money

A ten dollar mouse works fine for the basics; I keep one tucked into my laptop bag. If you spend a little more, you'll choose among these options:

✔ **Mechanical:** Stay away from these antiques. A rubber ball lives inside the mouse's belly; when you move the mouse, you also roll the little ball. The movement of the ball tells the computer the direction and speed to move the onscreen pointer. Unfortunately, mechanical mice need frequent cleaning.

✔ **Optical:** The much-preferred optical mice ditch the ball/roller mechanics for a small glowing light and a sensor. As you move the mouse, the optical sensor takes tiny snapshots of your illuminated desk, hundreds of times each second. By comparing differences between snapshots, the mouse knows how fast and far you're moving it, and it updates the pointer accordingly. If your desktop is glass or shiny laminate, your optical mouse requires a mouse pad because the reflections confuse the sensor. [Optical mice with lasers are slightly more accurate than light-emitting diode (LED) optical mice.]

✔ **Touchpad:** Prefer your laptop's touchpad to a mouse? Pick up an external touchpad that plugs into your desktop computer's USB port, eliminating the need for a mouse.

✔ **Scroll wheel:** This handy little wheel protrudes from the mouse's back, usually between the two buttons. Spin the wheel with your index finger, and your computer scrolls up or down the onscreen page, accordingly. Push down on the wheel to make it click; most scroll wheel mice let you program the wheel click to do just about anything you want.

✔ **Trackball:** Resembling an upside-down mouse, trackballs lie flat on your desk. By rolling the ball with your fingers, you control the mouse pointer. Trackballs are going out of style among everybody but a few gamers.

✔ **Wireless:** Wireless mice work just like their keyboard counterparts; in fact, some share the same receiving unit, which usually plugs into your computer's USB port. The mouse sends signals to the receiver, which sends them to your computer. Unlike wireless keyboards, wireless mice are battery hogs. Battery life is improving, but count on buying new batteries every three to six months. Or put rechargeable batteries in heavy rotation from the charger to your mouse and back again.

Upgrading Game Controllers

Many computer games perform just fine with the keyboard and mouse. Keyboards can handle both online chats and direction: Resting the fingers on the W, A, S, and D keys often lets you tell the computer whether you're moving up, left, down, or right. That leaves the mouse free for shooting, or other activities.

But for advanced gaming, many people prefer dedicated game controllers. All modern game controllers insist upon a USB port. (Some garage sale models don't, but they won't work with today's games.)

Because so much of the controller's appeal comes from its feel, take notice of what controllers your friends use when you're visiting. Find one you like, make sure it's compatible with your favorite games, and then buy it.

Some games work better with one kind of game controller over another, and not all controllers work with every game. Serious gamers acquire a serious collection of controllers.

So, how much do you want to spend? It boils down to the features you're looking for, as described here:

✔ **USB:** All game controllers, from simple joysticks to foot-controlled rudder pedals, come with a cable that plugs into your computer's USB port. If your computer lacks a front-mounted USB port, or you're running out of unused USB ports, pick up a USB hub: A small USB-port-filled box with a cable that plugs into your computer's remaining USB port.

✔ **Joystick/game pad:** Joysticks hail from the older school of gaming and use a movable stick for controlling onscreen action. Game pads skip the joystick in favor of a flat surface with many buttons. Some controllers combine both: a joystick surrounded by buttons.

✔ **Analog:** Analog game controllers measure the direction the joystick moves on a scale of 0 to 255. They send the number to the game, which interprets the joystick's direction and speed, moving the machine gun accordingly. They're best when subtle controls are needed — gently adjusting a flight path, for example.

✔ **Digital:** Digital controllers, by contrast, work on an on/off basis. Most simply inform the game which of nine directions the joystick is moved: top, top-right corner, right, bottom-right corner, bottom, and so on. The ninth direction? Centered, meaning it's not being moved at all. Game pads, with their many on/off buttons, usually hail from the digital camp.

✔ **Analog/digital:** Because both analog and digital controllers have their advantages and problems, many controllers combine both: An analog joystick sits next to a digital controller.

Game controllers all have their own particular feel. When you tell the computer to calibrate the controller, the computer measures the device's movements and corrects its settings to allow smoother and more accurate game play. I explain how to calibrate a controller in this chapter's last task, "Installing or Replacing a Game Controller."

Replacing a Monitor

Monitors, unfortunately, can't be repaired. When they're starting to die, they either blank out completely, lose their colors, or start sending odd lines down the screen. Sometimes it's the buttons that give out, keeping you from adjusting the display.

When your monitor's dying, you can almost always tell it's time for a replacement. Before shopping, though, check these steps to rule out a quick fix:

✔ Check to make sure that you plugged the monitor's power cord securely into the wall or power strip, and make sure that your power strip is turned on.

✔ Wiggle the connection where the monitor's video cable plugs into the back of your computer.

✔ Check where the video cord plugs into the back of your monitor. Some cords aren't built into the monitor, leading to loose connections. Push the cord hard to make sure that it's plugged in tight, and screw it down, if that's an option.

✔ Check where the power cord leads to the back of your monitor. Like video cables, some power cords plug into the monitor.

✔ Check your monitor's resolution, a task described later in this chapter.

If that still doesn't fix the problem, it's time to find a monitor that's fits both your computer's video connector *and* your budget, a journey described in the next two sections.

Buying a monitor that's compatible with your PC

Monitors grab their video signals from the video circuitry in your computer, so you can tell what type of monitor you need by looking at your computer's *video port* — the little connector on the back of your computer where you plug in the monitor's cable.

Fortunately, many computers come with several video ports, so they're compatible with several types of monitors. Here's the rundown on the ports you're likely to find on your computer, and the types of monitors they accept:

✔ **Analog (VGA):** The most common video ports found on computers, these look like the ones shown in the margin. They're called VGA (Video Graphics Array) ports, and they work with a wide variety of monitors. (Look for the words "VGA compatible" on the monitor's box.) Unfortunately, VGA monitors rank lowest on the quality scale.

Some manufacturers test your patience by claiming their monitor has a "15-pin mini D-SUB connector." That's a fancy term for "VGA port." The most common video port, it's found on nearly every PC and laptop.

✔ **Digital (DVI):** More expensive computers come with DVI (Digital Video Interface) ports, which resemble the one shown in the margin. Many digital monitors come with both VGA and DVI ports, letting you connect whichever one meshes with your monitor. By all means, connect with the DVI port, if given a choice, as it's much better quality.

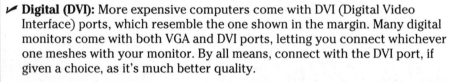

✔ **High-Definition Multimedia Interface (HDMI):** The newest computers come with HDMI ports, which let them connect to newer consumer electronics like HDTVs and Blu-ray DVD players. These send both sound and video through a single cable for easy hookup. They're the same quality as DVI.

Have a Digital (DVI) port on your computer, but an HDMI port on your monitor, or vice versa? Buy a cable with a digital connector on one end for your computer, and HDMI on the other for your monitor. The cables cost less than ten dollars on Amazon.

Some monitors don't come with any cable, but offer two ports, VGA and DVI. That lets you buy whichever type of cable that fits into your computer's video port. Most DVI monitors include a cable adapter that lets them plug into a VGA port, if necessary, but the display won't be as crisp.

Deciding what features are worth your money

After you decide on your monitor's required connector, VGA, Digital (DVI), or HDMI, you can concentrate on your own budget. Smaller monitors are cheaper;

larger monitors are more expensive. And the extra-wide monitors with built-in speakers cost the most of all. You'll find these choices when shopping:

- **LCD:** Nearly all monitors sold today are LCD (liquid crystal display), which pretty much translates to "flat panel." You won't find many, if any, old-school CRT (cathode ray tube) monitors still for sale. In fact, if a friend offers you an old CRT monitor, don't take it. Like old televisions, CRT monitors are qualified as hazardous waste in many areas, so they're difficult to dispose of. (That's why your friend's trying to pawn it off on you.)

- **Widescreen:** These LCD monitors boast a wide screen that's similar in proportion to a movie theater screen. That gives you extra desktop real estate in Windows, as well as letting you watch wide-screen movies in all their glory. (They're great for making home theaters, described in Chapter 11.) Some widescreen monitors even tilt vertically, letting you see an entire page onscreen, not just a choice between the page's top or bottom half.

- **CRT TV sets:** Old-style CRT televisions are designed for moving images, not text, so they make lousy computer monitors. Their low resolution can barely display an icon. Don't bother.

- **HDTV set:** HDTV sets, by contrast, make superb monitors that excel at showing digital photos, movies, computer games, or TV shows recorded in Windows 7 Media Center. Many HDTV sets come with digital video and HDMI ports, letting you plug them into whichever port your computer accepts.

Shopping buzzwords

Much as a sticker on a new car's side window breaks down the car's features into a few words, monitors sum up their features with these buzzwords:

- **Screen size:** A diagonal measurement from one corner of a monitor to the other. Don't be fooled, though: A TV-style monitor's screen size *includes* the plastic surrounding its edge; an LCD monitor's size measures the actual screen you see. That's why a 17-inch LCD monitor will have more usable space than a 17-inch CRT monitor.

- **Pixel:** A single little square dot on your screen. Computer pictures are merely collections of thousands of little colored dots. You need to know about pixels mostly in connection with dot pitch.

- **Dot pitch:** The distance between pixel dots onscreen. The smaller the dot pitch, the clearer the picture. Magic number: Buy a monitor with a dot pitch at .28 or smaller.

- **Resolution:** Your monitor stacks pixels across the screen in a grid, like tiny bottles in a wine rack. The more rows and columns your monitor and video card can display, the higher its *resolution* and the more images you can crowd onto your screen. Resolution is adjustable through the Windows Control Panel, so choose the highest available resolution that still reads comfortably.

Try to match your monitor's highest resolution — sometimes called its *native resolution* — with the highest resolution of your computer's video circuitry, as that's when the screen will look the best.

Installing a Keyboard

Stuff You Need to Know

Toolbox:

✔ A new keyboard
✔ A flashlight, if necessary, for finding the right port on the back of your computer

Time Needed:

Less than an hour

Buy a replacement keyboard that fits your computer's port, either USB or PS/2. If a keyboard says it works with both types of ports, then it's a USB keyboard with a tiny adapter: To plug it into the PS/2 port, slip the adapter onto the USB plug.

Some USB keyboards sport an extra USB port or two on their side, but those USB ports usually aren't *powered*. That means they'll work fine with low-power gadgets like tiny USB flash drives. But they can't charge an iPod, cellphone, or any other device that needs power through the USB port.

To install a new keyboard, follow these steps:

1. Before installing anything, save your current work and close your programs. If you're installing a PS/2 keyboard, turn off your computer first. (You don't need to turn off your computer to install a USB keyboard.) Remove your old keyboard by pulling the cable's plug from its socket on your computer. Examine the end of the cord; a rectangular plug with a pitchfork symbol on it is a USB plug (left). A smaller, round plug is an older-style, PS/2 plug (right).

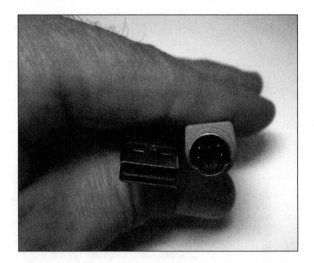

When you're unplugging any type of cord, pull on the plug, not the cord, to save the cord a little wear and tear.

2. Plug the new keyboard into the correct port. USB ports slide in pretty easily. Doesn't fit? Turn over the plug, and try again, as it fits only one way. If the USB keyboard is wireless, plug its receiver into the USB port. PS/2 plugs need their pins to match up with the notches of the PS/2 ports. Most computers have two PS/2 ports, one for the mouse and the other for the keyboard; if you're lucky, they're labeled with the appropriate icon. They won't do any harm plugged into the wrong port, but they won't work until pushed into the correct port. Push the PS/2 plug firmly into the PS/2 port with the keyboard icon until the plug sits firmly inside.

3. Turn your computer back on (if you've turned it off). If the computer doesn't complain and your new keyboard works, your computer found the keyboard and liked it. If necessary, install your keyboard's drivers or software: Insert the CD and double-click the Setup program, if necessary. (If the software doesn't work well, visit the manufacturer's Web site to download the latest set of drivers, a task described in Chapter 17.)

4. Adjust your keyboard's settings in Windows by choosing Control Panel from the Start menu and typing **keyboard** in the Control Panel's Search box in its top-right corner. When the Keyboard option appears, double-click it to see the Keyboard Properties dialog box shown in the figure. Here, you can change options like a key's repeat rate — how long it waits before repeating when you hold down a letter. Your keyboard's manufacturer may have tossed in a few options for your specific model, as well. (To adjust your keyboard settings in Windows XP, choose Start⇨Control Panel⇨Printers and Other Hardware⇨Keyboard.)

Installing or Replacing a Mouse

A mouse comes with its own software, if needed, and cord. You needn't buy any extras. If you're buying a fancy mouse for your Windows 7 computer, visit the manufacturer's Web site to see if it offers downloadable Windows 7 drivers. (Because you rarely find up-to-date drivers in a new product's box, I describe how to download and install the latest drivers in Chapter 17.) Windows can use pretty much any old PS/2-style mouse. Just plug it in, turn on your computer, and Windows knows it's there.

To replace or add a mouse, follow these steps:

1. If you're installing a PS/2 mouse, turn off your computer. Be sure to exit any of your currently running programs first. Examine where you currently plug in your mouse, and make sure your replacement uses the same type of plug, either USB or PS/2. Then unplug your old mouse if it's still plugged in.

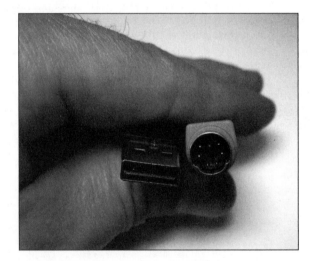

 If your mouse just died, here's the magic set of keystrokes to shut down Windows in a gentle way, without reaching for your computer's power button: Press your Windows key (or press Ctrl+Esc). Then press the right arrow key once and press Enter. (In Windows XP, press your Windows key or press Ctrl+Esc; then press the press the U key twice.)

 If your cursor is jumpy when you move your mouse, you probably need to clean your mouse. If you're using an optical mouse, use some screen wipes to clean the shiny lens on its undersurface. A pair of tweezers can remove a stuck cat hair or small fiber that's confusing the sensor.

2. Push the plug from the new mouse (or from the wireless mouse's receiving unit) into the correct port on your computer. USB plugs slide into USB ports pretty easily. If it's not fitting, turn it over; the connector fits only one way. PS/2 connectors plug into the PS/2 port with a little mouse icon next to it. (The adjacent keyboard PS/2 port won't work.) Make sure the notches and pins line up and push firmly until it's all the way in.

3. Add batteries to the wireless mouse, if necessary, and run the mouse's installation program. Windows usually provides a basic driver for your newly installed mouse. To use the mouse's fancier features, though, stick its CD into your drive. If the installation program doesn't start automatically, browse the drive's contents for a program named Setup to start things rolling. (For best results, download the mouse's latest drivers at the manufacturer's Web site, described in Chapter 17.) If the mouse cord isn't long enough, buy an extension cable at an office supply or electronics store.

Left-handed users can switch their mouse buttons through the Buttons tab in Windows 7's Control Panel: Click Start, choose Control Panel, choose Hardware and Sound, and select Mouse.

Installing or Replacing a Game Controller

Stuff You Need to Know

Toolbox:

- A game controller
- A computer's USB port

Time Needed:
Less than an hour

A game controller comes with its own software, if needed, and cord. You needn't buy any extras. Simple ones don't need any software; the fancier (and more expensive) models sometimes require software before all the features will work. Windows 7 supports game controllers with USB ports only; old-style joysticks won't work.

To replace or add a game controller, follow these steps:

1. Find a vacant USB port on your computer, preferably in the front. If you're currently using all your USB ports, buy a *USB hub* — a box that plugs into any USB port and dishes up several more ports. Push the plug from the game controller into an empty USB port. USB plugs slide into USB ports pretty easily. If it's not fitting, turn it over; the connector fits only one way.

Logitech Dual Action properties

Settings | **Test**

Test the game controller. If the controller is not functioning properly, it may need to be calibrated. To calibrate it, go to the Settings page.

Axes

Z Axis

Z Rotation

X Axis / Y Axis

Buttons

Point of View Hat

OK | Cancel | Apply

---

2. Run the game controller's installation program, if necessary, and then calibrate the controller within Windows by clicking the Start button, choosing Control Panel, and typing **Game Controller** in the Control Panel's Search box (in the upper-right corner). Choose Setup USB Game Controllers to bring up the Game Controller's window. (For the best gaming experience, visit the gamer controller manufacturer's Web site to download the latest drivers, described in Chapter 17.) In Windows XP, click Start⇨Control Panel⇨Printers and Other Hardware⇨Game Controllers.

3. Click the name of your game controller, and click the Properties button. Click the Test tab and move the controller's joysticks and press its button, watching the onscreen action. If it doesn't seem to be working correctly, click the Settings tab and choose Calibrate to calibrate the game controller.

Connecting a Monitor to a PC or Laptop

If you're installing a new video card along with your new monitor, flip to Chapter 9 first for instructions on installing the card. After the new card rests inside your PC, head back here to hook up the monitor.

To install a new monitor, perform the following steps:

1. Laptop owners can avoid this step. But desktop computer owners should shut down Windows, turn off your computer, and unplug and remove your old monitor. Unplug your old monitor's power cord from the wall before you unplug the monitor's video cable from its little port on the back of your computer's case. Then remove the old monitor from your desktop. Don't throw your old monitor into the trash because many monitors contain noxious chemicals. Check Chapter 13 for tips on finding recycling programs.

DVI | VGA | HDMI

2. Remove the new monitor from the box, place the monitor on your desk, and push the plug on the end of its cable into your computer's video port on the back of your computer. The cable should only fit into one port, be it DVI, VGA, or HDMI (shown here from left to right). If the cable doesn't fit right, you're either trying to plug it into the wrong port, or your monitor isn't compatible with your computer. (Or, if your monitor has a DVI connector, look amidst the packaging for an adapter that lets it slip into your computer's VGA port, if necessary.) If the monitor's not compatible, you need to upgrade your computer's video card to match your monitor, a chore tackled in Chapter 9. Make sure that the cable is fastened securely on the monitor's end.

DVI   VGA   HDMI

 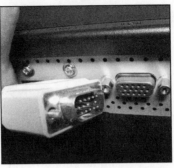 

3.   Plug the cable's other end into your monitor's matching port, be it DVI, VGA, or HDMI. Plug the monitor's power cord into the wall or a power strip. Turn on your monitor and then turn on your computer. Can you see words on the screen as the computer spews its opening remarks? If so, you're done. If it doesn't work, however, go through some of the fixes in the "Replacing a Monitor" section earlier in this chapter.

4.   If you bought a fancy monitor with speakers, cameras, or other goodies, you have to perform two more tricks: Plug the cords from the monitor's speakers or camera into their spots in the back of your computer. (The Appendix shows pictures of all your PC's ports and what plugs into them.) Then, if Windows doesn't recognize your new monitor's special features, you probably have to install the drivers that came on the CD that came with the monitor. (Or, for the newest drivers, visit the monitor manufacturer's Web site, a task described in Chapter 17.)

 WARNING!

Monitors are usually one of the quietest parts of your PC. If your monitor ever starts making noise, something is wrong. If those noises are ever accompanied by an odd smell, don't wait for smoke: Turn off your monitor immediately.

 TIP

If you install a new video card and the monitor screams, the card is trying to make the monitor do something cruel and unnatural. Chances are that the two aren't compatible. To fix the problem, right-click the desktop, choose Screen Resolution, move the Resolution slider toward the bottom, and click Apply.

Connecting a TV to a PC or Laptop

Stuff You Need to Know

Toolbox:
- A TV
- A cable that fits between the TV and your computer

Time Needed:
Less than an hour

You can connect a computer to only a High-Definition TV; older TV sets just don't work well. If you plan on using the TV as a second monitor, finish this task, and then proceed to the next, "Adding a Second Monitor to a PC or Laptop."

Here are the jacks found on both computers and TVs, listed in order of video and sound quality:

- **DVI:** Many HDTV sets come with a DVI port — the same one found on most LCD monitors and PCs. That makes the connection as easy as with an LCD monitor: Just connect a DVI cable between your PC's DVI port and the HDTV set. (You may need to unplug your PC's monitor when you plug in the TV.)

- **HDMI:** The latest HDTVs include one or more HDMI ports for connecting to Blu-ray DVD players, as well as computers.

Follow these steps to connect your computer to your TV:

1. Make sure your computer and TV have matching ports, and a cable that connects the two, and then set your computer and your TV within a few feet of each other. Most video cables are less than six feet long, which doesn't give you much room.

2. Find the matching TV ports on your monitor and your computer, and then connect the appropriate cable between them. The cables and ports will be identical to the ones in the preceding task, "Connecting a Monitor to a PC or Laptop." After all, an HDTV set is just a large monitor.

3. Adjust your computer's video so it fits on the TV's screen: right-click the desktop, choose Screen Resolution, and move the Resolution slider to the appropriate resolution. Start with a resolution of 1280 x 720. If that works, try bumping up the resolution to 1920 x 1080 to take full advantage of the TV's highest quality.

Unless you're using an HDMI cable, these steps connect only your PC's *video* to your TV, not its sound. If your PC's built-in sound isn't good enough, connect your PC's sound to your home stereo, a project I cover in Chapter 11.

Not hearing sound through your HDMI cable? Make sure you've attached a cable from your PC's digital sound output to the video card's digital sound input. (Most of them are tiny wires that run from two-pins on the video card to two pins on the sound card.)

Attaching a Second Monitor to a PC or Laptop

Stuff You Need to Know

Toolbox:

- A second monitor
- A laptop with a video port, or a desktop PC with two video ports
- A flashlight, if necessary, for finding the video port on your computer or laptop

Time Needed:
Less than an hour

Until you've added a second monitor to your computer, you won't realize what all the fuss is about. Adding a second monitor gives you the benefits of owning two computers, without the cost. For example, you can do your work as usual on your first monitor. The second monitor can devote itself to showing all those items that used to require shuffling a pile of windows.

For example, a second monitor lets you do these things:

- Keep your e-mail program visible for researching old e-mail, or checking for the latest one.
- Extend your netbook or laptop's tiny monitor onto your second monitor, doubling your desktop space.
- Keep open a Web page with constantly changing information about the weather, news, or research about what you're currently writing.
- View files on a networked computer while comparing them with your own.
- Keep two Word documents open simultaneously, letting you move or copy paragraphs between them.

To attach a second monitor to a computer, follow these steps:

1. Plug the second monitor's cable into the monitor and into a second video port on your desktop PC, or into your laptop's single video port. No second video port on your desktop PC? Then you need to buy and install a video card with two ports, one for each monitor, as I describe in Chapter 9. Conveniently, many newer video cards come with two video ports.

TIP

If you're feeling green, recycle the monitor from your old computer by putting it to work as your second monitor.

2. Tell Windows 7 about your second monitor: Right-click a blank part of the desktop and choose Screen Resolution to see both displays listed onscreen. Click the Detect button if Windows can't find the second monitor. Then click the icon representing your main monitor and choose Make This My Main Display to choose which monitor should display your Start button and taskbar. (In Windows XP, right-click the desktop, click Properties, and click the Settings tab. In Windows Vista, right-click the desktop, click Personalize, and click Display Settings.)

3. Tell Windows how to extend your desktop. Windows can extend your desktop above, below, to the left, or to the right of your current monitor. To tell Windows where you've placed your second monitor, drag the monitor's onscreen outline to the appropriate position, and click Apply. (I like placing the monitor to the right, extending my desktop in that direction.) To test it, move your mouse pointer off the screen in that direction; the mouse pointer should show up on the second monitor.

When in doubt, click Identify; Windows will place a huge number 1 on the screen of your main monitor, and a huge number 2 on the screen of your second monitor.

Adjusting Your Monitor's Settings

Stuff You Need to Know

Toolbox:
- A monitor
- Windows 7

Time Needed:
Less than an hour

Monitors and video circuits can display information in several different *resolutions,* meaning how much information they can squeeze onto the screen. A high resolution shrinks everything to pack as many windows onscreen as possible. Lower resolutions enlarge everything, limiting what you can fit on your desktop.

To find the resolution that's right for you, follow these steps:

1. In Windows 7, right-click a blank part of your desktop and choose Screen Resolution. (In Windows Vista, right-click your desktop, click Personalize, and click Display Settings. In Windows XP, right-click the desktop, click Properties, and click the Settings tab.)

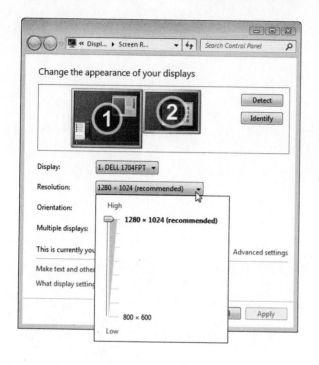

2. In the dialog box that appears, click the Resolution menu to see the Resolution drop-down list and use your mouse to drag the little bar between High and Low. Then watch the little preview screen near the window's top change as you move the mouse. The more you slide the bar upward, the larger your monitor display grows. Unfortunately, the more information Windows 7 can pack onto your monitor, the smaller that information appears.

3. View your display changes by clicking the Apply button, and then, if asked, click the Keep Changes button to authorize the change. Click OK when you're done tweaking the display. After you change your video resolution once, you'll probably never return here. Unless you plug in a second monitor, that is, as described in the preceding section.

There's no right or wrong choice here, but try the resolution Windows lists as "Recommended." That's the resolution your monitor will display best. Your monitor will still be able to display the other resolutions, but they won't look as crisp.

Chapter 4

Printers and Scanners

Installing printers and scanners has never been easier. Most printers and scanners now come combined as one unit. You install the printer or scanner's software, plug in the new printer or scanner, and Windows automatically recognizes it and introduces your new printer or scanner to all your programs.

This chapter walks you through the steps you need to take, from buying the right printer or scanner for your needs, to fixing the problems when Windows' world of automation somehow leaves something stuck.

Updating Your Printer

Printers have never been so inexpensive. Unless you're a graphic arts professional, it makes sense to buy a combination printer/scanner, known in the business as an "all-in-one." By combining the two, stand-alone models not only simplify printing and scanning, but also morph into a stand-alone copy machine.

Unlike other computer parts, the *vast* majority of printers work with every PC. Some wireless printers appear in your network (Chapter 15) as soon as they're plugged in and turned on. Almost every other printer plugs in through the ubiquitous USB port, a staple on every PC, laptop, and netbook.

Unfortunately, you'll probably have to supply your own USB cable: Most manufacturers leave out the cable in order to cut the price a few more dollars.

When you're shopping for a printer, compare the same letter and/or photo printed from several different printers. For example, one printer may be better for photos but lousy for letters. Other printers may be just the opposite. Consider your personal printing needs and compare several printers that meet those needs before making a final decision.

To help you decide, here's a list of the types of printers available, and their particular niches.

✔ **Inkjet:** Popular for their low price and high quality, inkjet printers (shown in Figure 4-1) squirt ink onto a page, creating surprisingly realistic images in color or black and white. Although the printers come cheap, their expensive ink cartridges wear out much faster than the typewriter ribbons of yesteryear. For low-to-medium level work and digital photography, these versatile printers provide the best buy for the buck. (Most all-in-one printers, discussed next, rely on inkjet technology.)

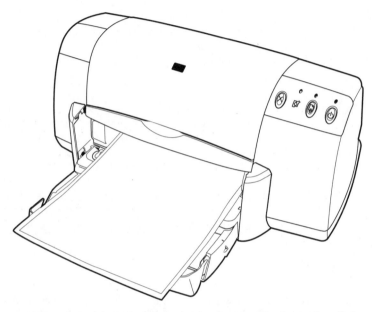

Figure 4-1: Inkjet printers handle photos as well as regular printing chores.

✔ **All-in-one (AIO):** The most popular printer today, this combines an inkjet printer, copy machine, scanner, and occasionally a fax machine into one compact package. (Sorry, no coffee maker.) The quality of all-in-one machines has risen dramatically in the past few years. As shown in Figure 4-2, their small footprint makes them perfect for small, one-person offices. The downside? If one component breaks — the scanner, for example — you've lost your copier and fax machine, as well. They also cost a little more than a plain old printer — but not much.

✔ **Photo printer:** Many color inkjet printers do a fair job at printing digital photos, but photo printers contain several extra colors, letting them print with more finesse. Some photo printers print directly from your camera or its memory card, letting you print without firing up your PC. Photo printers work best as a second printer, keeping you from wasting your expensive color photo ink on shopping lists, schoolwork, and Web pages.

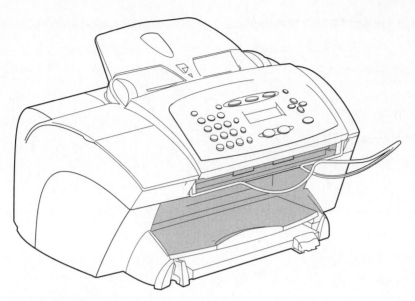

Figure 4-2: This all-in-one printer combines an inkjet printer, a scanner, a fax machine, and a copy machine into one package.

When buying a printer to print photos, pick up some photo-quality or glossy inkjet paper. It's not cheap, but it makes all the difference when printing photos.

Photo printers offer the utmost convenience, but they can't compete with professional developers for both quality and price. Drop by your local photo developer with a memory card or CD full of photos and compare the difference. Most photo developers like Costco even let you upload your digital photo files from your computer, and then pick up the prints at the store.

✔ **Laser:** Laser printers may sound dangerous, but these printers (shown in Figure 4-3) use technology similar to their ho-hum equivalent, copy machines; they sear images into the paper with toner. Black-and-white laser printers cost a little more than inkjet printers; double or triple that price for color laser printers. Although laser printers can't print digital photos, they're cheaper in the long run for general office paperwork.

Laser printers are *supposed* to heat up. That's why you shouldn't keep dust covers on laser printers when they're running. If you don't allow for plenty of air ventilation, your laser printer may overheat. After you turn off your laser printer, let it cool; then put on the dust cover to keep out lint and small insects.

Figure 4-3: Laser printers provide better quality than inkjet printers but at higher prices.

Fixing Common Printer Problems

Replacing an inkjet printer is usually more cost-effective than repairing it, unfortunately. Some new printers cost less than the price of replacing their ink cartridges! The more expensive laser printers, by contrast, require regular servicing to ensure a long lifespan. Some printers simply need to be cleaned in the right places, so get an estimate on repairs before giving up.

All-in-one printers vary widely in price and quality, so there's no clear answer about the cost-effectiveness of repairing versus replacing. If your printer cost more than $200, get an estimate.

To test whether it's your computer or your printer that's acting up, plug the printer into a friend's computer or test it on a computer at work. (Have a coworker blindfold the network administrator first.) If the printer works fine on other computers, your *own* computer is the culprit. If the printer has the same problems when connected to other computers, though, your printer is the hitch. To fix your printer, run through the fix-it tasks dealing with printer problems later in this chapter.

Updating Your Scanner

Scanners work like tiny copy machines. But instead of printing paper copies of what you place onto the scanner's bed, a scanner stores a copy of your item as a computer file. The popular all-in-one printers, which include a built-in scanner, work as copy machines, as well.

Like printers, today's scanners all connect to your computer the same way, through a USB port, making them compatible with nearly every computer made in the past ten years. Luckily for you, nearly any scanner on the store shelf will work with your computer.

Your biggest decision when shopping for scanners becomes the size of your wallet. To help you choose between quality levels, here are some words you'll find on the boxes of most scanners. You'll be familiar with many terms if you've shopped for a digital camera because the two items are basically the same: Scanners are digital cameras that specialize in close-ups of large, flat items. Because of this specialization, scanners include their own specialized words, making you wade through awkward acronyms like dpi and TWAIN.

Turning a standalone scanner into a copy machine

Although scanners look and work much like a copy machine, they differ in one frustrating way: They have trouble reproducing your image at the same size on the same-size sheet of paper. The software included with some scanners lets you turn it into a copy machine, but if your scanner's software is giving you trouble, try this trick to make a printed copy of something:

1. Place your item facedown in the top-right corner of the scanner bed.

2. Place a sheet of 8.5-by-11-inch office paper on top of it, in the same corner.

3. Preview your image on the scanner, being careful to crop the scan to the *same size* as the 8.5-by-11-inch office paper. Then make your scan.

4. Open your scanned image in a graphics program and print it on a standard sheet of 8.5-by-11-inch paper.

You can use any graphics program for the last step, but choose Page Setup from the program's File menu and tell the program to print your scan on a single sheet of 8.5-by-11-inch paper. Since that's also the size of your scan, you'll end up with an actual-size printed reproduction of your scan.

When you find yourself sinking into a scanner's vocabulary, use this rope to help pull you out.

- **dpi (dots per inch):** Choosing a higher dpi setting tells the scanner to collect more detailed information about your image. That translates to a larger image on your monitor, a larger-sized file, and a higher-resolution image with higher quality when printed out.

  You'll scan the majority of your photos and documents at between 75 to 300 dpi, although 2400 dpi comes in handy for archiving family photos.

- **Optical/Enhanced:** Many scanners have two dpi ratings: one for "optical" and another for "enhanced." The difference? The enhanced mode is a blurry computerized exaggeration of the optical mode, which is what the lens actually sees. For a true look at your scanner's quality, rely on the optical figures. (Digital cameras and camcorders, discussed in Chapter 12, use similar computerized exaggerations with their digital zooms.) A higher optical dpi means a higher price.

- **OCR (optical character recognition):** Scanners take high-quality, up-close pictures, usually of flat surfaces. Since they're taking photos, you can't view (or edit) the *text* from a scanned magazine in a word processor. But wouldn't it be nice if you *could* do just that? Well, some brainiac invented OCR software that analyzes images for recognizable characters. Then it dumps the characters into a text file as words. That lets you scan a document, run OCR software on the image, and save the text into a file for importing into a word processor.

  Windows doesn't include OCR software, although some scanners toss it in for free on higher-priced models. If you need it, look for the acronym OCR on a scanner's box or specifications list.

  When using OCR software, be sure to align your document or book's top edge with the top edge of the scanner's glass plate. Then scan at 300 dpi. Finally, most OCR software doesn't understand grammar, spelling, or etiquette. That's up to you and your word processor to fix.

- **TWAIN:** A not-for-profit group decided to liberate scanners from their complicated bundles of software. So the group created a set of standards for manufacturers to incorporate into their scanners. Thanks to TWAIN, many programs — as well as Windows — can easily bypass your scanner's bundled software and access your scanner directly.

  The initials TWAIN don't stand for anything. The TWAIN organization says it lifted the name from Rudyard Kipling's poem with the line, "and never the twain shall meet." However, one of TWAIN's founders (Hewlett Packard's Bob Gann) said they coined the term from "technology without an interesting name" after frustration at finding a name for a rather dry topic.

  TWAIN is a *device-specific* driver. You need to install the specific version of TWAIN that comes with your device. The TWAIN driver that comes with one scanner, for instance, won't necessarily work with other scanner models.

- **WIA (Windows Imaging Architecture):** WIA incorporates portions of TWAIN into Windows, letting you control scanners from nearly any graphics program, including Windows' Paint, covered at the end of this chapter, or most other graphics programs, using the same commands for every brand or model of scanner. From Paint's File menu, you can choose From Scanner or Camera to control the scanner directly with Windows 7's built-in software.

Most graphics software can also control your scanner directly. Turn on your scanner, insert the material to be scanned, and load your graphics program. Choose Acquire or Import from the program's File menu. The program tells your scanner to grab the image and dump it directly into your graphics program, conveniently bypassing your scanner's bundled software. (The Acquire/Import trick works through the scanner's TWAIN driver, so it works only with TWAIN-compatible scanners.)

✔ **24-bit color and 48-bit color:** Computers use *bits* — states of being turned on or off — to process information. Any item boasting 24-bit color means it can handle 16,777,216 colors, a standard known as True Color or photo quality. It's fine for most needs. (Some design and printing professionals scan at 48-bit color mode.)

Dealing with scans that look awful

A look at all the options in a scanning program should make anyone realize that scanning is a fine art. (If that's not enough, then look at the menus in Adobe Photoshop — or just look at the software's price tag.) Like any other art, scanning takes lots of practice before things look exactly the way you want.

Luckily, scans are free, just like digital photos. Take several using different settings and delete the ones you don't like. You're not wasting any paper — just temporarily filling space on your hard drive.

Follow these steps to get the most out of your scanner:

✔ Always clean your scanner's glass surface with a lint-free rag (never paper towels, which can scratch) and some glass cleaner. Spray the cleaner on the rag, not the glass, or the glass cleaner could seep between the glass and the scanner's sides. Any dust, lint, cat hairs, or fingerprints will show up in full detail when you scan something. Keep the glass as clean as possible

✔ Make sure your monitor displays as many as or more colors than your scanner's current setting. (I explain how to change your monitor's color settings in Chapter 3.)

✔ If your scanner's not performing properly, visit the scanner manufacturer's Web site and download the latest versions of the software and drivers. Most manufacturers update them on a regular basis to repair problems discovered by other annoyed users. The warehouse workers stuffed the scanner's box several months before it arrived on store shelves, and its software and drivers are usually out of date.

Installing or Replacing a Printer's Ink Cartridge

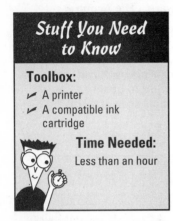
Printers need ink to place images onto a page. When you buy a new printer — or when your current printer's pages start to look blotchy or faint — you probably need a new ink cartridge.

Changing cartridges differs among printer models, but here's the general rundown:

1. Leaving the printer turned on, open its cover. Printers usually have a hood-release type of latch that pops up the cover. (You may need to remove the paper tray first.) Before you may install the cartridge, most inkjet printers must be turned on first, so their cartridge-bearing arm slides out of its hiding place. On most printers, the ink cartridges slide into view when you open the cover.

2. Remove the old cartridge, if necessary. The cartridge usually pops or slides up and out. While the cartridge is out, wipe away any dust or dirt you see inside the printer. Pull off the plastic strip that protects the new cartridge's ink nozzles and electrical contacts, as shown in the figure.

3. Slide in the new cartridge. Look for a sticker on the inside of the case with illustrated instructions for your particular printer model. When the cartridge is in place, you'll hear it lock in tight. When the new cartridge snaps in place, close the printer's cover. You may need to put the paper tray back on the printer.

4. Run your printer's software, if it has any. Some inkjet printers, for example, come with software that aligns a newly installed cartridge. The software prints several coded designs and then asks you to examine them and choose the best-looking ones. The printer then knows the best way to print. New cartridges can be a tad blotchy for the first few pages, so don't print any résumés right off the bat.

Color printers usually come with two ink cartridges, one for black and the other for colored ink. (Photo printers sometimes have four cartridges.) Luckily, the plastic ink cartridges are usually labeled to avoid confusion. If you're in doubt, the smaller cartridge probably holds the black ink.

Installing a Printer

Here's a secret: You don't have to install your printer's software. Windows 7 automatically recognizes and lets you print to hundreds of different printer models. So, try plugging in your printer *without* installing the printer's software. If you're not happy with the results, unplug the printer, install its software, and plug it back in.

To install a printer, follow these steps:

1. Remove the new printer and accessories from the box and install its software, if necessary. Remove the printer's cover and extricate any packaging from inside the printer. Many printers come with cardboard or plastic holders to protect moving parts during shipping. Check the manual to be sure you've located and removed them all. Also, make sure that you can account for any installation CDs, cables, paper, and cartridges that came with the printer.

2. Find the printer's USB cable and the cable's matching USB ports on your printer and on your computer. Then connect the cable between your PC (left) and your printer (right). The slightly rounded plug usually goes into your printer, as printers rarely use the most popular-sized USB cables. USB cables just need a slight push; if they're not going in, turn the plug upside down and try again.

3. Plug in the printer, turn it on, and install the printer's ink cartridges, as described in the preceding task. (Many new printers come with cartridges installed, but they're often only half full.)

4. Add about 25 sheets of cheap or previously used paper; you don't want to waste your expensive photo paper on your first few tests. Rustle the paper to get some air between the pages before placing it in the tray. That reduces paper jams and expletives.

5. Turn on your monitor and PC, if you'd turned them off. As your PC awakens, Windows notices that you've attached a new printer. Give Windows time to sniff your printer thoroughly and add the printer's name to your programs' printer menus. Finally, print a test page on your newly installed printer: Click the Start button, choose Devices and Printers, right-click your newly installed printer's icon, and choose Printer Properties. Click the General tab, if necessary, and click Print Test Page. The test page looks like gibberish, but it's a Rosetta Stone for tech support should things not go well.

Fixing a printer that doesn't print

Are you *sure* that the printer is turned on, plugged in to the wall, and a cable connects it securely to your computer? Then run through these steps until you find the fix.

1. Make sure the printer has paper. Some printers have a little readout or blinking light that announces a paper shortage. With other printers, you have to ogle the paper supply yourself.

2. Update the printer's drivers. Windows comes with drivers for most printers, but they often lean toward the generic, meaning that they don't support a printer's more advanced features. Upgrading to the manufacturer's current printer driver that's written for your particular model sometimes fixes problems. It's fairly easy to make sure that your printer is using the most up-to-date driver, and it's all explained in Chapter 17. (That chapter also explains how Windows can return to your older driver if your new driver makes things even worse.)

3. Check for jammed paper. Open the printer's top and carefully remove any offending sheets of paper. Keep your eyes peeled for little shreds of paper that might be getting caught in the printer's gears. When you're adding paper, hold the paper stack loosely at the bottom, and flick the top edges as though they were one of those little flip-page cartoons. This loosens up the paper and makes it flow through the feeder more easily.

4. Visit the printer manufacturer's support page on the Internet, or try searching for the printer's model name or number on Google. I describe Internet sleuthing for technical support in Chapter 21.

Keeping Words from Running off the Page

Stuff You Need to Know

Toolbox:
- A document that won't fit on the paper correctly
- Paper, plus scrap paper for tests, if needed

Time Needed:
Less than an hour

Sometimes an image or document refuses to align itself onto a single page: The printer cuts off lines or images along the right side. To avoid this problem, choose a program's Print Preview mode before you actually print the page. The computer displays a picture of the paper with your image or text printed on it. If the image doesn't fit onto the page, try these things to fix the problem:

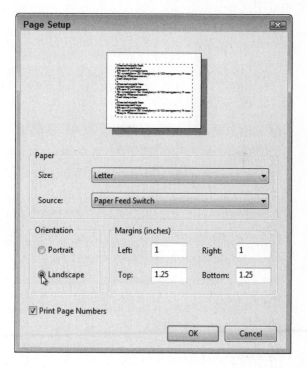

1. Switch to Landscape mode, which prints the text sideways. Printers usually print onto paper in Portrait mode: The paper is positioned vertically. If you're printing a spreadsheet or something that extends off to the right, look for a place in the Print window's Preferences or Page Setup area to switch from Portrait to Landscape mode. Then the printer prints the information horizontally, like a landscape.

2. Choose the Reduce to Fit Page option. Some printers and programs offer an option to shrink the image so that it fits onto the page. This works nicely for photos, but not so well for things with lots of fine print. Give it a test on cheap paper or the back of a page that didn't print correctly.

3. Use templates. The label-maker Avery (www.avery.com) and other manufacturers offer free templates from their Web sites. By calling up a template in your software and filling out the template's boxes, your program positions the text perfectly on the page. It works great for address labels, greeting cards, certificates, name tags, and other impossibly hard-to-configure spots. Avery has an online version, as well.

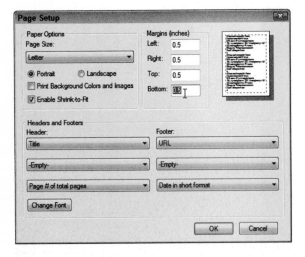

4. Change the margins. Use your program's Page Setup area and make sure you've set the margins to within a half-inch of the paper's edge. You might need to move out the right margin until everything fits.

Installing a Scanner

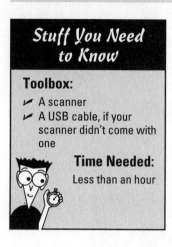
Installing a scanner works much like installing a printer, except that you needn't worry about ink nor toner cartridges. Installing the scanner's fairly easy. (The hard part comes when trying to figure out all the confusing options offered by the scanner's bundled software.)

Follow these steps to install a scanner:

1. Remove the scanner and its accessories from the box. Be sure to search the scanner's box for a cable — probably USB — the software, the manual, and any weird-looking plastic holders for negatives or slides. Some scanners come with their lids detached, so you may need to rummage around for that.

2. If required, install the software before installing the scanner. Better check the manual on this one. Some scanners require their software to be installed *before* the scanner is plugged in.

3. Remove any tape securing the scanner's lid in place.

4. Unlock the scanner. Some scanners come with a lock that holds their mechanism in place during transport. Look for a round plastic area with a notch along the scanner's side. Rotating that round piece of plastic usually unlocks the scanner. (Sometimes there's a little slot to insert in the lock; a coin often works in the slot as a makeshift screwdriver.)

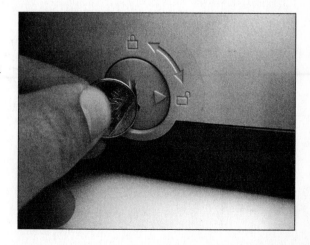

5. Put on the scanner's lid and fasten its connecting cable, if necessary. Most lids don't have a firm hinge. Some have two prongs that slide in and out of holds, and others have spring mechanisms.

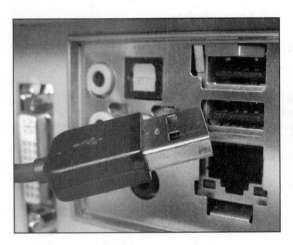 

6. Plug your scanner into the power outlet and plug its cable into the scanner and into your computer. The slightly rounded USB connector (right) usually goes into the scanner; the rectangular USB connector (left) plugs into your computer.

7. Press the power button. After a second or two, Windows recognizes your new scanner. If it doesn't, try fiddling with your bundled software to see if it recognizes your new software. If your computer doesn't seem to notice all your work, it's time to head to the next section.

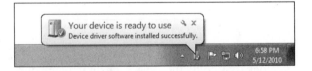

Scanning with Windows 7 Software

Stuff You Need to Know

Toolbox:
- A scanner
- Windows 7

Time Needed:
Less than an hour

Most scanners come with oodles of bundled software, yet Windows 7 already comes with its own simple software for scanning images. Follow these steps to hand the scanning reins to Windows 7. Windows 7's built-in software is so simple, you might find yourself using it for quick tasks, like scanning an item for a fax, e-mail, or party flyer.

Before scanning anything, always clean the item to be scanned and the scanner's glass thoroughly with a lint-free cloth. Any dirt or residue will show up on the scan.

1. Lift your scanner's cover, place the item to be scanned on the glass, and close the cover. Most scanners prefer that you nestle the scanned item in the top-right corner.

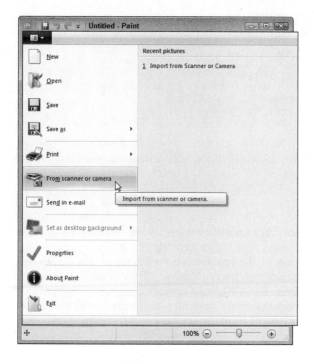

2. Open Paint from the Start menu, click Paint's File menu, and choose From Scanner or Camera. Paint comes with every version of Windows, so I'm using that as an example here. But almost every graphics program offers a similar option under the File menu. If you prefer a different graphics program, click its File menu and choose Acquire or Import to start scanning. Windows' built-in scanning software jumps in, shown here, with your scanner's name listed along the window's top edge. If the scanner's name doesn't appear, then it isn't WIA and TWAIN compatible, and you're stuck with its bundled software. If you own more than one scanner, choose your model from the pop-up menu.

TIP

Like cooking grills and tennis rackets, some inexpensive scanners have sweet spots, where the picture scans the most clearly. If you're having trouble with poor optics, light leaks, or uneven light along the scanner's edges, search the manufacturer's Web site to see if your particular model of scanner has a sweet spot. (Chapter 21 covers Web searches.) You may need to experiment by moving your item to different corners of the scanning bed.

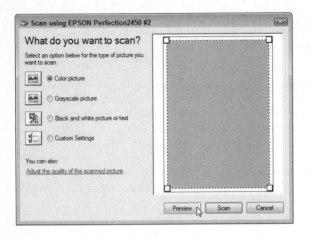

3. Choose your Picture type. Windows offers four choices. Choose Color for anything with color or being sent to a color printer. Choose Grayscale for black-and-white photos. Choose Black and White only for scanning line art — that is, drawings made with a pen or pencil. Choose Custom only to change the resolution or fiddle with the brightness/contrast settings. Finally, click the Preview button, which tells Windows to scan the picture and place it on the screen.

4. The dotted lines surrounding the image on the screen show the exact area being scanned. See the black squares in each corner? Drag them in or out until the crop marks surround exactly what you want to scan — not the entire scanner area. Spend a little time adjusting them so you don't accidentally lose part of the image.

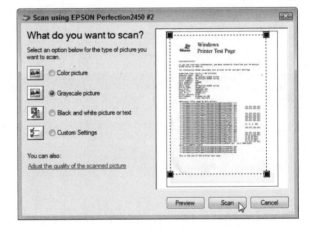

5. Click the Scan button, and save the image in Paint. When you click the Scan button, Paint scans your image and brings it into the program. From there, you can save the image as either a JPG or TIF file. Choose JPG format if you're saving a photo. Choose TIF for something you'll print, like a party flyer. The TIF format creates a larger file, but preserves the highest quality image. Save all your images in Windows 7's Pictures library, accessible from the Windows Start menu.

Chapter 5

Adding More Memory

Topics and tasks in this chapter

✔ Buying the right memory

✔ Installing memory into a computer or laptop

✔ Diagnosing failing memory

Adding memory is one of the most popular upgrades today, especially for people upgrading to Windows 7. It's also one of the easiest and cheapest upgrades around. Years ago, memory cost more per ounce than gold; computer stores doled it out to the highest bidder. Today, you'll find cheap memory chips sold at your local discount warehouse store, hanging next to the bulk-pack blank CDs.

What exactly *is* memory? When your computer's CPU (central processing unit) tells your computer what to do, it needs a scratch pad for taking notes. Memory works as that scratch pad. The more memory you stuff into your computer, the larger the scratchpad, letting you run more programs more quickly.

This chapter explains the many types of memory, their unfortunate acronyms, how to buy the specific type of memory your computer needs, and how to snap the new memory into the right spot inside your computer.

Deciphering Memory Advertisements and Packaging

Although manufacturers have created many types of memory over the years, all the memory today looks pretty much the same.

For a desktop computer, memory comes on a fiberglass strip about four inches long and an inch tall, with little notches in its sides and edges. Most computers hold from two to four strips.

Laptop memory is about half the size of a desktop computer's memory; most laptops can hold one or two strips.

Different types of memory fit into different types of *sockets* — little slots that hold the strip's bottom and sides. The notches on the memory module must mesh with the dividers and holders on their sockets. If they don't line up, you're inserting the wrong type of memory into the socket.

You'll probably encounter the following words when shopping for those types of memory or browsing the ads:

- ✔ **Stick:** A piece of memory, also called a *module*. Memory looks more like a *strip* than a *stick,* but many people still call it a stick.

- ✔ **Sockets:** This describes the number of memory slots (sometimes called *banks*) living inside your computer. Each socket holds one stick of memory.

- ✔ **Matched pairs:** Some computers require you to install memory in *matched pairs*. That means you need to buy and install *two identical* sticks of memory at a time. Also, those two memory sticks must be placed in *matched pairs* of memory sockets inside your computer. Not all computers are this picky. But if your computer requires memory to be installed in matched pairs, be sure to buy *two identical* sticks.

- ✔ **Free slots:** If every one of your memory sockets contains a stick of memory, you don't have any free slots. That also means you don't have room to insert any more memory sticks. So, how do you upgrade your memory? You need to remove some low-capacity memory — a 512MB stick, for example — and replace it with a higher-capacity memory stick — 1GB, for example. Unfortunately, that tactic leaves you with a leftover-and-useless 512MB stick.

- ✔ **DDR400, DDR533, DDR2-4200, DDR2-6400:** Numbers after an acronym describe the speed of a particular DDR SDRAM or DDR2 SDRAM module. (Those names refer to different types of memory, adding to the confusion surrounding memory.) The larger the number, the faster the memory – if your motherboard's equipped to handle it. You can usually install faster memory in slower motherboards without problem, but putting slower memory in faster motherboards will slow down your computer.

- ✔ **Laptop memory:** Laptop computers use smaller parts for everything, and that includes memory. Regular sticks of memory won't fit into a notebook, and vice versa. Buy memory designed specifically for your brand *and* model of laptop.

Buying the Memory Your Computer Needs

Stuff You Need to Know

Toolbox:
- An Internet connection
- A credit card or PayPal account

Time Needed:
Less than an hour

When faced with the unpleasant task of buying the right type, speed, and size of memory for a computer, most people give up and take it to the shop. Do-it-yourselfers often turn to online memory vendors because they've made the process so easy. Follow these steps for the quickest and easiest way to figure out how much memory's already inside your computer, and the best type of memory to add to your particular model.

This computer has 2GB of memory and 4 slots.

The site recommends adding two 1GB memory modules.

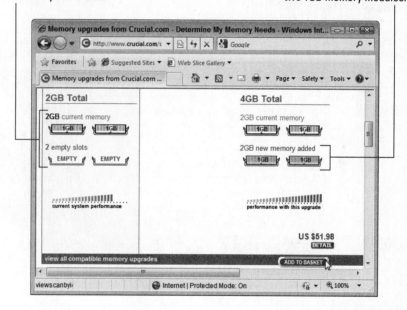

1. Visit the Web site of Crucial (www.crucial.com) or another online memory vendor. Most online memory vendors, including Crucial, offer special programs to scan your computer's memory requirements and offer recommendations. Tell the Web site to find out what memory's inside your computer and to recommend compatible upgrades. On Crucial, for instance, click Scan Your Computer, and choose Download the Scanner. The Web site sends a small program to your computer to scan its memory, and then presents the results.

2. The Web site revealed these three things about my computer: My computer has four slots of memory; two slots are filled with 1GB memory modules, and two are empty. My computer currently has 2GB of memory, and the scanner recommends I double my memory from 2GB to 4GB, at a cost of $51.98. When you've identified the type and amount of memory you need, you're ready to make your purchase.

TIP

Feel free to make a printout of what you've learned about your computer- and memory-buying strategy at Crucial, and compare prices at other sites (or local stores) before buying. Or simply buy it from Crucial.

Installing Memory in Your Computer or Laptop

Stuff You Need to Know

Toolbox:
- ✔ Your hands
- ✔ New memory
- ✔ Screwdriver
- ✔ Antistatic wrist strap (optional)
- ✔ Plastic baggie for storing old memory (optional)

Time Needed:
Less than an hour

If you live in a static electricity-prone environment, buy a grounding strap that wraps around your wrist and attaches to the computer. Even if you don't have static electricity problems in your area, you should still ground yourself by touching a metal part of your computer's case before touching its innards. If you're working in a dry area with lots of static, take off your shoes and socks. Working barefoot can help prevent static buildup.

After you buy your new memory modules, follow these steps to install them.

1. Turn off the computer, unplug it, remove the case, and locate the memory sockets on your motherboard.

2. Remove any old memory sticks, if necessary, to make room for a higher-capacity memory stick. Pull the socket clasps away from the existing memory module on each side, and then pull the module up and out. Place the extracted memory into a plastic baggie for safekeeping.

To open a laptop or notebook computer, turn it off, and remove the panel from the bottom of the laptop. (Check your notebook's manual to see exactly where its memory modules live.)

3. Add the new memory. Look for the notched sides and bottom of the memory stick. Align the memory stick's notches with the socket's dividers and clasps. Then push the memory stick straight down into its socket, and push its little locking clips toward its edges to hold it in place. (Or if you're adding memory to a laptop, skip to Step 4.)

4. On a laptop, push the smaller memory stick into a smaller socket. Two clips then hold the memory stick flat.

5. Double-check your work. Then plug in and turn on your computer. Are all the memory modules firmly in position? Wiggle them a little bit and make sure their clips hold them firmly. Are any of their pins showing? The pins should be deeply embedded in the socket. Your computer might greet you with an error message about memory mismatch or something weird. The message sounds scary, but it's good news! Your computer found the new memory chips and was startled to find more memory than the last time you turned it on.

6. Put the case back on your desktop PC, or the small panel back onto the laptop. Windows should run faster, more smoothly, and be able to juggle more programs at once.

TIP

If your computer doesn't recognize your new memory chips, turn it off and push those chips into their sockets a little more firmly. That may do the trick.

Diagnosing Failing Memory

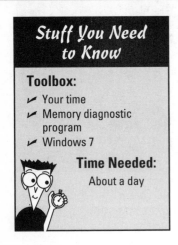

**Stuff You Need
to Know**

Toolbox:

✔ Your time

✔ Memory diagnostic
program

✔ Windows 7

Time Needed:

About a day

Memory rarely fails. But if your computer's sending a strange error message and somebody suggests you check your memory, it's an easy enough job. You simply copy a memory-testing program to a CD, stick the CD in your drive, and restart your computer. Your computer loads the program, instead of Windows, and proceeds to test your memory thoroughly. So thoroughly, in fact, that I suggest you run it before you go to bed so that you can wake up the next morning to see the results. Follow these steps to test all your memory, or one stick at a time:

1. Download a free memory testing program like Memtest86 Memory Diagnostic (www.memtest86.com; click Free Download) or Microsoft's Memory Diagnostic utility (http://oca.microsoft.com/en/windiag.asp). The programs come in the format of an ISO file, ready to be burned to a CD.

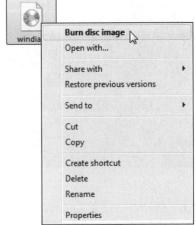

2. To burn the ISO to a CD, insert a blank CD into your CD or DVD burner, right-click the ISO file, and choose Burn Disc Image. After you've created the CD, keep it in the disc tray, and restart your PC by clicking the Start button and choosing Restart.

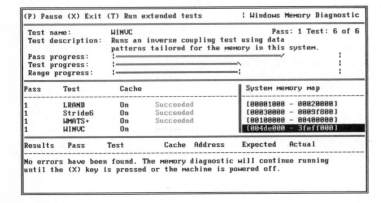

3. When your computer restarts, it will load the memory-testing program instead of Windows. Tell the program to run all night. In the morning, check the results to see if the program caught any memory errors. If it's found errors, you need to replace your memory stick. No errors? Then the memory is okay.

Not using Windows 7? Then you'll need to download an ISO burning program, or use a third-party disc burning program to burn the memory-testing program to a CD or DVD.

Chapter 6

Adding or Replacing a Hard Drive

People pile their junk into closets, garages, and kitchen drawers. Computers stuff everything onto their humming hard drives.

Unfortunately, hard drives suffer from the same problem as their household counterparts. They're rarely large enough to hold everything, especially after a few years of accumulating odds and ends.

Every new Windows version consumes more hard drive space than the previous version, and new programs always grow larger, too. The Internet keeps dishing up stuff that's fun to store. E-mail keeps piling up. And those digital camera photos are larger than ever.

To deal with the constant information flow, some people add a second hard drive, either inside their PC or by plugging a portable hard drive into one of their PC's USB or FireWire ports. Others take the plunge and replace their Windows drive with a faster, larger hard drive.

This chapter shows you how to add more storage to your PC by adding a second hard drive, or by upgrading your Windows drive. As a bonus, it explains how to back up your Windows drive and store it on another drive as a system image for safekeeping.

Upgrading a Hard Drive

Upgrading a hard drive isn't as difficult as it sounds. First, you discover what type of hard drive you need by peeking inside your computer. Armed with that knowledge, you decide how much you want to spend. Faster drives that hold oodles of information, for example, cost much more than slower drives with less capacity. And laptop drives cost a premium because of the mechanics of stuffing all that information into such a small space.

This section explains how to buy a compatible hard drive without spending more than necessary. Finally, it explains the best way to juggle hard drives inside your PC, keeping the newest, fastest drive for your Windows drive, and relegating the slower ones to extra storage.

Buying a compatible drive

The vast majority of today's PCs use SATA drives, described in this section. Older PCs, by contrast, usually require IDE drives, an older technology also described in this section.

And how do you tell whether your PC needs a SATA or an IDE drive? The surefire way is to peek at the drive itself, as described in the upcoming task, "Identifying Your PC's Drive Type."

You'll find that your PC uses one or more of these types of drives:

- **SATA (Serial ATA):** Found inside almost all PCs and laptops sold in the last few years, SATA drives transfer their information through sleek, thin cables that easily route around your PC's innards.

- **IDE (Integrated Drive Electronics or Intelligent Drive Electronics):** Found inside older desktop and laptop PCs, these drives will still work with SATA-style computers if you pick up a cheap adapter. (You can also buy an adapter to install a new SATA drive into a PC that accepts only IDE drives.) The latest breed of IDE drives is sometimes called EIDE rather than IDE, but for your purposes, they're the same.

- **Laptop:** Unless a drive specifically says "laptop" somewhere in its specifications, it's meant for a desktop computer. Laptop drives, by contrast, are built specifically for laptops: They're about four times smaller than drives for desktops. Just as with desktop computers, new laptops use SATA drives; older ones used IDE drives.

- **SSD (Solid State Drive):** Built with no moving parts, these speedy, low-capacity drives exist mostly for netbooks and specialty PCs. The hard drives of many netbooks can't be upgraded; others can. Only your netbook's manual, the manufacturer's Web site, or, sparing that, a tiny screwdriver and a removal of your netbook's case, can tell for sure.

- **Portable USB:** Compatible with any computer, these drives live inside their own little cases, and they plug into any available USB port. Some people call portable drives "external drives."

✔ **Portable SATA:** Like USB drives, portable SATA drives are also portable, living outside your PC. Instead of plugging into a USB port, though, these plug into an external SATA port, a rare feature found on some newer PCs. Because few computers come with an external SATA port, portable USB drives are much more versatile.

Deciding what features are worth your money

After you've decided what type of drive your computer needs, either SATA, IDE, laptop, SSD, or portable, you must decide how much to spend. The following items found on a drive's fine print will all affect that drive's price tag:

✔ **Capacity:** The more information a drive can store, the higher the price. A drive's capacity is its most important feature: Buy the largest capacity drive you can possibly afford.

✔ **Access or seek time:** This measures the amount of time the drive takes to locate stored files, measured in milliseconds (ms). The smaller the number, the faster the drive, and the more it will cost.

✔ **DTR (data transfer rate):** This measures how quickly your computer can transfer the files after it finds them. Usually measured in RPM (revolutions per minute), larger numbers are better, and cost more.

✔ **Cache:** Your drive stashes recently accessed information in a special, extra-speedy spot called a *cache,* where it can dish it out quickly if you need it again. The larger the cache, the faster the drive, and, of course, the more expensive.

✔ **Laptop:** You pay a premium for laptop drives. They not only cost more than their desktop PC equivalents, but they don't hold as much information.

✔ **Portable drives:** These are regular, internal hard drives stuffed inside a box with some electronics and a USB cable. They cost about the same as a regular, internal drive, but with a $20 to $30 premium for their casing, electronics, and cable.

✔ **SSD (Solid State Drive):** Living on the cusp of developing technology, these drives cost more than their SATA or IDE counterparts, and they don't hold nearly as much information. But they're small, fast, and don't slurp up batteries, so they're often found in netbooks and some specialty PCs. Avoid them unless you have a pressing reason for one.

✔ **Reliability:** Before settling on a particular make and model of drive, read that drive's customer reviews on sites like Amazon (www.amazon.com) and NewEgg (www.newegg.com). Sometimes it's a good idea to trade some speed or capacity for reliability.

When you're purchasing a drive for everyday work or sound/video editing, spend extra to buy a very fast drive with a large cache. If you're looking to simply store large amounts of data, such as music, videos, or other large files, save money by buying a slower drive with a smaller cache.

Choosing how to add more storage space

You usually know when it's time for a new hard drive. Windows constantly complains about needing more room. Programs refuse to install, complaining of not enough available space. Or, worse yet, your C drive begins grinding noisily, Windows no longer loads, or you see error messages mentioning the words "disk error" or "disk failure."

You have three options, listed in order of preference:

- ✔ **Replace your C drive (the drive inhabited by Windows and most of your files) with a bigger drive.** This is your only solution if your C drive dies. But even if your Windows drive still works fine, replacing it will add storage space *and* speed up your PC. Windows 7 makes this task easier than ever before. After replacing the drive, recycle your old C drive as a second drive inside your PC, which adds even *more* storage for your music and videos.

- ✔ **Add a second internal drive.** This adds storage but doesn't solve the problem of an overcrowded C drive. You'll still need to transfer your large files from your C drive to your second drive. Plus, Windows will still live on its old drive, not the speedy new drive with the latest technology.

- ✔ **Add a portable drive.** A quick and easy upgrade, this leaves you with the same problems mentioned above. But at least the drive is portable: a handy trait when copying large files between computers, or saving off-site backups.

The tasks in the rest of this chapter cover each of those three options, walking you through each upgrade.

All computer owners should start by backing up their computer. It's easily done when you complete the next two tasks: buy a portable hard drive and create a system image backup on that drive. Armed with a freshly made system image backup, you won't lose any information when your computer's hard drive dies. (And *all* hard drives will eventually die.)

Installing a Portable Hard Drive

Less expensive than ever before, a portable hard drive comes in very handy for several reasons:

✔ You can make a backup of your computer's files and store the drive off-site — an important fact should your computer be stolen or, heaven forbid, catch fire.

✔ It works easily with Windows 7's built-in backup program.

✔ You can easily move the drive between computers, backing up each one in turn.

✔ It simplifies transporting large files from home to work, and vice versa.

✔ It greatly simplifies upgrading your C drive to a larger, faster hard drive.

✔ It's often the only way to add more storage to a laptop or netbook.

Follow these steps to buy and install a portable hard drive that you can use for backups.

1. Find the size of your Windows drive, also referred to as your *C partition* by clicking Start, choosing Computer, and looking at the number beneath your C drive's icon. A partition is simply a sectioned-off portion of a hard drive. A hard drive can have one partition that fills the entire drive; a drive can also be divided into several separate partitions, each with a different letter.

2. Buy a portable hard drive *at least* as large as your C partition. Because my drive, for example, is 279GB, I'd want to buy a hard drive of at least 300GB, preferably 500GB. Portable hard drives can often connect through several different ports, but buy one that includes a USB port. That ensures the drive will connect to your own computer.

3. Plug the portable hard drive into its power adapter, if needed. Some portable hard drives don't require any power; others require a power adapter connected between the drive and an outlet. (Geeks call their little black power adapters *wall warts*.)

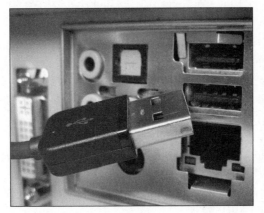 

4. Plug the portable drive's USB cable into both your computer and the drive itself. The cable's large plug fits into your computer's or laptop's USB port (left); the small end fits into the drive's own, smaller USB port (right).

5. Most portable drives work as soon as you plug them in: Windows immediately recognizes the drive, assigns it the next available drive letter, and lists it in the Start menu's Computer program. If you have a hard drive labeled C, for example, and a DVD drive named D, then your new drive will be named the next available letter: E. (Some drives need to be formatted, covered in the "Partitioning and Formatting a Second Internal Drive in Windows" section, later in this chapter.)

6. Double-click the new drive's icon in Computer to see the drive's contents. That's it. Once you've opened its window in Computer, you can start moving files to and fro just as with any other drive. It's also ready to store a system image backup, covered in the next task.

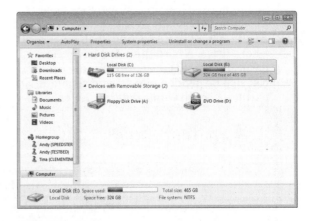

To easily identify your portable hard drive in Windows, rename it: Right-click its icon in Computer, choose Rename, and type in **Portable** or **PortHardDrive** or something similar. That new name distinguishes it from other hard drives, which are usually named "New Volume" or "Local Disk."

Backing Up Your Windows Drive with a System Image

Stuff You Need to Know

Toolbox:

- ✔ A computer
- ✔ Windows 7
- ✔ A second hard drive, preferably a portable one

Time Needed:

Less than an hour

Windows 7's Backup and Restore program lets you create a *system image:* a single file that contains everything on your computer's C drive: Windows, your installed programs, and the files you've created with those programs. A portable hard drive, described in the previous task, is the perfect receptacle for the system image you create in this task, because you can keep the portable drive in a safe location, safe from any hazards that may befall your PC.

A system image takes longer to create than a regular backup, so you should make a system image once a week, and daily regular backups. But when your C drive eventually dies — or you want to upgrade to a faster, larger Windows drive — a system image is your best friend. Here's how to create one:

1. Connect your portable hard drive, if you have one, as described in the previous task. No portable hard drive? You can still choose to save your system image to either a second internal drive in your PC, a few DVDs, or to a network location. Those areas aren't perfect backup locations, but they're better than nothing.

2. Click the Start button, choose Control Panel, and choose Backup Your Computer from the System and Security section. Then choose Create a System Image from the left pane.

A system image versus a regular backup

So, how does a system image differ from the Backup and Restore program's regular backup? The regular backup copies only your *files,* mostly from Windows 7's libraries: Documents, Music, Pictures, and Videos. If you accidentally delete a file or two, your regular backup lets you cherry-pick the lost files you want to restore.

A system image, by contrast, copies the *entire* Windows drive, storing everything in one large file. Restoring a system image is an all-or-nothing affair: You can return to the exact setup you had when you made the system image — but, unlike a regular backup, you can't quickly grab a file you accidentally deleted from your Documents library.

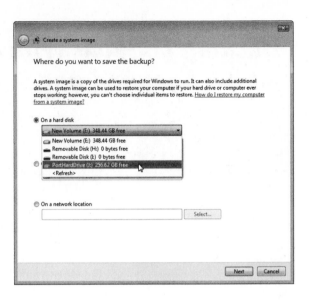

3. Choose where you want to save the system image file: a hard drive, a handful of blank DVDs, or on a network location. To choose your portable hard drive, click the On a Hard Disk drop-down menu, choose your portable hard drive, and click Next. (Your portable drive will probably have a different letter than the one in this figure.)

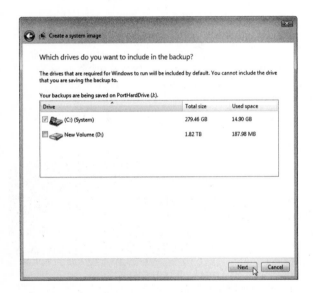

4. Click Next in the following window, which confirms that you're creating a system image of your (C:) (System) drive — the home of Windows, your programs, and your files. In the next window, click Start Backup to start copying the system image to the drive. Depending on your drive's speed, the backup consumes roughly an hour for each 200GB of files, but you can continue working while backing up.

5. When the backup finishes, take Windows up on its offer to create a *new* type of disc: A system repair disc: Insert a blank CD or DVD into your CD/DVD burner, click Yes, and follow the onscreen instructions. Later, if your C drive dies or you've replaced it with a larger hard drive, you can insert that repair disc into your CD or DVD drive, and turn on your PC. Your PC boots from the repair disc and offers an option to restore your system image backup. I walk you through the process in the "Reinstalling Windows from a System Image" task later in this chapter.

Identifying Your PC's Drive Type

Your computer or laptop needs one of two types of drives: SATA or IDE. The most foolproof way to see what type of drive your PC uses is to open its case and peek at the drive or drives inside. You'll need to carry out this task before you can buy a compatible drive for your computer or laptop.

To do that, follow these steps:

1. Remove your computer's case, as described in this book's Cheat Sheet, downloadable from www.dummies.com/cheatsheet/upgradingandfixingcomputersdiy. Or if you have a laptop or netbook, turn it upside down and open the panel covering its hard drive. (You may have to check your laptop or notebook's manual to find the panel's location.)

2. Examine the data cables that move from your computer's *motherboard* (the large, flat circuit board filled with chips and cables) to your hard drive or drives. If the drive's cable is small (left), then your computer uses SATA drives. (The SATA connector is often labeled "SATA," as well.) If you see a wide, flat ribbon cable (right), then your computer uses IDE drives. It's that simple.

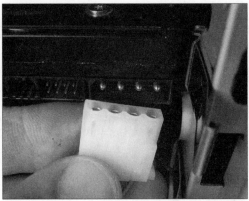

3. Examine the power cables that move from your computer's *power supply* — that massive box in the corner that sprouts all the wires — to your drive. Your drive uses either a SATA power cable (left) or a *Molex* power cable (right). SATA power connectors are almost always black; Molex connectors are almost always white. Both of them fit only one way — the right way. You can buy SATA-to-Molex or Molex-to-SATA power adapters at your computer store, if necessary. They're only a few dollars, and RadioShack often carries them.

If your desktop computer uses IDE drives, you can still add a SATA drive, or vice versa. The key is buying and inserting the right adapter: IDE to SATA or SATA to IDE. These small adapters fit between the drive and the cable and cost from $10 to $20. Their performance isn't the best, but they'll work in a pinch. Don't try the adapters in a laptop or netbook, though, as they won't fit.

Upgrading or Replacing Your Windows Drive

Stuff You Need to Know

Toolbox:

✔ A computer or laptop
✔ A compatible replacement hard drive
✔ A system image of your Windows drive
✔ A screwdriver

Time Needed:
Less than an hour

Today's hard drives are larger and faster than the drive currently living inside your computer. So, one way to speed up your computer comes from installing Windows onto a newer, faster drive. (You can even recycle your old drive as a second drive for storage.) Windows 7 makes this seemingly complex task easier than ever.

You'll also need this task when your Windows drive crashes — taking with it all your programs and your work. (All drives eventually crash.) The loss can be *devastating* unless you've created a system image, a task I describe in this chapter's first two tasks.

The key point with this upgrade is making sure your replacement drive uses the same settings and cable as your old one, as I describe in the preceding task.

1. Identify your old drive, described in the preceding task, and buy a replacement of the same type, either SATA or IDE. You can buy new hard drives at office supply stores, computer stores, or online at places like Amazon (www.amazon.com) or NewEgg (www.newegg.com). (I buy almost all of my computer parts at NewEgg.) I describe purchasing strategies in this chapter's "Deciding what features are worth your money" section.

2. Remove your computer's case, as described in this book's online Cheat Sheet, find your hard drive, and examine where the cables currently plug into your dead hard drive, as described in the preceding task. Those same cables will plug into the same places on your new drive; you needn't buy new cables. (Take a close-up digital photo, if you want something to fall back on.)

Upgrading a laptop or netbook's hard drive? Look in your laptop or netbook's manual and find the plastic compartment housing the drive. (Or just examine the drive's bottom for a plastic plate that's screwed in place.) Remove the plastic compartment with a small screwdriver, pry off the plastic cover, and find the drive awaiting inside. If your netbook's drive can't be replaced, the best you can do is buy a large-capacity SD card for its memory slot.

3. Remove the screws and/or trays holding the old drive, saving the screws. Then slide the new drive in the old one's place, and screw it back into place. Installing an old IDE/ATA drive? Then set the new drive's master/slave jumper to Master. (See this chapter's task, "Setting an IDE Drive's Jumpers" for more detailed information.)

4. Plug in the new drive's data cable and its power cable. The cables from the old drive fit into their new drive's connectors only one way — the right way — on both ATA/IDE (right) and SATA drives (left). Screw the drive back into place inside your computer's case, and replace the plastic cover if you're performing surgery on a laptop.

5. Head to the "Reinstalling Windows from a System Image" task, described next. When Windows reinstalls your information, it will automatically partition and format your new drive, if necessary. If your system image's partition is smaller than your new drive, you can expand it to fill the entire drive, as described in this chapter's "Extending a Partition to Fill a Drive" task.

Reinstalling Windows from a System Image

Here's where your work in this chapter's first two tasks pays off. You've created a system image of your Windows drive, and you've stored it on a portable hard drive. You're now ready to place that system image onto a new, larger, and faster hard drive that you've just installed to replace your tired, old, or, gulp, stolen Windows drive.

In any of those cases, follow these steps to make your desktop computer or laptop wake up with that system image in place and ready to work. (If you're trying this on a netbook, you need a portable CD or DVD drive to read the system repair disc you created in an earlier task.)

1. With your computer turned off, plug in your portable USB drive that contains the system image you made in this chapter's earlier task, "Backing Up Your Hard Drive with a System Image." (Or, if you saved the system image to DVDs or a network location, go to the next step.)

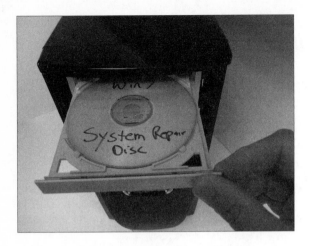

3. When the System Recovery Options window appears, click Next. (That chooses "US" as your keyboard layout. If you're not in the United States, choose a keyboard layout in a different language from the drop-down menu.)

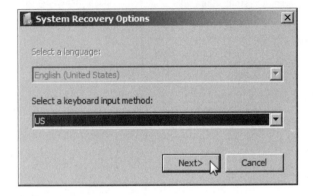

2. Turn on your computer, and quickly insert the system repair disc you made in the earlier task, "Backing Up Your Hard Drive with a System Image." When your computer asks, press any key — the spacebar will do — to tell the computer to load from the system repair disc. You'll see a message that Windows is loading files.

4. The system repair disc will search your newly installed hard drive for a previously installed version of Windows, but come up empty. Choose Restore Your Computer Using a System Image That You Created Earlier, and click Next.

5. The Reimage Your Computer window automatically finds the system image on your portable hard drive, listing the date and time it was made. Click Next to tell it to reinstall that image onto your new drive. Saved your system image on DVDs? Then when the program says it can't find a system image, eject the system repair disc from your disc drive. Insert the first DVD of your system image, and click Retry. The program will then find your system image on the DVD.

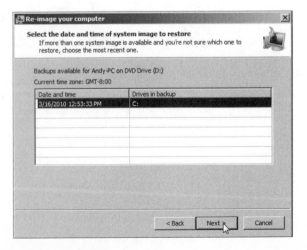

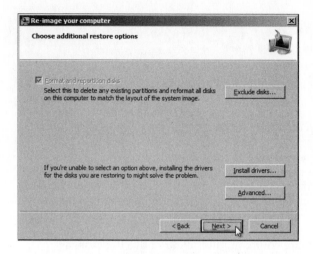

6. Click the Format and Repartition Disks option, if asked, and click Next. That tells the program to prepare your newly installed hard drive to receive the system image, install it, and make your computer wake up in the same state it was when you created the system image.

7. Click Finish to approve the date and time of the system image you'll be restoring. Then click a final Yes for approval, if necessary, and Windows goes to work. It partitions and reformats your newly installed hard drive to the same size as your system image. Then it fills that space with the system image, returning your computer to the way it was when you first created that system image. If your copy of Windows was activated, it should remain activated — even though it's installed on a new hard drive on the same computer.

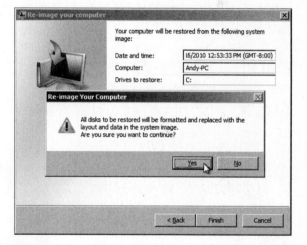

If you're restoring a system image onto a newer, faster C drive, recycle your old Windows drive as a second internal drive, described in this chapter's "Partitioning and Formatting a Second Internal Drive" task. That lets you put it to use as a backup drive or for extra storage. You can even use it to store system images, now that you know how handy they can be.

Adding a Second Internal Drive

This task doesn't apply to laptops or netbooks; they're too small for a second internal drive. If you need more space, add a portable drive or upgrade the existing drive. No, a second internal hard drive is a perk reserved for desktop computers. Some can even hold three or four extra drives. Depending on your computer's type of case, you may need special rails or an adapter to mount your hard drive inside your computer. Some drives and cases come bundled with mounting rails and/or an adapter; others don't. Rails and adapters are fairly inexpensive, and you can pick them up at the computer store, buy them online, or buy them from your computer's manufacturer.

1. Turn off and unplug your computer and remove the case, as described on this book's downloadable Cheat Sheet. If you live in a static-electricity-prone environment, buy a grounding strap that wraps around your wrist and attaches to the computer. Even if you don't have much static electricity in your area, remember to touch your computer's case to ground yourself before touching its innards.

2. Buy a compatible drive for your computer, as covered in the "Identifying Your PC's Drive Type" task. Drives usually live in a *mounting bay:* a collection of slide-in compartments inside your computer. Your existing hard drive takes up a mounting bay, for example. Look at how it's fastened inside the mounting bay; your hard drive will fasten in the same way. Find an empty bay — you can often find a spot adjacent to your existing hard drive — and slide the new drive in place.

3. Attach the data cable between your new hard drive and your motherboard. Follow the cable of your existing drive to see where it plugs into a motherboard connector marked "SATA." Then plug your new drive's SATA cable into one of your motherboard's adjacent SATA connectors. Plug the other end of this thin cable into your new SATA drive's connector (left). The plug fits into only one connector, and only right-side up. Installing an IDE drive? Attach the ribbon cable (right), and see the "Setting an IDE Drive's Jumpers" task later in this chapter.

4. Attach the power cable to the drive. A SATA power cable looks like a wider SATA data cable (left); an IDE drive's Molex connector has four pins (right); both cables lead from your PC's power supply.

5. Slide in the drive and screw it in place, if necessary. Cables attached? Master/slave jumpers set, if you're installing an older IDE drive? If your two hard drives are in the same large bay, sometimes loosening the existing drive's screws helps you slide the new drive into place. Sometimes it's easier to attach the cables *after* the drive is in place. Use your own judgment.

6. Replace the PC's cover, plug in your computer, and turn it on. Windows awakens with its new drive installed. Partition and format your new hard drive, and then assign it a drive letter so you can put it to work. You find this information in the "Partitioning and Formatting a Second Internal Drive" task, described next.

Partitioning and Formatting a Second Internal Drive

Stuff You Need to Know

Toolbox:
- A desktop computer
- A second internal hard drive
- Windows 7

Time Needed:
Less than an hour

When you first install a second drive into your PC, Windows doesn't go out of its way to tell you about it. In fact, it ignores your installation handiwork because that brand-new drive is *empty:* You haven't prepared the drive to receive any data, nor have you assigned it a drive letter. To introduce your computer properly to its new drive in Windows 7, follow these steps:

1. Click the Start button, right-click Computer, and choose Manage.

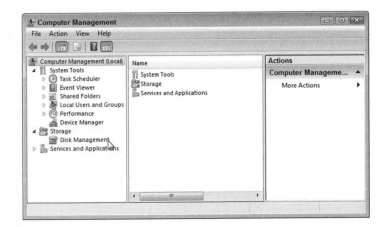

2. In the Computer Management window that appears, you see advanced controls few mortals dare to see. Click Disk Management from the left pane of the Computer Management window.

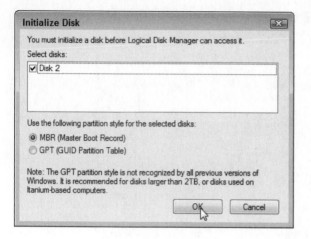

3. Windows pops up the Initialize Disk window, which lists your newly installed drive and asks your permission to *initialize* it — prepare it for Windows to start stuffing it with information. Without changing any other settings, click OK to start the process.

4. When Windows finishes, the drive is recognized, but still *unallocated,* meaning it needs to be given a drive letter and told to begin accepting files for storage. To do that, back in the Computer Management window, right-click your newly-installed-but-still-unallocated drive and choose New Simple Volume.

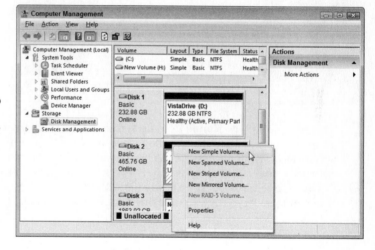

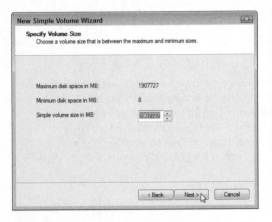

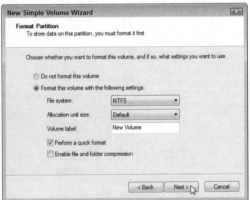

5. Thankfully, the New Simple Volume Wizard appears, ready to prepare your drive. And, as with most wizards, your journey's much easier from here: Click Next at every screen, and Windows assigns the next available letter to your drive, and *formats* it, the computer equivalent of setting up shelves so you can finally begin storing files. And, finally, you're through. Your newly installed second drive now has a letter, and the drive appears in your Computer program when you click Start and choose Computer.

Defragmenting a Hard Drive

Stuff You Need to Know

Toolbox:
↳ A computer

Time Needed:
Less than an hour

When your computer first copies a bunch of files onto a hard drive, the computer pours them down in one long strip of information. As you begin working, you inevitably delete a few files, leaving gaps in that once-pristine strip. As you begin adding new files, the computer begins filling in those gaps. If an incoming file won't fill an entire hole, the computer breaks up the file, stuffing in bits and pieces wherever it can find room.

After a few months, your files can have their parts spread out all over your hard drive. Your computer remembers where to find everything, but it takes longer because the hard drive must work harder to find and grab all the parts. To stop this *fragmentation,* a concerned computer nerd released a defragmentation program. The program picks up all the information on your hard drive and pours it back down in one long strip, putting all the files' parts next to each other.

Windows 7 is smart enough to defragment your hard drive automatically once a week. However, you may want to defragment your drive immediately before changing a partition's size, described in the upcoming "Expanding a Partition to Fill a Drive" task. To defragment your drive immediately in Windows 7, follow these steps:

1. Click the Start menu and choose Computer. Right-click your hard drive's icon and choose Properties.

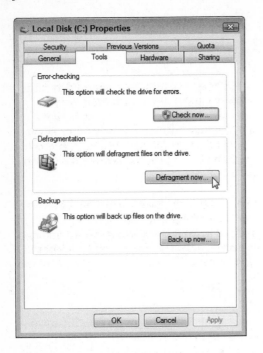

2. When the Properties window appears, click the Tools tab, and click the Defragment Now button. Windows brings the Disk Defragmenter dialog box to the screen.

3. Click Defragment Disk to start the process. When Windows finishes defragmenting, it issues a report on its results. Some files can't be defragmented, so don't worry if you see that message. If a file is being used at the time, Windows can't defragment it. Some files will always be in use, as Windows needs them to keep running.

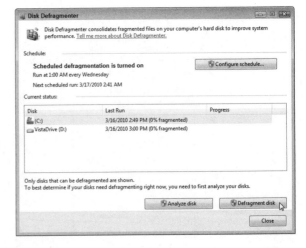

Checking for Disk Errors

Stuff You Need to Know

Toolbox:
- ✔ A computer
- ✔ A suspicion it might have disk errors

Time Needed:
Less than an hour

Ever lost your train of thought after somebody snuck up and tapped you on the shoulder? The same thing can happen to your computer.

If the power goes out or a program crashes while a computer is working, the computer loses its train of thought and forgets to write down where it put stuff on the hard drive. (That's why you should always close your programs before turning off your computer.)

These lost trains of thought result in *disk errors,* and Windows fixes them pretty easily when you follow these instructions. In fact, Windows 7 usually senses when it has crashed and automatically fixes any resulting errors. Still, if your computer is running strangely, checking for disk errors is often the first step toward a fix.

1. Click the Start button, open Computer, right-click your hard drive's icon, and choose Properties. Then click the Tools tab from the top of the Properties dialog box, just as in the previous task. Click the Check Now button.

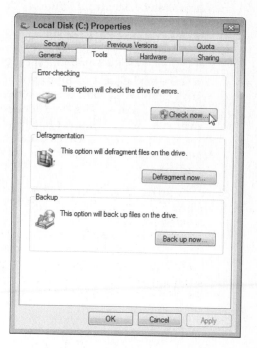

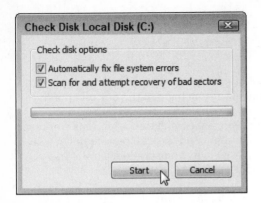

2. When the Check Disk Local Disk window appears, select both options and click the Start button.

3. If you're checking your Windows drive, Windows asks to reschedule the scan for the next time you start your computer. Click the Schedule Disk Check button and restart your computer so that the scan can begin. If you're checking a different disk, Windows doesn't restart, but begins examining your drive, looking for suspicious areas and fixing the ones it can. The process can take a *long* time; feel free to let it run overnight. When Windows finishes the process, the proud little program leaves a dialog box on the screen, summing up the number of errors it found and fixed, if any.

Extending a Partition to Fill a Drive

Stuff You Need to Know

Toolbox:

- A computer
- A hard drive with unpartitioned space

Time Needed:

Less than an hour

Windows stores information on drives, but before Windows can store any information on a drive, you need to put "shelves" on the drives, known as *partitions*. Although often a partition fills an entire drive, some drives contain several partitions, each with its own letter. And, just as you occasionally need to rearrange your bookshelves, sometimes you need to change your drive's partitions, moving, deleting, creating, extending, or shrinking them.

For example, you may upgrade your old 150GB Windows drive to a faster, 300GB drive, as described in the "Upgrading or Replacing Your Windows Drive" task. Then, when you place your Windows system image back onto that new 300GB drive (described in the "Reinstalling Windows from a System Image" task), your Windows partition will still be a 150GB partition on a 300GB drive.

How do you give your Windows partition access to the *entire* drive? That's where this task comes in: You can *extend* that 150GB partition to fill the entire drive, all with Windows 7's built-in Disk Manager. Here's what to do:

1. Click the Start button, right-click Computer, and choose Manage. The Computer Management window appears, a launching point for lots of technical tasks. (You'll revisit here to see Device Manager when you want to update your computer's drivers, covered in Chapter 17, as well as for troubleshooting, covered in Chapter 19.)

2. Choose Disk Management from the Computer Management window's left pane, and the window's right side displays your disk drives and their partitions. Your C partition is identified by the characters "(C:)", along with the words "System," "Boot File," "Page File," and other technical verbosity. (It also has a blue line across its top.) The space to the right on your C drive is listed as "Unallocated," meaning it's not being used. (It has a black line across its top.) So, your mission is to extend your C partition's boundaries to grab that unused space.

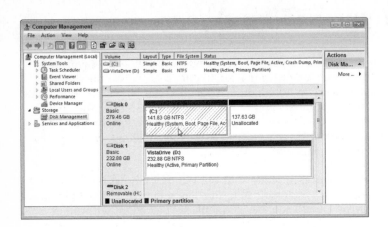

3. Right-click your C: partition and choose Extend Volume. The Extend Volume Wizard appears, ready to walk you through the process of extending your C partition to fill the entire drive. Click Next to start the Wizard.

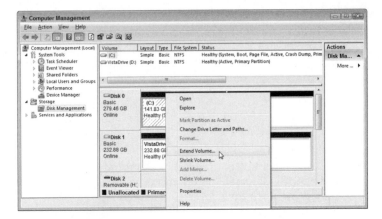

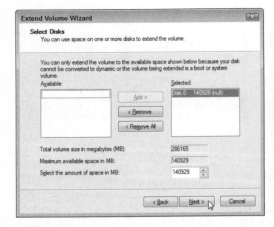

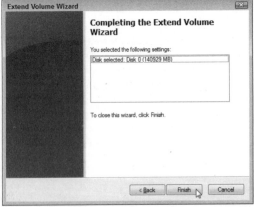

4. The wizened Wizard is sharp enough to know you want to extend your drive into the vacant space, so it offers you that option with its first screen. Click Next (left) to confirm that you want to extend the partition to fill the entire drive. Then click Finish (right) to confirm that you've chosen the right drive to extend. A few seconds later, your partition fills the entire drive.

Setting an IDE Drive's Jumpers

Stuff You Need to Know

Toolbox:

- ✔ A computer
- ✔ An IDE drive
- ✔ A pair of tweezers or needle-nose pliers

Time Needed:
Less than an hour

Hailing from days gone by, IDE drives take more cajoling than today's SATA drives. SATA drives each have their own cable that connects to the computer's motherboard. Yesterday's IDE drives, by contrast, share a single cable. When two drives share one cable, how does the computer know which drive is which? Well, just as when you have two cats, you give them different names. And in the archaic world of IDE drives, those names are "Master" and "Slave."

And you can't simply flip a Master/Slave switch on the drive. No, in the dark ages of IDE drives, you assign the drive's names by manually moving little tiny jumpers over tiny rows of pins. I'm not joking.

With IDE drives, the Master/Slave relationship has three rules:

- ✔ If you're *replacing* an IDE drive, set its jumpers to match the old drive's settings, either Master or Slave.

- ✔ If you're adding a *second* drive, set its jumpers to Slave, and leave the other set to Master.

- ✔ Here's the clincher: Drive manufacturers set different rules for their pins. A setting of Master for one drive model might be a setting of Slave for another — even though you're placing the little jumper over the same set of pins on both drives. Luckily, most drives come with labels telling which pins to cover to set them as Master or Slave.

Here's how to set the jumpers on an IDE drive:

1. Find the drive's Master/Slave identification chart, usually printed in black on a sticker attached to your drive. The sticker in the figure, for example, says to cover the middle pair of pins for Slave, and the right pair of pins for Master. No sticker on your drive? Visit the drive manufacturer's Web site and search for their downloadable Master/Slave pin settings for that particular model of drive.

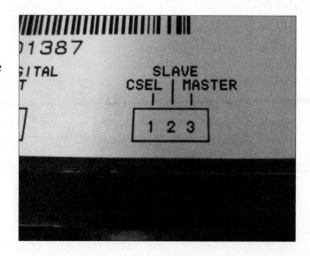

2. Locate the drive's Master/Slave pins (left). These both live near where the data and power cables plug into the drive. You'll find six or more pins, but they're always set in *pairs* like the ones in the photo. You'll also find a jumper (middle) — a little plastic thingy — resting on or near the pins. With a pair of tweezers or needle-nose pliers, place the jumper across the correct pair of pins (right), either Master or Slave.

Set an IDE drive to Master if it's the *only* drive; choose Slave if it's the *second* drive on an IDE computer cable.

Chapter 7

Adding a DVD Drive

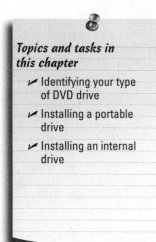

Computers with DVD drives once drew envious looks. No longer were laptoppers simply cramming in more work during long flights. No, they were reclining the seats and watching their *own* in-flight movies.

Today, nearly every computer or laptop comes with a DVD drive. Windows 7 even requires a DVD for installation.

If your computer still doesn't have a DVD drive — or the drive's too slow or not working well — take heart: DVD drives are particularly easy to install. Netbook owners can simply plug a portable drive into their USB port, for example. Or, if your desktop's DVD player is acting slow or cranky, it's simple to upgrade it to something faster, or that plays the latest DVD lust word: *Blu-ray*.

This chapter explains how to buy the right DVD drive for your desktop computer, laptop, or netbook, as well as how to install it.

Choosing a Compatible DVD Drive

Just like hard drives, DVD drives come in three main types:

✔ SATA (new style)

✔ IDE (old style)

✔ Portable (which plugs into a USB port)

Most computers can handle all three types without much problem.

Unlike earlier models, today's drives can handle nearly *any* type of blank DVD. You needn't worry about buying the wrong format.

In fact, upgraders need only ask themselves one question: Do I need *Blu-ray?*

Blu-ray, the sucessor to DVD, holds enough information to store a high-definition movie. (That's about 25GB or 50GB, if you're curious, compared to a normal DVD's capacity of either 4 or 8GB.) Blu-ray discs look just like regular DVDs, but with the words *Blu-ray* written on them.

So, when you need a DVD drive, here's what to do:

✔ If you're replacing a dead DVD burner, buy a Blu-ray DVD *drive,* not a Blu-ray *burner.* Blu-ray drives cost the same as regular DVD burners, and they can still burn regular CDs and DVDs. As a perk, they can play Blu-ray DVDs. However, they can't *burn* Blu-ray discs.

✔ If you simply *must* burn Blu-ray DVDs, stretch open that wallet: Blu-ray burners cost several times more than Blu-ray players. (Wait until the price drops in a few months.)

✔ If you want to watch Blu-ray DVDs on your desktop computer, install a Blu-ray drive next to your existing DVD burner. There's nothing extravagant about putting two DVD drives in one computer. A pair of DVD burners make it easier to duplicate discs, either CDs or DVDs.

Finally, a laptop's DVD drive is notoriously difficult and expensive to replace. If your laptop's DVD drive dies, do as the netbookers do: Buy a portable DVD burner that plugs into a USB port. (Some companies even sell portable Blu-ray burners or players, but for a steep price tag.)

Identifying Your Computer's CD/DVD Drive Type

Stuff You Need to Know

Toolbox:
- A screwdriver

Materials:
- A computer
- A CD or DVD drive

Time Needed:
Less than an hour

Just as with hard drives, your computer or laptop needs one of two types of CD/DVD drives: SATA or IDE. The most foolproof way to see what type of drive your computer can take is to open it up and take a look at the drive or drives it's currently using. You'll need to carry out this task before you can replace or add any disc drive in your desktop computer.

To do that, follow these steps:

1. Remove your computer's case, as described in this book's Cheat Sheet, downloadable from www.dummies.com/cheatsheet/ upgradingandfixingcomputersdiy.

2. Examine the data cables that move from your computer's *motherboard* (the large, flat circuit board filled with chips and cables) to your CD/DVD drive or drives. If the drive's cable is small (left), then your computer uses SATA drives. (The SATA connector is often labeled, too.) If you see a wide, flat ribbon cable (right), then your computer uses IDE drives.

TIP

If your computer uses IDE drives, you can still add a SATA drive, or vice versa. The key is buying and inserting the right adapter: IDE to SATA or SATA to IDE. These small adapters fit between the drive and the cable, and they cost between $10 and $20. Their performance isn't the best, but they'll work in a pinch.

 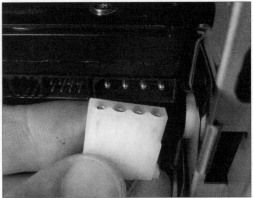

3. Finally, examine the power cables that move from your computer's *power supply* —
that massive box in the corner that sprouts all the wires — to your drive. Your drive
either uses a SATA power cable (left) or a *Molex* power cable (right). SATA power
connectors are almost always black; Molex connectors are almost always white. Both
of them only fit one way — the right way.

You can buy SATA-to-Molex as well as Molex-to-SATA power adapters at your computer store, if necessary.
They're only a few dollars, and RadioShack often carries them in a pinch.

Installing an External CD/DVD Drive

Installing an external CD/DVD drive is as simple as plugging in a mouse or keyboard. Here goes:

1. Remove the new drive and its cable from the box. Some bulky external drives come with power supplies, as well. Save the manual, as it often comes in handy later.

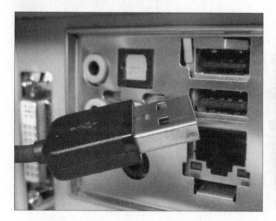

2. Plug the drive's power cable into the wall, if necessary, and turn on the drive. Some tiny drives skip the outlet, instead grabbing their power straight from your computer's USB port. Some really hoggy drives plug into *two* of your computer's USB ports in order to draw enough power.

3. Plug the drive's USB cable into its own port and your computer's USB port (two USB ports, for the hoggy drives). Windows automatically recognizes your drive when it's plugged into the USB port, and it will appear in your Computer folder, ready to play your CDs and DVDs, and burn blank discs, as well.

Installing an Internal CD/DVD Drive

Stuff You Need to Know

Toolbox:
- A screwdriver
- Tweezers, if necessary

Materials:
- A compatible replacement drive

Time Needed:
Less than an hour

Internal CD/DVD drives install nearly the same way as installing hard drives, discussed in Chapter 6: Just slide in the drive, screw it in place, and plug in the same two cables (power and data). Here are the steps:

1. Remove your computer's case, as described in this book's Cheat Sheet, downloadable from www.dummies.com/cheatsheet/upgradingandfixingcomputersdiy.

2. Remove the old drive, if necessary. Unplug its power and data cables, shown in this chapter's "Identifying Your Computer's CD/DVD Drive Type" task, unscrew the drive from the case or pull on its rails, and slide it out of the front of your computer case.

3. If you're installing a SATA drive, jump to Step 4. If you're replacing an existing IDE drive, set its jumper to match your old drive's setting, either Master or Slave. If you're adding a second IDE drive, set its jumper to Slave. (You'll find an illustrated guide to setting master/slave jumpers in the last task of Chapter 6.)

4. Attach rails to your DVD drive, if your case uses them. Slide the new DVD drive into the front of your computer. You need a vacant drive bay, which is an opening where your disk drive normally lives. You may need to pry out a rectangular plastic cover from the front of your computer before the drive slides in. (Sometimes you must pry out a thin foil protector from behind the plastic cover, too.) Screw the drive in place, if it doesn't use rails.

5. Connect the drive's data and power cables, as shown in this chapter's "Identifying Your Computer's CD/DVD Drive Type" task. The plugs fit only one way, so don't force them.

6. Replace your computer's cover, plug in the computer, and turn it on. When Windows boots up, it should recognize the new or replacement DVD drive and automatically list it in your Start menu's Computer program. Some drives come with free disc-burning software that's more powerful — but more complicated — than the disc-burning tools built into Windows 7. However, the software often lets you duplicate music CDs, a task Windows 7 still lacks.

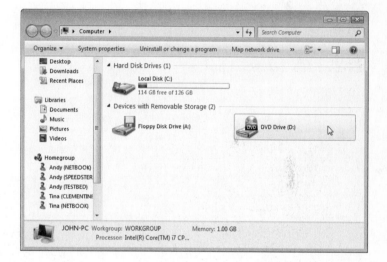

Blu-ray and DVD drives may need updates to their *firmware* — built-in software that helps them write to discs. Visit your drive manufacturer's site, download the latest firmware for your drive, and run the installation program to bring your drive up-to-date.

Chapter 8

Fine-Tuning Your Computer's Sound

Years ago, computers simply beeped when you turned them on. A few early games managed to strangle the computer's little speaker into making squawking noises. Engineers eventually created *sound cards:* circuit-filled gadgets that plug inside your computer to add music and explosions to computer games. A few years later, the cards grew sophisticated enough to power speaker-filled home theaters.

Today, however, sound cards are slowly fading away. What once took a large circuit-filled card now lives on a single chip built into many computers' motherboards.

Some folks still shell out the cash for the higher-quality sound available only through an add-on card. Gamers still buy sound cards, for example, as do musicians, who turn their computers into full-fledged recording studios.

This chapter explains how to upgrade the sound on your computer, laptop, or netbook; plug the right cables into the right spots; and route the sound to your computer's speakers or to your home stereo.

Choosing a Compatible Sound Card

Today, nearly every computer, from netbooks to desktops, includes a ⅛-inch stereo speaker jack, and a ⅛-inch microphone jack. Plug in your headphones or a small microphone, and you're ready to hear music or record your own podcasts.

But when you're looking for more quality or volume, you can upgrade your computer's sound in either of two ways: Plug in a USB sound device, or slide a sound card into a slot inside your computer.

Every desktop computer comes with both USB ports and either a PCI or PCI-Express 1x slot. (The first task in this chapter lets you know whether you have one or both of those two slots.) The small size of laptops and netbooks, by contrast, limits them to USB port add-ons. Still, that's hardly a concern, with the wide variety of USB sound options available.

So, when it comes to sound, your biggest decision is really how much to spend. These items influence the price the most:

- ✔ **Line Out:** Even the most basic sound card comes with a Line Out jack, so you won't need to pay extra for this perk.

  To hear the best sound your PC has to offer, connect a stereo cable between this ⅛-inch stereo jack and the Line In jack of your home stereo, a task described later in this chapter.

- ✔ **Line In:** All sound cards include a Line In jack. Built to accept amplified sounds, this ⅛-inch stereo jack lets your PC record music that comes from a small radio, tape recorder, mixing board, or an amplifier's Line Out jack.

- ✔ **¼-inch jacks:** Those tiny ⅛-inch stereo ports work fine for amateur work. But professionals use larger, ¼-inch jacks that aren't as prone to damage. Add in the higher-quality circuitry found on these cards, and the price increases.

- ✔ **MIDI:** MIDI stands for Musical Instrument Digital Interface, a system widely used by musicians. Run a MIDI cable from your music synthesizer's MIDI Out port into your sound card's MIDI In port to record the sounds. Or plug a MIDI cable from your computer's MIDI Out port to your synthesizer's MIDI In port, and your PC can tell your synthesizer what sounds to play.

- ✔ **Dolby 5.1:** Stereo normally has two speakers: left and right. Dolby 5.1 stereo builds on that by controlling *six* separate speakers. You place your normal stereo speakers up front, along with one center speaker for dialogue. Add two rear stereo speakers for sound effects, and a booming subwoofer to shake the room during explosions, and you've created home-theater-level sound.

- ✔ **Subwoofer:** The coolest sound cards come with a way to send sound to a *subwoofer* — a big box with a large speaker that plays the bass rumbles of explosions and drums. Because of their physical size and large magnets, subwoofers cost more than regular speakers.

- ✔ **5.1, 7.1:** These numbers refer to the number of speakers. The ".1" part of the number refers to the subwoofer, so a 5.1 system has six speakers: One lives atop the monitor for the center channel, two live on each side of the monitor, a pair sits behind the listener, and a subwoofer shakes the rafters from the room's corner. A 7.1 system works like 5.1, but adds an extra pair of speakers, one on each side of the listener. Many low-cost chips include this, so it's not as expensive as you'd think.

- ✔ **Audio-processing software:** Because many PCs already come with built-in sound, audio-processing software is now a rising star. Look for software that lets you easily digitize your old vinyl collection, for example. Some software tricks the ear, making your headphones sound as spacious as a movie theater. Don't be surprised if the software bundled with your device completely replaces Windows 7's built-in sound processing.

- ✔ **Amplified speakers:** Most sound cards don't crank out enough power to drive a traditional set of bookshelf speakers. To increase the volume, most computer speakers come with a tiny amplifier hidden inside their box. If your speakers require batteries or an AC adapter for power, they're amplified speakers, which drives up the cost. Also, to hear 7.1 sound you need *eight* speakers, further upping the price.

Installing a Sound Card

Stuff You Need to Know

Toolbox:

✓ One screwdriver

Materials:

✓ Sound card
✓ A PCI or PCI-Express 1x slot

Time Needed:
Less than an hour

Every computer sold in the past ten years comes with PCI slots. Chances are, your PC also has the PCI-Express slots preferred by some new sound cards. Follow these steps to locate one or both of those slots inside your computer so that you know exactly which sound cards will work inside your PC. Then proceed to install your new sound card into the correct slot.

To install a sound card, follow these steps:

1. Turn off your PC, unplug it, and remove your computer's case, as described in this book's Cheat Sheet, downloadable from www.dum mies.com/cheatsheet/upgradingandfixingcomputersdiy.

2. Find the slots for your sound card — the row of parallel slots inside your PC. The tiniest slots, about an inch long, are PCI-Express 1x slots. The adjacent slots, about three times as long, are usually PCI slots. The longest slot is probably a PCI-Express 16x slot, almost always reserved for video cards, which I cover in Chapter 9.

PCI-Express 1x slots   PCI slots

 Take a digital photo of the inside of your computer before taking things apart or replacing them. You can always turn to the photo for later reference.

If you find both types of slots, you're exceptionally lucky: You can install a sound card built for either PCI slots or PCI-Express 1x slots, and you can install USB options, as well. No little PCI-Express 1x slots in your PC? Then you're limited to PCI slot cards or USB add-ons. Also, if you have two compatible slots, you can insert the card into either of them. You don't need to fill the slots in any particular order, just make sure the PCI card goes into a PCI slot, and the PCI-Express 1x card goes into a PCI-Express 1x slot.

3. If you're replacing your old sound card, find and remove the old card. To find it, look at the back of your computer for a row of ⅛-inch jacks. (Your speaker cable plugs into one of them.) Those jacks live on the back of your old sound card. Remove the single screw holding that card in place, and then lift the card up and out of its slot. If those jacks aren't in a long row, then the jacks are built into your computer's motherboard. (Don't worry about it; Windows lets you choose to use your newly installed sound card, instead.)

4. If you're placing a new card in an empty slot, remove the empty slot's metal backplate by removing the single screw that holds the backplate in place. Then lift out the little plate. (Save the screw, as you need it to secure the new sound card in place.)

5. Push the card into any empty slot, either PCI-Express 1x or PCI. Hold the card by its edges and position it over the appropriate empty slot, either PCI or PCI-Express 1x. The edge with the shiny metal bracket faces toward the *back* of your computer. Line up the tabs and notches on the card's bottom edge with the notches in the slot. Push the card slowly into the slot. You may need to rock the card back and forth gently. When the card pops in, you can feel it come to rest. Don't force it!

TIP

If the screw accidentally drops into your PC, pick up your computer and shake it until the screw falls out.

6. Secure the card in the slot with the screw you removed in Step 3 or 4.

7. Plug the computer's power cord back into the wall and PC, turn on your PC. Windows usually recognizes a newly installed card, displays a message saying it recognizes the new device, and automatically sets the card up to work correctly. If something goes wrong, install the software that came with your card. No software? Then head for Chapter 17 for tips about installing drivers. If everything's working, however, put your PC's cover back on.

Whenever you install a new sound card or any other card, visit the manufacturer's Web site. Find the site's Support or Customer Service section, and then download and install the latest drivers for that particular model and your version of Windows. Card manufacturers constantly update their drivers and software to fix bugs.

Plugging the Right Sound Cable into the Right Jack

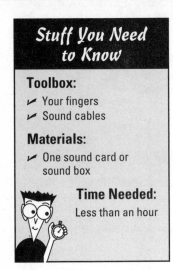

Stuff You Need to Know

Toolbox:
- Your fingers
- Sound cables

Materials:
- One sound card or sound box

Time Needed:
Less than an hour

Most sound cards offer a long row of almost identical ⅛-inch jacks for plugging in your speakers, microphones, and other goodies. How do you know what plugs in where? If you're lucky, your computer comes with a little label explaining the purpose of each jack. If you're not lucky, follow these steps:

1. Examine the colors of each jack, and look for tiny lettering. Then consult Table 8-1 to see which cables plug into which colored jack:

2. Plug the appropriate cable into the appropriately-colored-and-labeled jack. (A flashlight often helps.) Be sure your speakers are turned way down before plugging in any cables. Then, slowly turn up the volume to make sure you've plugged the right cable into the right spot.

Table 8-1	Deciphering a Sound Jack's Color-Coding
The Jack's Color	*What Usually Plugs Into It*
Pink	Microphone
Blue	Line Input (iPod, VCR, tape deck, or other unamplified source)
Green	Stereo speakers (two front speakers or headphones)
Black	Stereo speakers (two rear speakers)
Silver	Stereo speakers (two side speakers)
Orange	Center speaker and subwoofer

Installing a Sound Box

A *sound box* is any sound-related item that plugs into a USB port. It can be as simple as a tiny USB plug with a headphone and microphone jack — a handy solution to a laptop with a broken headphone or microphone jack. Or it can be a desk-sized home studio for making professional recordings.

Prices range from $20 for a USB flash drive-sized model to $500 for home theater models. Plan on spending between $100 to $200 for a good one.

Follow these steps to install a sound box to a PC or laptop:

1. Plug the USB cable into the USB ports of both the sound box and your computer or laptop. (Some tiny laptop adapters plug right into the USB port without a cable.) Some sound boxes require power from a wall outlet.

2. Install the sound box's software. Most sound boxes come with excellent software, but manufacturers also dump borderline-useful software onto your hard drive — trial versions of software with rapid expiration dates, for example. Be prepared for that bit of rudeness with a post-installation trip to the Control Panel's Uninstall a Program area to remove any unwanted software.

3. Connect your gadgets to the sound box. Many sound boxes come with only one cable: A USB cable for plugging into your PC. That means you'll have to buy cables for everything else you want to connect to the sound box: speaker cables, a microphone, optical cables for hooking up to a surround sound system, and similar items. Now's the time to make a trip to RadioShack or an office supply store.

Some sound cards and boxes add their own icon to the Control Panel. If you spot a Control Panel icon named after either your card or its manufacturer, open it with a double-click. It usually offers many more options than Windows' standard settings area.

Connecting Your PC's Sound to Your Home Stereo

To hear your PC or laptop at its best, hook it up to a home stereo. There's just no comparison in sound. To hear how good your PC's sound can be, spend less than ten dollars on a cable and try it yourself. (No, you don't need those extraordinarily expensive cables sold at stereo stores. Do your shopping at computer stores or online, instead.)

If you're connecting your sound to a home theater system and want surround sound through five speakers and a subwoofer, flip ahead to Chapter 11, where I explain how to hook up a surround sound system.

But if you're connecting your PC through an amplifier to a set of stereo speakers, follow these steps:

 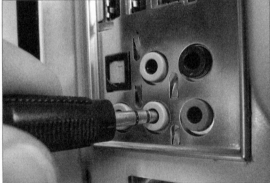

1. Buy a ⅛-inch stereo plug to stereo RCA port cable. This handy cable plugs into your sound card's ⅛-inch jack and offers two handy RCA ports on its other end, one for each stereo channel. Plug the cable's ⅛-inch jack into your computer's headphone or speaker port.

This same handy cable also lets you plug your iPod and most other portable music players into your home stereo, as well. Just unplug it from the back of your PC and plug it into your iPod or music player. Plug it back into your PC when you're through.

2. Connect the stereo audio cable's two RCA connectors to your stereo's two Line In ports. If your stereo lacks a free pair of Line In jacks, connect the cable to any other jacks designed to accept sound: a CD or DVD player, for instance.

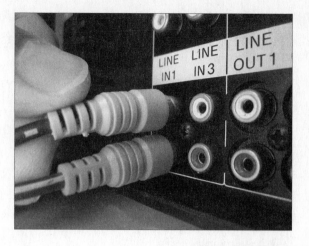

3. Set your stereo's front sound input to Line In. Most stereos let you hear sound from a variety of gadgets: CD/DVD players, radios, digital video recorders like TiVO, or record players. To hear your PC, turn the stereo's input to Line In — or the name of the jack you've plugged the cable into in Step 2.

4. Adjust the volume. Play music through your PC at a low volume, and then slowly turn up the volume on your stereo. You'll probably want to control the volume at your PC because that's within reach. So turn the volume up on your stereo, and leave your PC set fairly low. Then, as you turn up the volume on your PC, your stereo will grow louder, as well. Slowly tweak the volume settings until you find the right mix. If the PC's too loud and the stereo's too low, you'll hear distortion. If the PC's too low and the stereo's too loud, you'll blast your ears when you turn up your PC's sound.

The *red* jack connects to the stereo's *right* channel. The other jack (usually white) connects to the left channel.

Routing Sound Through an HDMI Cable

Follow this rarely undertaken task only if all three of these conditions are met:

- Your monitor (which might double as your TV set) includes built-in speakers, and you want to listen to sound through them.

- Your monitor connects to your video card through an HDMI cable.

- You want to route the sound through the HDMI cable rather than through a separate sound cable.

If you meet those narrow guidelines, follow these steps to route your sound through your video card's HDMI cable, into your monitor, out of your monitor's built-in speakers.

1. Turn off your PC, unplug it, and remove your computer's case, as described in this book's Cheat Sheet, downloadable from www.dum mies.com/cheatsheet/upgradingandfixingcomputersdiy.

2. Locate the S/PDIF (Sony/Philips Digital Interconnect Format) pins that carry sound from your sound card or motherboard. Then slide one end of the jumper cable onto the two pins. And just where *are* these "S/PDIF pins"? Well, sometimes they're labeled with tiny print on the circuit board, right next to the connector. But if they're not labeled, you'll have to pull out the manual, unfortunately. Don't have the manual? You can almost always download the manual online from the manufacturer, described in Chapter 21.

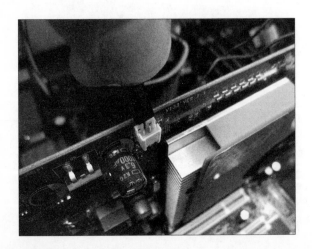

3. Slide the other end of the jumper cable onto the S/PDIF pins on your video card. Secure the jumper cable with a twist tie to keep it from being caught in any nearby fans.

4. Replace your computer's case and turn on your computer. You may have to adjust the volume on your monitor to hear the newly flowing sound running through the HDMI cable.

Chapter 9

Beefing Up Your Computer's Video Card

When engineers sat down at their poker table many years ago to design computers, they decided on a quick and easy way to upgrade their many parts.

Upgrades would come on *cards,* they decreed. To upgrade the computer, owners would simply slide the card into one of several standard-sized slots built into every computer. Simple.

And today, that's still how you upgrade your computer's video: You slide a video card into your computer's video slot. This chapter covers that specific task in minute detail by covering these things:

✔ Discovering what type of video card works with your computer's video slot.

✔ Choosing a more powerful video card that both fits into that slot and matches the video ports on your monitor.

✔ Installing the new video card and plugging a cable between the card and your monitor.

Dig in — unless you own a laptop and netbook, unfortunately. Only desktop computers can upgrade their video.

Buying the Right Video Card

Video cards require two things to be compatible with your computer:

✔ The card must physically fit into your computer's video slot.

✔ The card's *ports* — its connectors — must match the ones on your monitor.

Let's tackle the slot issue, first.

Finding a compatible video slot

Also known as *buses,* slots sit together in a long row on your motherboard, like rake marks left in dirt. When you plug in a card, the card's flat silver end rests against the back of your PC, allowing its ports to protrude from the back of the PC's case. Different types of slots support different types of computer gadgets.

Your computer most likely comes with one of two types of video slot: PCI-Express or AGP. In fact, your PC probably comes with a PCI-Express 16x slot, because that slot has been built-into most computers for the past five years.

✔ **PCI-Express (Peripheral Component Interconnect-Express):** Found on nearly every PC sold since 2005, PCI-Express slots dominate the video card world. PCI-Express slots come in several sizes; most video cards require the largest size, shown in Figure 9-1, which is called *16x.* Conveniently, most newer computers come with a 16x slot.

PCI-Express cards and slots come in several version numbers, but they're *backward compatible.* That means that a PCI-Express "version 2.1" card will work fine in a "version 2.0" slot.

PCI Express slots are *longer* than the PCI slot that lives next to it.

Figure 9-1: Most PCs include a 16x PCI-Express slot like this one. PCI-Express slots are *longer* than the adjacent PCI slots.

✓ **AGP (Accelerated Graphics Port):** Venerable PCs hailing from the late 1990s through 2005 often came with an AGP slot, shown in Figure 9-2. An AGP slot is usually chocolate brown. Although the slot's been through several revisions, most AGP slots accept either 4X or 8X AGP cards. You can still find a few AGP cards sold online at NewEgg and Amazon.

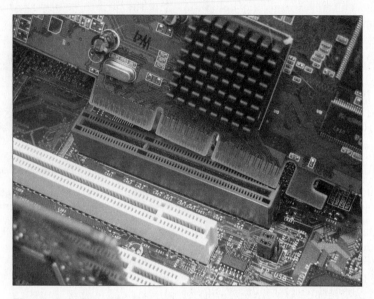

Figure 9-2: Older PCs come with an AGP slot like this one. AGP slots are smaller than the adjacent PCI slots.

Still not sure what type of video slot you have? Look closely at the motherboard's lettering near the slots. In tiny letters, you'll usually see either the words "AGP" or "PCI-Express."

Don't want to open your PC's case just yet? Then download CPU-Z (available at www. cpuid.com), a popular free utility that reveals lots of boring information about your computer's innards. Run CPU-Z, click the program's Mainboard tab, and you'll see your type of video slot listed in the Graphic Interface section's Version area.

Finding a compatible video port

After you know what video slot lives inside your computer, your mission is nearly complete. Your new goal is to buy a video card with at least one port that matches a port on your monitor. (Most video cards come with two or more ports.)

Examine the connectors on your monitor, and you'll find any combination of these four.

   ✔ **VGA (Video Graphics Array) or D-SUB:** Created in the late 1980s, this early video connector simply won't die. It's still found on nearly every computer, laptop, netbook, monitor, and flat screen TV. A VGA port, shown in Figure 9-3, works fine as a last resort to stay compatible, but the next three ports provide better-quality video.

Figure 9-3: A VGA port found on a video card (left), cable connector (middle), and monitor (right).

   ✔ **DVI (Digital Visual Interface):** Born around 2000, this port, shown in Figure 9-4, sends numbers to a flat-panel monitor, which converts those digits into pictures. For extra compatibility, many flat panel monitors include both a VGA *and* a DVI port, letting you plug your monitor into one. When given a choice, always use the DVI port for a better picture.

Figure 9-4: A DVI port on a video card (left), cable connector (middle), and monitor (right).

   ✔ **HDMI (High-Definition Multimedia Interface):** Heralded in mid-2000 as a "single cable" solution for the unsightly dangling cords plaguing home theaters, HDMI cables carry both video *and* surround sound. As computers began turning into mini-home theaters, they began carrying those ports, as well. An HDMI port, shown in Figure 9-5, is handy if you plan on watching your computer on a High Definition TV set.

Figure 9-5: An HDMI port on a video card (left), cable connector (middle), and monitor (right).

✔ **DisplayPort:** Newly emerging at the time of this book's printing, DisplayPort, shown in Figure 9-6, will soon be replacing the VGA, Digital, *and* HDMI ports on computers, leaving HDMI to its original market: home theaters. When shopping, look for a card and monitor with a DisplayPort adapter to keep them compatible with as many new products as possible. (Adapters let you convert DisplayPort to HDMI or DVI, if necessary.)

Figure 9-6: Look for the DisplayPort logo found on the newest video cards and monitors.

If you find yourself staring at a pair of video ports that don't match on your monitor and computer, there's a convenient solution: Computer stores sell adapters that convert nearly any connector to the one you need.

Deciding what features are worth your money

After you've decided what graphics card fits inside your PC and works with your monitor, your last choice is price. Video cards come with oodles of options. Here's a rundown on the things that drive a video card's price up or down:

- ✔ **Video memory:** Only your video card can touch its own "onboard" video memory; none of your programs can borrow any of it. More memory means more detailed images, leading to a higher price tag. Windows 7 runs best on video cards with at least 256MB of video memory; more memory is better.

  Cheaper cards come with very little of their own memory. Instead, the card robs some of your computer's memory, slowing down your computer in the process.

- ✔ **Brand:** Two companies battle it out for the graphic market: NVIDIA and AMD (ATI). However, those two companies license their chips to *lots* of other companies. Don't be surprised to see a wide variety of brands selling what appears to be the same type of card. Off-brand cards can save money, but sometimes ship with incomprehensible manuals, little documentation, and no technical support.

- ✔ **Graphics chip:** NVIDIA and AMD constantly introduce newer, more powerful chips. Because the latest chips carry a premium price, buy a slightly older model to save some money. For up-to-date tips, visit Tom's Hardware (www.tomshardware.com) and read their "Best Graphics Cards for the Money" article, updated monthly.

- ✔ **Ports:** As described in the previous section, make sure one of the card's ports matches the port on your monitor. If they don't match, you'll need an adapter or adapter cable, which can add anywhere from $5 to $50 to your purchase.

- ✔ **Dual-monitor support:** Most video cards now sport two ports, meaning you can plug two monitors into them. A few even offer three ports, making them compatible with the most monitors possible. Although additional ports rarely add more than a few dollars, they're a nice option for future compatibility.

- ✔ **DirectX:** Programmers use this special software to create advanced visual tricks. Many games use DirectX to display three-dimensional fire-breathing dragons and other spectacular effects. For the best experience, Windows 7 requires video that can handle DirectX version 11.

- ✔ **Noise:** Video cards generate a lot of heat, so most of them include built-in fans. Cheap cards often come with noisy fans, known as "leaf-blowers." Quieter cards cost more.

- ✔ **Resolution:** The higher the resolution, the more information you can pack onto your monitor at once. And, of course, the higher the price. To save money, check your monitor's manual (or do a Google search for its make and model) to see its highest resolution. Then buy a card that meets that resolution, because any higher resolution would be wasted.

- ✔ **Power:** If you're planning on playing lots of computer games or doing video-editing work, buy a powerful, more expensive card costing more than $100. If you're just word processing or crunching numbers, you can get away with a decent card for less than $50.

Installing a Video Card

Cards are particularly susceptible to static electricity. Tap your computer's case to ground yourself before touching the card. If you live in a particularly dry, static-prone area, wear latex gloves — the kind that doctors and dentists often wear.

Cards are also delicate, so don't bend them. Handle them only by their edges. Finally, those little silver dots on one side of the card can be sharp; don't scratch yourself.

To install a card, follow these steps:

1. Turn off your PC, unplug it, and remove your computer's case, as described in this book's Cheat Sheet, downloadable from www.dummies.com/cheatsheetupgradingandfixing computersdiy.

PCI-Express 16x slot

AGP slot

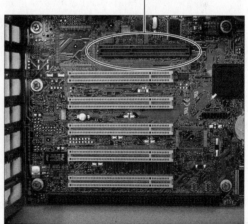

2. Locate the right slot for your card, either PCI-Express 16x or AGP, as I describe earlier in this chapter. The card won't fit into the wrong slot, so you can't go wrong. Don't confuse your computer's thin memory slots for its video card slot.

3. With a small screwdriver, remove the screw holding in the old card or the metal cover. Don't lose that screw! You need it to secure the new card in place. If you're replacing an old card, pull it up and out of the slot. If you're not replacing an old card, remove the metal cover from the back of your computer. (Unused slots have a little cover next to them to keep dust from flying in through the back of your computer.)

4. When you've identified the card's appropriate slot, hold the card by its edges and position it over the correct slot. The edge with the shiny metal bracket should face toward the *back* of your computer. (That shiny bracket replaces the cover you removed in Step 3.) Line up the tabs and notches on the card's bottom with the notches in the slot. Push the card slowly into the slot. You may need to rock the card back and forth gently. When the card pops in, you can feel it come to rest. Don't force it!

TIP

Dropped the screw inside your computer's case? Keep poking at it with a screwdriver or chopstick until you get it out. If you lose the screw inside the computer, your computer could electrocute itself. If the screw's still lost inside your PC, pick up your computer and shake it until the screw falls out.

Most video slots have a flexible plastic retaining clip that fits over a tab on the end of the video card. Bend out the clip slightly when inserting the card; when the card fits into the slot, release the clip, letting it hold the card in place.

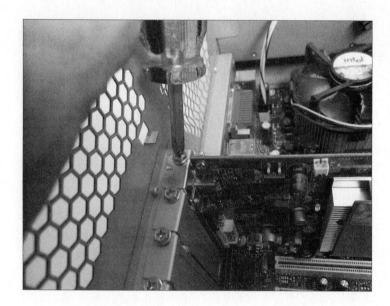

5. Secure the card in the slot with the screw you removed in Step 3. Then, plug the computer back in, turn it on, and see whether Windows recognizes and installs the card. Windows usually recognizes newly installed cards and sets them up to work correctly. If something goes wrong, turn off your computer, unplug it, and make sure you've seated the card correctly. If everything's working, however, put your PC's cover back on.

6. Some monitors come with built-in speakers. If you're connecting the monitor through an HDMI cable and want the HDMI cable to carry the video *and* the sound, you need to connect a small jumper cable between two pins on your sound card or motherboard and your newly inserted video card. I explain this bit of microsurgery in a task in Chapter 8.

Whenever you install a new video card or any other card, be sure to visit the manufacturer's Web site to download and install the latest drivers, a chore I describe in Chapter 17. Card manufacturers, especially video card manufacturers, constantly update their drivers to fix bugs.

Chapter 10

Replacing the Power Supply or Laptop Battery

You can't see it, but you can almost always hear it: Your desktop computer's power supply sits inside your computer's case in a corner with its cooling fan whirring away. Some fans add a pleasant, running-water ambience to the room. Others whine like a weed whacker.

Power supplies suck in the 120 volts from your wall outlet and reduce it to the lower voltages preferred by your computer's more sensitive innards. This seemingly simple task heats up the power supply, so it needs a constantly whirling fan to keep it cool.

The power supply's fan sucks hot air out of your computer's case and blows it out the hole in the back. In fact, if you keep your computer too close to the wall and don't move it for a while, the fan leaves a black dust mark on the wall.

Power supplies retire more quickly than many other computer parts. This chapter shows how to interview potential replacements and place the new one into its proper cubicle. (Power supplies are replaceable only on desktop computers. Laptops and netbooks grab their power from batteries, which I describe how to replace in this chapter's last task.)

Choosing a Compatible Power Supply

Almost all power supplies work fine with today's PCs. When choosing a replacement power supply, you need keep an eye on only these two things:

✓ **Watts:** Power supplies come rated by the amount of watts that they can deliver, and you need to choose a high enough wattage to power your PC. Just like brighter light bulbs, powerful computers require more watts. An average PC needs a power supply of at least 500 watts. A modern, powerful PC handling lots of video games or video editing work needs more, from 750 to 1,000 watts.

When in doubt, buy more watts than you need. Like light bulbs with self-adjusting dimmer switches, computers rarely run at full power. A 500-watt power supply, for example, may send only 200 watts to your PC most of the time. But when you fire up some demanding software, your power supply will be able to kick in the power your PC needs.

✔ **Dell:** For some reason, Dell computers break the rules with their power supplies, making them incompatible with most over-the-counter power supplies. If you're replacing a power supply in a Dell computer, buy the replacement from Dell. Or, if you shop at a retail store, make sure the power supply is built specifically for a Dell computer.

I've had good luck buying power supplies, both Dell and others, from PC Power & Cooling (www.pcpower.com).

Deciding How Much to Spend

Once you've chosen the amount of watts you need in a power supply, the sticker price varies according to these things:

✔ **Watts:** I'm throwing this in here again just to explain that the more watts you need, the more expensive your power supply will be.

✔ **Sound level:** Higher-quality power supplies come with quieter cooling fans, leading to a more relaxing computing experience. Look for fans with ball-bearings and rubber gaskets.

✔ **Durability:** To keep the price down, many PC manufacturers skimp on power supplies. After all, they need them to last only throughout the one-year warranty. Spending more on a power supply ensures a longer life, and strong, steady power. That steady, unfluctuating power helps extend the life of your PC and its components.

Curious as to how many watts your PC currently uses? I bought a Kill-A-Watt P4400 from Amazon for $20 to find out. You plug the meter into the wall, plug your computer into the meter, and the digital readout shows how many watts is being consumed. Try it on your PC while running different types of software, as well as your friends' PCs, to compare ratings. (Then try it on your refrigerator. Ouch!)

Setting Up an Uninterruptible Power Supply

When the power goes out in your home, so do the lights and everything else powered by electricity — including your desktop PC. And when your PC turns off unexpectedly, you lose any work you haven't saved. There's no way to recover it.

Laptops aren't affected by power outages; they simply switch to their battery to stay afloat. You can do the same for your PC with a UPS (uninterruptible power supply). Also known as a battery backup, a UPS is basically a big box with a heavy battery inside. You plug the UPS into the wall outlet, and plug your desktop computer into one of the UPS box's several outlets.

The UPS constantly powers your PC through the battery, simultaneously recharging the battery with power from the outlet. Then, when the power dips or dies, the UPS keeps sending battery power to keep your PC running. The power lasts for only a few minutes, but that's plenty of time to save your work, shut down your PC, and rummage for the flashlight. More expensive UPSs will work unattended. If the power dies while you're in the coffee room, they save your work and shut down your computer automatically.

Most uninterruptible power supplies also serve as a surge protector and power line conditioner, feeding your PC with the steady flow of power it craves. Here's how to buy and install a UPS in your home:

1. Buy a UPS, also called a "battery backup." Make sure it puts out enough wattage to power your computer, probably between 300 and 600 watts. They're sold at office supply stores, computer stores, and online.

2. Plug the UPS into the wall, and let its battery charge for 12 hours or the minimum specified by its manual. When the battery's charged, move to Step 3.

3. Plug your computer into one of the uninterruptible power supply's outlets; plug your monitor into another. (Without a monitor, you can't see how to save your work and turn off your PC.) Then turn on your computer and monitor.

Replacing Your Desktop PC's Power Supply

Power supplies can't be repaired, just replaced. Recycle your old power supply by finding a local or mail order recycling company, as I describe in Chapter 13. The power adapters for laptops and netbooks can't be repaired, either, but they're easily replaced. Just visit the manufacturer's Web site and order a new one.

To install a new power supply, perform the following steps:

1. Turn off your PC, unplug it, and remove your computer's case, as described in this book's Cheat Sheet, downloadable from www.dummies.com/cheatsheet/upgradingandfixingcomputersdiy.

2. Locate your PC's old power supply sitting in a corner of your PC's case. The power supply's back end fits snugly against the back of your PC so that its built-in fan can blow out the hot air. On its other side, dozens of colorful cables flow from a small hole.

3. Each cable ends with one of several types of plugs. The plugs are shaped differently to mesh with their particular connector. To make sure the new power supply's cables will plug into the same spots, put a strip of masking tape on the end of each plug and write down its destination. Better yet, make a foolproof roadmap by taking a few well-lit digital photos before unplugging *anything*.

Don't *ever* open your power supply or try to fix it yourself. The power supply stores powerful jolts of electricity, even when the computer is turned off and unplugged. Power supplies are safe until you start poking around inside them.

4. Start by unplugging the power cables from the motherboard (the large, flat, circuitry-and-slot-filled board). Two power supply cables plug into the motherboard: one pushes into a large, 20- or 24-pin connector (left), the other pushes into a smaller, 4-, 6-, or 8-pin connector (right). On motherboards set up to run *two* video cards (Chapter 9), you'll also remove a four-pin connector that looks just like the ones plugging into older CD/DVD drives, below.

5. Unplug the power cables from the hard drives and the CD/DVD burners (new on left, old on right), as well as any other places on the motherboard, usually small four-pin connectors for controlling switches and fans. Your old power supply will probably have some dangling cables that don't plug into *anything*. (Those cables are thoughtfully supplied to power any future upgrades.)

Power supply screws

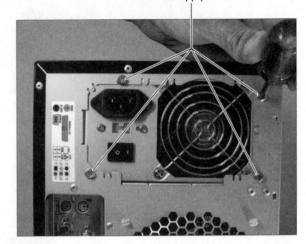

6. Remove the four screws that hold the power supply to the computer's case. Be careful not to remove the screws holding the power supply's internal fan. To see which screws are which, try loosening the screws slightly and wiggling the power supply from inside the case; that sometimes makes it easier to tell which screws are which.

7. Lift out the power supply. If the power supply is cramped, you may need to loosen the screws holding some drives in place and pull them forward a bit. If the power supply still won't come out, make sure that you've removed all the screws. Some power supplies have extra screws around their base to hold them down.

The screws that hold the power supply in place are generally closer to the outside edge of the computer's rear. The screws that hold the fan are generally closer to the fan's edge.

Plug your new power supply into the wall before installing it, just to listen for the fan. If the fan doesn't work, return the power supply for one that works. If you do hear the fan, though, unplug the power supply before beginning to install it.

8. Buy a replacement power supply. If you can't purchase a replacement power supply online, take the old one to the store and look for a replacement. If you're planning on adding more computer gear — a powerful graphics card, more hard drives, or more DVD burners — buy a power supply with a higher wattage. If you can't find a replacement for your particular power supply, head to your computer manufacturer's Web site and look for the replacement for your particular computer model. (It will be expensive.)

9. Make sure that the power supply's voltage is set correctly, if necessary. On the back of some power supplies, near the fan, a red switch toggles the power to either 120 volts or 220 volts. If you're in the United States, make sure that the switch is set to 120 volts. If your country uses 220 volts, flip the switch to the 220-volt setting.

10. Now, the steps (and figures) run in reverse, starting with Step 6. Place the new power supply in the old one's place, and tighten the screws. Then reconnect the cables to the motherboard, the drives, the fans, and the power switch. Grab your digital photo for reference, if necessary, or look at the masking tape labels you put on the old power supply's cables. Remember, some cables won't connect to anything; they're for future add-ons.

11. Reconnect the power cord. Plug your computer back in; its power cord should push into the socket near the fan. Turn on the power and see whether it works. Do you hear the fan whirring? Does the computer leap to life? If so, then all is well. If the fan is not spinning, though, something is wrong with the new power supply or your power outlet. Try plugging a lamp into the power outlet to make *sure* that the outlet works. If the outlet works, exchange the power supply for a new, working one.

12. Turn off the computer and put the case back on. Is everything still working right? If it is, put a cool glass of iced tea in your hands. Congratulations!

If your new power supply's cables don't fit your drives, buy adapters, either SATA to IDE or IDE to SATA. (I cover those in Chapter 6.) Be sure that you tighten down any disk drives you may have loosened.

Replacing the Battery on Your Netbook or Laptop

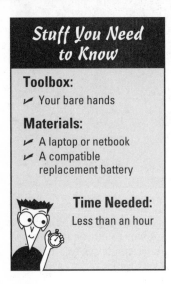

Stuff You Need to Know

Toolbox:
- ✔ Your bare hands

Materials:
- ✔ A laptop or netbook
- ✔ A compatible replacement battery

Time Needed:
Less than an hour

Even if they don't explode in a ball of flames, laptop batteries eventually die of old age. Most batteries last between 18 to 24 months, depending on how often they're used and recharged. Toward the end, you'll notice that it doesn't hold a charge nearly as long, and you're constantly prowling for power outlets.

When it's time to replace your old battery with a new one, start shopping online. Laptops accept only batteries made *specifically* for their make and model. Other batteries either won't fit or may not supply the right voltage. Buy batteries only from reputable retailers, and avoid prices that seem too cheap: They're often fakes with safety issues.

When your replacement arrives, install it by following these steps:

1. Save all your open files, close your programs, click the Start menu, and tell Windows to Shut down. You want to turn it off — *completely off*. Don't just choose hibernate or sleep modes.

2. On the underside of your laptop or netbook, release the battery lock lever by pushing it to the side marked "Unlock," or with an unlocked lock icon. Then slide the other lever to release the battery, sliding it out with your hands.

3. Slide in the new battery; it fits only one way — the right way. Then slide the latch closed and slide the second latch to Locked.

4. Turn your laptop back on. Your laptop will probably need to charge the new battery before running on battery power alone. Leave the laptop turned off but plugged in overnight to ensure a good charge.

Many states require that electronics stores take back old batteries for recycling. To check for recycling programs near you, visit Earth911.com at http://earth911.com.

Part III
Teaching an Old Computer New Tricks

The 5th Wave   By Rich Tennant

"I got this through one of those mail order PC companies that lets you design your own system."

In this part . . .

After twenty years of computing, just about everybody has an old computer, or three, lying around the house. This part of the book explains what to do with them.

You can upgrade them with a TV tuner to create a home theater, for example. Beef them up to edit those home movies sitting in the closet.

Or, if your computer's really old, give it a new lease on life by turning it into a backup machine for your newer computers.

I explain how to remove its hard drives, screw them inside a case, and create portable hard drives for your newer computers.

Or, if your old computer's no longer good for repurposing, I explain how to purge it safely of all your data, making it safe to donate to charity or give to a friend.

Chapter 11

Creating a Home Theater with Windows 7's Media Center

Determined to pry TiVo off the nation's TV sets, Microsoft tossed its *own* digital video recorder into Windows 7. Called Windows Media Center, the built-in program lets you automatically record movie and TV shows with your computer. The catch? Your computer needs three things to record television:

✔ A TV signal, which usually enters through a cable in the wall or an antenna

✔ A TV tuner, which plugs into your computer or lives on a card slipped inside it

✔ Any Windows 7 version but Starter, the stripped-down version sold mostly on netbooks

The three tasks above let you record and playback TV shows, but to hear the best sound, connect your computer's sound to your home theater, a task covered in Chapter 8.

This chapter explains how to install a TV tuner for recording and watching TV on your computer. It also explains how to connect your computer to your TV and home stereo, turning your computer into the backbone of a home theater.

Can't afford a TV tuner? Go ahead and fire up Windows Media Center, anyway. The program lets you watch many TV shows over the Internet, neatly bypassing the need to install a TV tuner.

Buying a TV Tuner

Your television signal may come into your home through an antenna, or through a cable in the wall. But before you can tell your computer to display or record a show, you need to tell it which channel to grab. And that's where a TV tuner comes in: It's a piece of electronics that separates your coveted TV channel from the dozens of other channels flowing down the wire.

TV tuners hail from two schools. Some plug into a USB port, making them handy for laptops, netbooks, and desktop PCs. Other tuners fit inside a desktop computer; designed for those willing to pick up a screwdriver, these internal tuners usually cost less and offer more performance.

Since nearly any TV tuner on the store shelves will work with your computer, which do you buy? Here's how to juggle your needs, your budget, and the fine-print on the TV tuner's box.

- **Dual-tuner:** Ever wanted to record two shows when they both air at the same time? Then you need a *dual-tuner* TV tuner. These let you grab an episode of *South Park* even when it's airing against *The Simpsons*. The most expensive cards come with four tuners; less-expensive cards include only one.

- **Hauppauge:** This company's been selling TV tuners longer than nearly anybody, so they provide more online support and better drivers than much of the competition. Give them a plus, even it if means a slightly higher price tag.

- **Windows 7 compatible:** Many older tuners won't work with Windows 7. Make sure you're buying one that's *guaranteed* to work with Windows 7. (A Windows Vista tuner might work, but you're taking chances.)

- **Remote control:** TV tuners that come with handheld remotes receive bonus points. You'll be watching the screen from a distance and need a handy way to control the action. Make sure the remote control works with Windows Media Center, though, or you'll be forced to use the TV-viewing software bundled with the tuner.

- **Video In:** Some cards toss this in for people who want to convert video from old VCRs or camcorders into computer files, which can be edited and burned to DVD. Don't want it? Don't pay for it. If you want it, though, make sure you buy one that supports your old VCR or camcorder's format, either S-Video or regular (also called "composite") video.

- **CableCARD:** All digital channels above channel 99 are encrypted, meaning you can't watch them. Unless, that is, you have a CableCARD: a slim card that slides into your TV tuner and works as a decryption box. CableCARDs come from your TV signal provider, and only the more expensive tuners accept them. And without them, forget about premium HDTV channels.

- **Antenna:** Local TV stations broadcast their HDTV signals over the airwaves. Some TV tuners come with a small antenna, which picks up a handful of local stations or more, depending on your geographic location. If you don't have a CableCARD, a rooftop digital antenna might help.

- **NTSC (National Television System Committee):** Television's old broadcast standard sent channels 2–99 through the airwaves for more than fifty years, so nearly every tuner still accepts it. This old analog standard is now replaced by ATSC.

- **ATSC (Advanced Television Systems Committee):** Tuners supporting this standard can tune in to digital broadcasts, which include high-definition channels.

✔ **Clear QAM (quadrature amplitude modulation):** ATSC channels are sent in this format. If your tuner can grab Clear QAM signals, it can handle nearly anything broadcast today. The most expensive tuners can grab NTSC, ATSC, *and* Clear QAM.

✔ **FM tuner:** Recording television is the main attraction, but some deluxe tuners also toss in an FM tuner for recording FM radio stations. Many FM stations come in on the same cable as your TV; others require an antenna.

Identifying the Cables and Connectors on Your Computer's Television Tuner and Your TV

Your computer's TV tuner comes with plenty of ports to grab video and send it to your TV screen in a variety of ways. Table 11-1 helps you identify the cables, their connectors, and their purpose in life.

Table 11-1		A Cadre of Connectors	
The Cable and Its Connectors	**Its Name**	**Its Location**	**Its Purpose**
	USB	Some TV tuners; all computers	External TV tuners plug into your computer's USB port.
	Coaxial (RF) cable	Almost all TV tuners and TV sets	Most TV tuners and TVs receive their signals through this cable.

(continued)

Table 11-1 *(continued)*

The Cable and Its Connectors	Its Name	Its Location	Its Purpose
	RCA (composite)	Some TV tuners and most TVs	Usually found in groups of three, these carry stereo sound and video. Yellow cables always carry video; the red (right channel) and white (left channel) cables carry stereo sound. Some TV tuners accept RCA for recording from VCRs.
	S-Video	Some TV tuners and some TVs	This cable, usually black, carries high-quality video, but no sound. Many TV tuners accept S-Video for recording from VCRs and DVD players.
	HDMI (High-Definition Multimedia Interface)	Some video cards, monitors, and TVs	This single cable carries both "surround sound" and high-definition video to a TV or monitor.
	DVI (Digital Visual Interface)	Some video cards, monitors, and TVs	This cable carries high-quality video from computers to monitors or TV sets.

The Cable and Its Connectors	Its Name	Its Location	Its Purpose
	Optical/ Toslink	Some sound cards and home stereos	This carries Dolby AC-3 sound (sometimes called *multichannel*, *surround sound*, or *5.1)* but no video.
	Digital RCA	Some sound cards and home stereos	Like Optical/Toslink, this also carries Dolby AC-3 sound (sometimes called *multichannel*, *surround sound*, or *5.1)* but no video.

The problem with recording digital cable and satellite channels

If you subscribe to premium digital cable channels or satellite TV, I've got bad news: Those providers *encode* their TV signals to thwart thievery. Unscrambling the signal requires a special decoder which comes in two forms:

✔ A cable box that connects to your TV.

✔ A TV tuner for your PC that accepts *CableCARDs:* little gadgets issued by your cable company that slip into your PC's TV tuner to unscramble the signal.

Without a box or a CableCARD-equipped tuner, Windows Media Center can't unscramble the channels.

You can still record nonpremium channels entering your home, which are channels 2 through 99, as well as some locally aired HDTV shows. But most digital channels, usually channels 100 and above, must go through a cable box or CableCARD before entering your TV or PC.

One solution comes in the form of an infrared radiation (IR) control cable — a little infrared transmitter on a cable. You tape the IR transmitter over your cable box's IR receiver and plug the transmitter's other end into your computer's TV tuner. Then, when it's time to change channels and begin recording, Media Center tells the IR transmitter to tell the box to switch channels. As the channel pours in, your computer's tuner starts recording the unscrambled channel straight from the decoder box.

Not all TV tuners come with the Infrared control cable, however, and if yours doesn't, you're stuck with channels 2-99 and local HDTV shows.

Installing a USB TV Tuner

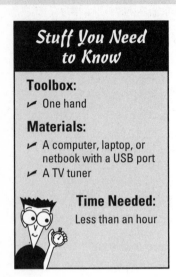

Stuff You Need to Know

Toolbox:
- One hand

Materials:
- A computer, laptop, or netbook with a USB port
- A TV tuner

Time Needed:
Less than an hour

TV tuners that plug into a USB port provide a great way to turn laptops into portable TV sets. USB tuners are also easy to install, and they're easily moved from one computer to another. (Keep an eye on your roommates.)

To install a USB TV tuner, follow these steps, and then head to an upcoming task, "Connecting Your TV Signal to Your Computer." Without a TV signal, you won't see any TV shows.

1. Unpack your TV tuner and find all the parts. The tuner itself has a USB plug on one end, and a coaxial cable port on the other. Look for a USB cable and a cable for connecting the tuner to your TV set, if desired. Some tuners also come with remote controls, as well as miniature antennas for pulling TV signals from the air.

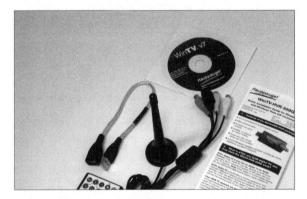

2. Slide the tuner's USB plug into a USB port. Windows usually recognizes newly installed USB devices and sets them up to work correctly. If you don't see the words "Device Installed Successfully," install the tuner's software, which should contain the right drivers. If you're still having trouble, head for Chapter 17 for quick-fix tips about installing drivers.

3. Visit the manufacturer's Web site and download the latest setup software for your model of TV tuner, and run that software instead of the CD included in the box. (It's more up-to-date.) Also, some TV tuners come with their own TV-viewing software. Instead of installing that bundled program, run a Windows Media Center Kit setup software, if you see one. The kit lets you control the tuner through Windows 7's Media Center, instead of the bundled viewer.

4. Set up the remote, if included. USB TV tuners usually have the receiver built into their box. Aim the remote control at the little box's built-in receiver when changing channels. (The built-in receiver is usually hidden by dark translucent plastic.) After you've installed the TV tuner, it's time to connect it to your TV signal, described in Chapter 3's task, "Connecting a TV to a PC or Laptop." (The video signal must come from your computer's *video card*, not the TV tuner.)

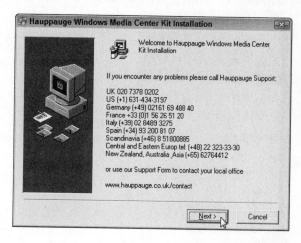

Finding Your PC's PCI-Express 1x and PCI Slots

Stuff You Need to Know

Toolbox:
✔ One screwdriver

Materials:
✔ A desktop computer

Time Needed:
Less than an hour

If you're planning on installing your TV tuner inside your desktop computer, you need to make sure your PC has the right slots — little plastic things where the card lives.

Every computer sold in the past ten years comes with PCI slots, so you're always safe buying that option. Chances are, your PC also has the slots preferred by the latest TV tuners, PCI-Express 1x. Follow these steps to locate one or both of those slots inside your computer so that you know exactly which type of tuner card you should buy for your PC.

1. Turn off your PC, unplug it, and remove your computer's case, as described in this book's Cheat Sheet, downloadable from www.dummies.com/cheatsheet/upgradingandfixingcomputersdiy.

PCI-Express 1x slots   PCI slots

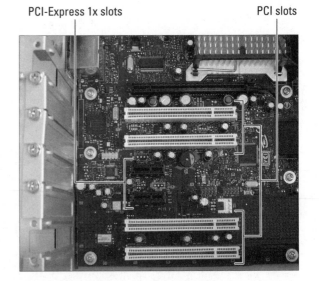

2. Examine the row of parallel slots inside your PC. The tiniest slots, about an inch long, are PCI-Express 1x slots. (They're often black.) The adjacent slots, about three times as long, are usually PCI slots. (They're often white.) The longest slot is usually a PCI-Express 16x slot, almost always reserved for video cards, which I cover in Chapter 9.

TIP

If you find both type of slots, you're exceptionally lucky: You can install a TV tuner card built for either PCI slots or PCI-Express 1x slots, as well as USB tuners. No little PCI-Express 1x slots in your PC? Then you're limited to PCI slot cards or USB add-ons.

Installing an Internal TV Tuner

The more powerful tuners, especially those with two or more tuners, usually come on cards. Before shopping, complete the preceding task, "Finding Your PC's PCI-Express 1x and PCI Slots," so you know which type of card to buy.

To install a TV tuner, follow these steps:

1. Turn off your PC, unplug it, and remove your computer's case, as described in this book's Cheat Sheet, downloadable from www.dum mies.com/cheatsheet/upgradingandfixingcomputersdiy.

2. Find an empty PCI or PCI-Express 1x slot to match your TV tuner card. Then remove the empty slot's metal backplate by removing the single screw that holds the backplate in place. Then, lift out the little plate. (Save the screw, as you need it to secure the new sound card in place.)

3. Push the card into the appropriate slot, either PCI-Express 1x or PCI. Hold the card by its edges and position it over the appropriate empty slot. The edge with the shiny metal bracket faces toward the *back* of your computer. Line up the tabs and notches on the card's bottom edge with the notches in the slot. Push the card slowly into the slot. You may need to rock the card back and forth gently. When the card pops in, you can feel it come to rest. Don't force it!

4. Secure the card in the slot with the screw you removed in Step 2. If you drop the screw, be sure to fish it out of your computer's case. You may have to pick up the case, turn it upside down, and shake it.

5. Plug the computer's power cord back into the wall and PC, turn on your PC, and see whether Windows recognizes and installs the card. Windows usually recognizes newly installed cards and sets them up to work correctly. If something goes wrong, head for Chapter 17 for tips about installing drivers. If everything's working, however, put your PC's cover back on.

6. Install the latest version of the card's drivers and software. When you turn on your computer again, Windows will announce that it's recognized the card, just as it does when you plug in a USB gadget, like an iPod. Whenever you install a new tuner card or any other card, visit the manufacturer's Web site. Find the site's Support or Customer Service section, and then download and install the latest drivers for that particular model and your version of Windows. Card manufacturers constantly update their drivers and software to fix bugs.

7. Install the IR receiver for the remote control, if needed. TV tuner cards that include handheld remote controls sometimes come with an IR receiver that give you something to aim at. The IR receiver is a thin cable with a jack on one end and little plastic receiver on the other end. Plug the cable's jack into the card's IR port, and then place the receiver within sight of where you'll point the remote. Once you've installed the TV tuner, it's time to connect it to your TV signal, described in the next task.

Connecting Your TV Signal to Your Computer

Stuff You Need to Know

Toolbox:
- Your hands
- A pair of pliers to loosen stubborn connections

Materials:
- A cable splitter
- Two coaxial TV cables

Time Needed:

Less than an hour

This part's easy, as the vast majority of TV tuners grab a TV signal only one way: through a *coaxial port* — a little threaded plug that lets you screw a connector onto it. If your room already has a coaxial cable poking out through the wall, screw it onto your tuner's coaxial port. That's it!

But if that coaxial cable's already being hogged by your TV or cable box, then you need a splitter — a little gadget that splits one cable into two, letting one end stay plugged into your TV or cable box, while the other plugs into your computer's tuner. They're available at nearly any store that sells TVs.

Installing a splitter is cheap, easy, and lets your TV work normally, even when your computer's recording a different channel.

Follow these steps to install a splitter, which magically turns one cable into two: One for your computer, and the other for your TV or cable box:

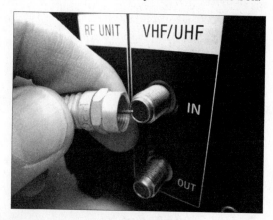

1. Unplug the coaxial cable from the RF or VHF\UHF "In" port on your TV or cable box. Found on the back of every TV and cable box, that port accepts the signal from a TV cable that runs from either the wall or an antenna. You may need a pair of pliers to loosen the connector from the port on the back of your TV or cable box; your fingers can handle the rest.

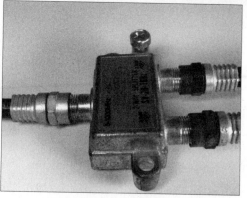

2. Screw the coaxial cable's connector into the end of the splitter with only one port (left). Coaxial cables should always screw onto a splitter; the push-on connectors tend to fall off. Then plug your two new coaxial cables onto each of the two ports on the splitter's other side (right).

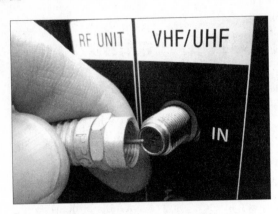 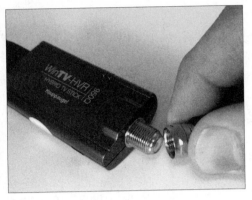

3. Plug one of your two new cables back into the spot where you unplugged it in Step 1, on either your TV or cable box (left). Then plug the other end into your TV tuner's coaxial port (right). The splitter then lets your TV keep its same connection, so it still receives the same channels. Plus, your computer receives all the channels, as well.

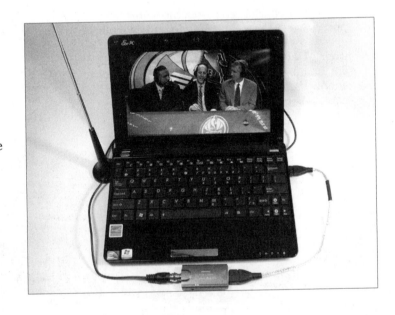

4. Fire up Windows Media Center, follow the setup screens to tell the program about your tuner, and start watching TV on your computer.

TIP

Want to watch your recorded shows on your television rather than your monitor? I describe how in Chapter 3's task, "Connecting a TV to a PC or Laptop."

Connecting Your Computer's High-Quality Sound to Your Home Theater

Most home stereos cost several hundred dollars more than the cheap desktop speakers sold with many computers today. If you watch a lot of DVDs on your computer and want surround sound — or you simply want higher-quality sound when listening to MP3s or playing games — this task explains how to connect your computer's sound to your stereo or home theater. (If you're connecting to your home theater through an HDMI cable, drop by Chapter 8, where you find a task that explains routing sound through an HDMI cable.)

Most of today's home stereos accept sound from up to three types of connectors: digital, optical, or analog RCA jacks. The key to success is finding the best sound source your sound card dishes up and connecting it to the best sound source accepted by your home stereo.

Follow these steps to connect your computer's sound to your home stereo:

1. Count the speakers connected to your home theater or stereo. If your stereo sends sound through a single pair of speakers, usually one speaker on each side of the TV, it's probably using *analog* sound. (I describe how to connect analog sound in Chapter 8's task, "Connecting Your PC's Sound to Your Home Stereo.") If your home theater pipes walls of sound through five or more speakers, however, it's probably using *digital* sound, which I describe how to connect here.

2. Discover the type of sound offered by your computer. Examine the sound jacks on the back of your computer. Most offer at least two of these three connectors: Optical/Toslink (digital, left) resembles a square hole. Sometimes it's called an *optical* connector. When not in use, the hole's usually plugged with a small plastic cover that pulls off with a little effort. Coaxial/RCA (digital, middle) is sometimes called an S/PDIF or digital coaxial connector. A ⅛-inch port (analog, right), like the kind you plug headphones into, is limited to stereo sound, which I describe in Chapter 8.

3. Examine the back of your stereo to find its Audio In jacks. If you have only two speakers connected to your home stereo, you'll probably spot a pair of RCA Audio In jacks (left). If you have more than two speakers, you'll probably find either a Toslink (middle) or a single RCA connector (right).

4. Connect the matching digital cable between the matching ports on your computer's sound card and your stereo. You'll need to buy whichever digital cable matches the digital ports on both your computer and home stereo, Optical/Toslink or RCA. Stuck with a Toslink connector on your computer's sound card and an RCA connector on your home stereo — or vice versa? Pick up a Toslink/RCA converter from RAM Electronics (`www.ramelectronics.net`) or a stereo store. For less than $30, the little converter box lets the two connect.

5. Most stereos let you hear sound from a variety of gadgets: CD/DVD players, radios, iPods, or even record players. To hear your computer's sound, turn your home stereo's input selector knob to Line In — or the name of the jack where you plugged in your computer's sound cable. If you've plugged in a digital connection, you may need to flip a switch on your stereo to Digital mode.

6. Play music through your computer at a low volume, and then slowly turn up the volume on your stereo. You'll probably want to control the volume at your computer because that's within reach. So turn the volume up on your stereo, and leave your computer set fairly low. Then, as you turn up the volume on your computer, your stereo will grow louder, as well. Play around with the volume settings for a while until you find the right mix. If the computer's too loud and the stereo's too low, you'll hear distortion. If the stereo's too loud and the computer's too low, you'll blast your ears when you turn up the sound on your computer.

Chapter 12

Upgrading a Computer for Editing Movies

No longer the shoulder-toted boxes of yesteryear, camcorders now live inside most digital cameras and cellphones, transforming everybody into a cinematographer. Old-school vacationers probably still have a few old camcorder tapes lying around.

But whether you created your movies yesterday or years ago, you're probably waiting for enough time to edit them into treasured keepsakes, storing them on DVDs for everybody to enjoy.

Editing takes a lot of time, but taking the essential first step — copying the video into your computer — doesn't take much time at all.

This chapter tackles the problem of moving your video out of its current receptacle and into your computer for storage. Actually, those old video tapes may be deteriorating, so your deadline for moving old video into your computer could be sooner than you think. See the sidebar, "Capturing sound and video from old camcorders," in this chapter. You also find help if you want to upgrade a computer so it can handle video editing.

Transferring Movies and Photos from a Camera or Camcorder to a Computer

Stuff You Need to Know

Toolbox:
- Your hands

Materials:
- Digital camera or camcorder
- USB or FireWire cable
- A computer

Time Needed:
Less than an hour

Digital cameras and digital camcorders cooperate with your computer quite easily. As you film the action, the digital camcorder packs both the video and sound into a single file; your digital camera does the same thing with your snapshots.

That leaves the problem of moving the file from the camcorder to the computer. Luckily, many modern camcorders store their images on a memory card, easily read by a memory card reader that plugs into a USB port.

Other camcorders plug into one of these two jacks on your computer:

- **USB cable:** Many digital camcorders and cameras use the ever-popular USB port, found on every computer, be it desktop, laptop, or even a tiny netbook.

- **FireWire:** Some techies refer to FireWire as "IEEE 1394," but both refer to the same port. Unfortunately, many computers lack a FireWire port. The solution? Buy a FireWire card and install it inside your computer. (FireWire cards install the same way as dial-up modem cards, covered in Chapter 14.) Laptop owners can install a FireWire adapter card that slides into a PCMCIA slot. Netbook owners, unfortunately, are left out of the FireWire camp altogether.

To copy digital video into your computer from a camera or digital camcorder, follow these steps:

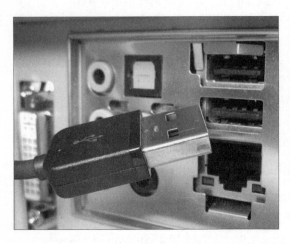 

1. Connect a cable between your digital video camera's or camcorder's Data or Digital I/O port and your computer's USB port (left) or FireWire port (right). Then set the camera to either Play or View mode rather than Shoot mode. When your camera connects for the first time, Windows may say it's installing drivers.

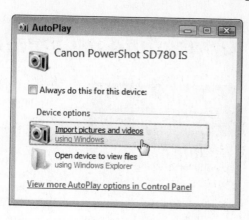

2. When the Autoplay window appears, click the words Import Video or Import Pictures and Videos.

3. When the Import Pictures and Videos box appears, click the words Import Settings to fetch the Import Settings window.

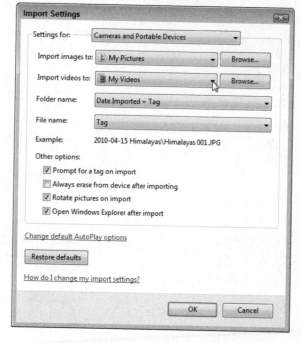

4. Make sure you approve of the settings in the Import Settings window. For example, Windows 7 normally dumps your camera's photos *and* videos into the same folder in your *Pictures* library. If you'd prefer to see your videos moved into a folder in your *Videos* library instead, choose that option from the Import Videos To drop-down menu. Also, to keep your camera from filling up with old images, feel free to select Always Erase from Device After Importing. Click OK to return to the Import Pictures and Videos window.

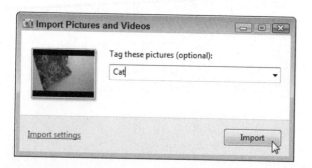

5. In the Import Pictures and Videos window's Tag These Pictures box, type a short name that describes the video or photos you're importing, and then click Import. Depending on the settings you've chosen, Windows 7 grabs the videos and photos from your camera and places them into your Pictures library — or Videos library if you chose that option — with your chosen name. After importing your files, the program ends by showing you a Search window displaying your newly imported videos and pictures.

Upgrading a Computer for Video Editing

If your computer's able to run Windows 7 with its 3-D graphics and transparent windows, then your computer can probably stand up to the rigors of video editing. Still, you can speed things up and make your work easier by upgrading a few key areas of your computer.

- **Two hard drives:** One drive stores Windows 7, of course, as well as your photo-editing program. But it should also be big enough to hold your imported video, which consumes 16GB for each hour. And if you plan on importing professional-quality, uncompressed high-definition video, count on filling up 40GB or more per hour. Then add a second drive to store your *edited* video, which also grabs a massive amount of hard drive space. Buy a drive with a fast *transfer speed,* as I explain in Chapter 6, so the drive will store the incoming video quickly, without gaps.

- **Video capture device:** Most modern camcorders connect to your computer through a USB or FireWire port. Older videos, however, need a video capture box. The box plugs into your computer's USB or FireWire port, and your camera plugs into the box. As you play back the video on your camera, your computer records it. (Some TV tuners, described in Chapter 11, can grab video coming in through an S-Video or RCA port, if your camcorder offers that option.)

- **Fast CPU:** The faster your computer's central processing unit (CPU), the faster your computer will be able to turn your edited video into a polished movie. When it's time for a new CPU, though, it's time for a new computer.

- **Video-editing software:** Microsoft's free Windows Live Movie Maker program at `http://download.live.com/moviemaker` works for editing small movies. For more creative control, Sony's Vegas Movie Studio software has a popular following. You may also find a deal on Adobe Premiere Elements, which often comes bundled with Photoshop Elements in special deals online or at discount stores.

The steps in this task let you see where your computer falls short so that you know what to upgrade.

1. Run Windows Experience Index by clicking the Start menu, right-clicking Computer, and choosing Properties.

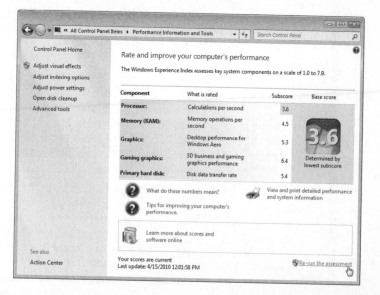

2. Then click the words Windows Experience Index. Meant as an easy way for showroom shoppers to assess a computer's strengths and weaknesses, the index tests your computer, and then rates its strengths on a scale of 1 to 5.9. (Windows Vista's index ranked computers on a scale of 1 to 7.9.)

3. If you've upgraded your computer lately, click Rerun the Assessment. Windows 7 will reassess your computer's performance and update the scores.

4. Look at the overall performance index — the large numbers in the square box. If your computer's rated 3 or below, it can probably play some high-definition video, but might have problems editing it. Consider this a warning flag.

5. Check the score for your computer's processor, also known as its CPU. If it's rated 4 or 5, you can edit most video without problems. But to edit *high-definition* video without problems, you'll want a processor rated at least 6 or 7. Unfortunately, it's usually cheaper to buy a new computer than upgrade your computer's processor or motherboard.

6. Look for your lowest score in any of the five categories. Your computer's lowest score in any of the five categories — Processor, Memory (RAM), Graphics, Gaming Graphics, and Primary Hard Disk — drops your computer's overall score to that level. After all, your computer's only as strong as its weakest link. So, find the lowest score, and start upgrading those parts first. (Don't worry about your computer's Gaming Graphics score, though, as that rates something called 3D Acceleration, which isn't used in video editing.) I describe how to upgrade memory in Chapter 5, graphics in Chapter 9, and hard drives in Chapter 6.

Can't afford a new computer or upgrades? Your old computer will still be able to import and edit video, but at a slower pace. Be prepared for delays while you work, waiting for your computer to catch up. When you've completed your edits, you might need to let your computer run all night to compile your edits into a finished video, ready for burning to DVD.

Capturing sound and video from old camcorders

Windows 7 doesn't offer a built-in way to grab video from older DV (digital video) tape camcorders. That requires a separate video-editing program for controlling the camera through a digital video cable, either USB or FireWire.

To grab those old digital movies, Microsoft's free Windows Live Movie Maker program at http://download.live.com/moviemaker might be all you need. I describe how to download, install, and use the program to import, edit, and burn your video to DVDs in *Windows 7 For Dummies* (Wiley).

If you have an even older 8mm or Hi8 camcorder, then you're in for even more work. Unlike digital camcorders, those older camcorders didn't convert their video into numbers as they recorded your vacations. That makes it harder to move the camcorder's

video onto your number-lovin' computer. The solution is a *video capture device* — a box that plugs into your computer's USB port. (Some TV tuners include a Video In option for camcorders and VCRs, as I describe in Chapter 11.)

Another option, welcomed by people with footage recorded by parents or grandparents, is to drop off the film reels or tape cartridges at a film conversion service. Many film developers and digital photo processors offer the service.

Don't delay. Those older formats don't last forever, and neither does the equipment required to play them back. By bringing them into a modern, digital format, you're helping ensure their enjoyment by your children and relatives.

Chapter 13

Repurposing an Old Computer

State laws classify computers as hazardous waste and forbid tossing computers into the trash. So, what do you do with the old computer after you buy a new one?

You can donate it to charity, of course, and take a tax deduction. But with a little creativity, you can also salvage a lot of its parts and functionality, which is where this chapter comes in. It turns you into a recycler in the truest sense of the word, taking your old computer's pieces and giving them a new life.

The tasks in this chapter describe how to add a second monitor for your desktop, and how to create a portable hard drive, a second drive for your main computer, or a backup unit to keep your work safely duplicated.

If you'd rather donate the computer to a friend or to charity, a final task describes how to cleanse your hard drive of all traces of your personal information: passwords, credit card numbers, and other things you don't want falling into the wrong hands.

Adding a Second Monitor to Your New Computer

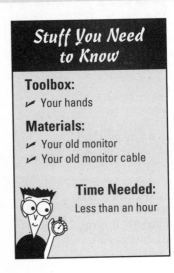

Stuff You Need to Know

Toolbox:

✔ Your hands

Materials:

✔ Your old monitor
✔ Your old monitor cable

Time Needed:

Less than an hour

Just as a larger closet can hold more goodies, an expanded desktop lets you place more information within your view. Adding a second monitor lets you double your desktop, letting you work on one monitor while eyeballing your reference materials on the other. You can double the size of your cockpit in the latest flight simulator. Or you can keep Facebook or Twitter running on your spare monitor to keep up with your friends.

Here's how to put your old monitor to work as a second monitor on your main computer or laptop:

1. Unplug the old monitor from your old computer. I describe monitors and their connectors in Chapter 3's task on connecting a monitor to your PC or laptop.

2. Plug your old monitor into your new netbook, laptop, or computer, which I describe in the Chapter 3 task about attaching a second monitor to a computer or laptop. No video port for it on your other computer? Then pluck your old monitor's video card and install it into your new computer, too. Or upgrade to a new video card that has two video ports (I describe both chores in Chapter 6).

3. Tell Windows about your second monitor: Right-click a blank part of the desktop and choose Screen Resolution to see both displays listed onscreen. Click the Detect button if Windows can't find the second monitor. Then click the icon representing your main monitor and choose Make This My Main Display to choose which monitor should display your Start button and taskbar.

4. On that same screen, drag and drop the onscreen monitors until they resemble the way you've arranged them on your real desk. You can tell Windows to spread the desktop to the left or to the right, depending on how you've arranged your two monitors. Or, if you work on long spreadsheets, stack the two monitors on top of each other with a shelf to double your rows of numbers. Then click OK to save your monitor arrangement.

Creating a Portable Hard Drive from Your Old Hard Drive

Portable hard drives are *very* handy to have around. They're great for backing up files, moving information from one computer to another, or simply serving as storage spots for those large files you don't want cluttering up your main computer's hard drive.

This task explains how to remove your old computer's hard drive, slip it into a small case, and turn it into a portable hard drive, all for the cost of the case (usually under $30). Your new portable hard drive will work with any type of computer, be it a netbook, laptop, or desktop. (It will even work with an Apple computer, if you've walked down that path.)

You can reuse the hard drive from either a desktop computer or laptop.

To create a portable hard drive from your old computer's hard drive, follow these steps:

1. See whether your old hard drive uses SATA (right) or IDE (left) connectors so that you can buy the right type of case. I describe how to determine your type of hard drive in Chapter 6.

2. Buy either a SATA or an IDE portable hard drive enclosure that fits the size of your drive, either desktop or laptop. If you're using a laptop's drive, buy a case meant for the smaller 2½-inch drives; desktop drives need cases for the standard 3½-inch drives. (They're always a bit larger than that, so don't fret if yours aren't exactly 2½ or 3½ inches.) More expensive enclosures come with more padding, saving them from the hard knocks of travel. Cooling fans add to the cost, as well, but help the drive last longer, especially if it's meant to run constantly.

3. Remove your old computer's hard drive; it's held in place by two cables and either two or four screws. I describe how to remove a hard drive in Chapter 6, in the task about upgrading or replacing your Windows drive.

4. Take apart the portable hard drive enclosure. The enclosure consists of two main parts: A long rectangular box and a detachable connector on one end. It will also come with a power supply and a USB cable that plugs between the box and your computer's USB port. Plus, you'll find a few screws for holding the drive in place and putting the enclosure together.

5. Connect your old drive to the enclosure's connectors, fastening both its power cable and its data cable. The two cables fit into their proper spots only, and they fit only one way — the right way. I describe how to plug in a drive's cables in Chapter 6, in the task about adding a second internal drive.

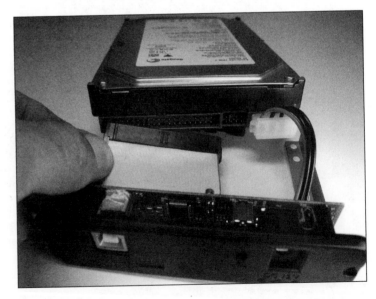

6. Screw the drive into place on the connector's rails, slide the drive into the large enclosure, and screw the enclosure together with the bundled screws.

7. Plug your new portable hard drive's adapter into the wall, plug the power adapter cable into the portable drive box, and then plug the portable drive's USB cable into your computer's USB port. Finally, turn your drive on with the enclosure's On switch. The drive will soon appear as a new letter and drive icon in your Start menu's Computer window. Double-click it to see inside.

If the drive doesn't show up, it's probably a new drive that hasn't been partitioned or formatted. That problem's easily cured by following the steps in Chapter 6, in the task about partitioning and formatting a second internal drive.

Recycling your old computer equipment

It's just not right to throw your unwanted computer parts into the trash anymore. In fact, it's illegal in some states.

To stem the flow of toxic trash, many cities offer recycling centers where you can drop off or mail in your unloved gadgetry. It could be as simple as dropping off your old cell phone at a local library.

For the most up-to-date information about recycling programs in your area, visit the US Government's Environmental Protection Agency's Web site at `http://www.epa.gov/wastes/conserve/materials/ecycling/donate.htm`.

There, you'll find lists of recyclers in your area, ways to recycle old batteries, and local retailers who accept parts for recycling.

Removing the Old Hard Drive and Adding It to Your Main Computer

Stuff You Need to Know

Toolbox:
- Your hands
- A screwdriver

Materials:
- Your old hard drive
- An IDE to SATA adapter, if necessary

Time Needed:
Less than an hour

If you don't want to bother with a portable hard drive enclosure, take a simpler route: Remove your old computer's hard drive and install it into your new computer. It's easy, involving a screwdriver and unplugging and plugging two cables.

With your old drive inside your new computer, you can easily fetch any important files you want to transfer to your new computer's main drive. And after you've transferred everything that you need, you can erase the old hard drive and use it for extra storage or backups.

This task explains how to remove your old computer's hard drive and install it into your new computer with a total project cost of zero dollars.

1. Remove your computer's old hard drive as described in Chapter 6, in the task about upgrading or replacing your Windows drive.

2. Examine both your old hard drive's connectors and your new computer's connectors to see if they match. If they don't, you need an adapter. Because older computers came with IDE connectors and most new computers use SATA connectors, you might need an IDE-to-SATA adapter, which costs about $15 from Amazon (www.amazon.com) or NewEgg (www.newegg.com).

3. Install the old drive into your new computer, as described in Chapter 6, in the task about adding a second internal drive. If necessary, plug an IDE-to-SATA adapter into your old drive's connector so it can plug into a SATA cable.

Turning Your Old Computer into a Backup Unit

Stuff You Need to Know

Toolbox:
- ✔ Your hands

Materials:
- ✔ Your old computer
- ✔ Your new computer
- ✔ A network linking the two

Time Needed:
Less than an hour

Still using your old computer occasionally? Then don't scrap it for parts. Instead, set up a network between your old and new computers. Then, back up your new computer onto your old computer's hard drive. That gives you not only a backup plan, but leaves you with a second computer for light computing tasks.

To back up your main PC to your old computer, follow these steps:

1. Set up a network between your new and old computers (as explained in Chapter 15). You can connect them either with cables or wirelessly, depending on the distance between your two computers and your broadband Internet source.

2. After transferring your files from your old computer to your new computer (explained in Chapter 20), free up as much space as possible on your old computer: delete your old files, purge any unneeded user accounts from your old computer, and empty your Recycle Bin.

3. Set up Windows Backup on your new computer, telling it to store the backup on your old computer. (I explain how to create a system image backup in Chapter 6, in the task about backing up your Windows drive with a system image.)

4. Check your backup to make sure it's successful.

TIP

Backups grow larger as you create more information with your new computer. Make sure your old computer has enough space to store it all; you may need to add a larger hard drive, as described in the Chapter 6 task about adding a second internal drive.

Cleansing Your Old Computer's Personal Information Before Passing It On

Stuff You Need to Know

Toolbox:

⟋ Your hands

Materials:

⟋ A copy of Darik's Boot and Nuke free software
⟋ Your Windows 7 computer
⟋ A blank CD
⟋ Any computer with personal data you want to delete from its hard drives

Time Needed:

Less than half a day

After a few years, you've filled your computer with passwords, credit card numbers, and other information you'd rather not share with the world. And in these days of quickly copied Internet information, giving your old computer to a charity, a friend, or simply leaving it in the alley is the same as giving that information to the world.

Simply deleting all your drive's files or even reformatting the drive won't irrevocably delete all its information. Data recovery specialists, including thieves, can still recover the files.

To purge your drive of all its information, you need to overwrite your old information with new information. The best data killers overwrite your data *seven* times, but that's probably overkill unless you're James Bond. The solution is a free program called Darik's Boot and Nuke. Burn the program to a CD, insert the CD into your old computer, and push the restart button: When your old computer comes to life, the program will purge all traces of your data on your old computer's hard drive or drives.

If you can find your old computer's copy of Windows, dig it out and reinstall Windows after wiping your old computer's hard drive clean. (That makes the computer much more valuable to charities.)

If you're ready to donate or sell your old computer and its hard drives, follow these steps to create the Darik's Boot and Nuke CD with your Windows 7 computer. Then you'll run the program on your old computer to wipe away all your old information:

Don't use this program unless you're ready to wipe out any and all information stored on *all* the hard drives inside your computer. There's no going back from this point.

1. With your Windows 7 computer, download a copy of Darik's Boot and Nuke (`www.dban.org/download`). The program erases all the information on any hard drive it finds inside your computer. It says it won't erase information stored on *external* hard drives — drives plugged into a USB port, for example — but unplug them anyway, just to be safe.

2. Unzip the Darik's Boot and Nuke program by right-clicking it and choosing Extract All from the pop-up menu. (The program was called `dban-2.2.6_i586.iso` on my computer; its name will probably have changed slightly.)

3. Create the Boot and Nuke bootable CD: Open your Downloads folder, right-click the extracted Boot and Nuke file (`dban-beta.2006 042900_i386.iso`), and choose Burn Image. Insert a blank CD into your CD or DVD drive, click Burn, and then wait until the computer finishes creating the bootable disc. When it's done, label the disc "Darik's Boot and Nuke" so you won't use it accidentally.

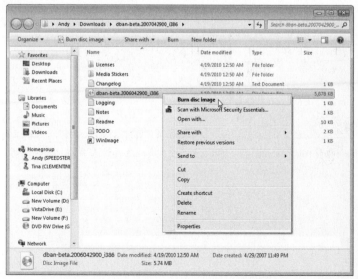

4. Insert the bootable CD into your old computer's disc drive, and restart your old computer.

```
Darik's Boot and Nuke

Warning: This software irrecoverably destroys data.

This software is provided without any warranty; without even the implied
warranty of merchantability or fitness for a particular purpose. In no event
shall the software authors or contributors be liable for any damages arising
from the use of this software.  This software is provided "as is".

http://www.dban.org/

* Press the F2 key to learn about DBAN.
* Press the F3 key for a list of quick commands.
* Press the F4 key for troubleshooting hints.
* Press the ENTER key to start DBAN in interactive mode.
* Enter autonuke at this prompt to start DBAN in automatic mode.

boot: autonuke
```

5. When your computer boots from the Boot and Nuke CD, type **autonuke** and press Enter. The program begins overwriting your entire drive, leaving it completely covered with random numbers. After you wipe the drive clean, reinstall your copy of Windows, if you have one, place your original Windows CD into the box with your PC, and ship them both to a charity, knowing your TurboTax files won't fall into the hands of strangers.

Part IV
Communications

The 5th Wave   By Rich Tennant

"So I guess you forgot to tell me to strip out the components before drilling for blowholes."

In this part . . .

Windows 7 loves to chat. As soon as you install or upgrade to Windows 7, it tries to connect with the Internet and announce its presence.

Windows 7 is ready to talk to any other computers sitting in your home or office, as well. Don't want to string networking cables around the house? Windows 7 is content to chatter through the airwaves — it includes built-in support for wireless networking.

This part of the book shows you how to install or upgrade your modem for dialup Internet access, as well as send and receive faxes. You find out how to set up your own home network, and add wireless access so that you can check your e-mail while you're gardening.

And if you're ready to sooth your paranoia level a notch, Chapter 16 shows you how to make sure Windows 7's firewall keeps your computer safely protected with a burning ring of fire.

Chapter 14

Adding or Replacing a Modem

Windows keeps a constant finger on the Internet's pulse, so the Internet is no longer a luxury but a necessity. As soon as you turn on your computer, Windows eagerly downloads security patches, as well as updated drivers and help menus. Windows even drops by Microsoft's Web site occasionally to make sure you've paid for your copy of Windows.

Because Windows clings to the Internet so tightly, it's understandable that nearly every computer sold in the past few years includes some type of *modem* — a gadget that sends and receives digital information.

Dialup Internet subscribers are no strangers to modems. Subscribers to speedy broadband Internet service providers (ISPs), both cable and DSL, need slightly different types of modems.

This chapter explains how to choose and install a modem that's compatible with your type of Internet service. As a bonus, it tackles the modern-day survival issue: How to fire up your computer's old dialup modem in times of desperate Internet need.

Choosing a Compatible Modem

Internet service providers — the companies you pay for the privilege of connecting to the Internet — come rated largely by how quickly they spew information to and from your computer. Unfortunately, you can't simply pick the fastest: You're stuck with whatever services are offered in your area, and the modems those services require.

Here's a rundown of the three most common types of Internet connections available today: dialup, cable, and DSL, as well as their required modems.

After you connect to the Internet, you can share that connection with all of your household's computers with a *router* and a *network,* both covered in Chapter 15.

Dialup or POTS (Plain Old Telephone Service)

Three types of people still cling to dialup modems: those living in rural areas with no alternatives, those living on very low budgets, and survivalists who can't find connections any other way.

Dialup Internet service doesn't cost much, it's slow, and the modem hogs a phone line, keeping others from calling in or out when you're online. But when Wi-Fi or network hookups aren't around, you can almost always find a telephone. In fact, when the power's out, dialup might be the *only* Internet connection that still works: Phone lines don't require power, so they usually stay alive during power failures.

Any modem sold today that says "dialup" on the box will work with dialup Internet service providers, and most of today's dialup modems also offer the perk of being able to send and receive faxes. They come in two models: External dialup modems plug into either a USB port (common) or a serial port (rare). Internal modems plug into a PCI slot inside your PC. I describe how to install both types in tasks later in this chapter.

Cable modems

Your cable company sends the Internet rushing into your home through the same coaxial cable that carries your TV shows.

In most areas, setting up cable service works like this: A cable techie drops by your house or office to install a network card in your computer (if it needs one), split your cable TV signal, and hook one end of the cable to a cable modem, which you rent for a monthly fee. After the cable modem is connected to your computer's network card, your computer can connect to the Internet at blistering speeds.

Best yet, the family can still watch cable TV or listen to cable radio at the same time you're blazing around the Internet.

If you want to buy your *own* cable modem to avoid the monthly rental fee, you must buy a cable modem that's guaranteed to work with your cable company, as cable companies are picky. The only way to see which modems are approved is to call the cable company or browse its Web site for compatible modems.

Don't buy used modems at garage sales or auctions; modem technology changes quickly, and cable companies require newly updated modems every few years.

After you've bought a compatible modem, it lives outside your computer, plugged into a power outlet, connected to the cable company's cable, and connected to your computer through a network port. I describe it all in this chapter's task, "Installing a Broadband (Cable or DSL) Modem."

DSL (Digital Subscriber Line)

DSL offers a different broadband modem that attempts to squeeze more information through your home's tiny copper phone lines. DSL modems work more than ten times faster than dialup modems, which run through the same phone lines.

The downside? DSL modems are usually slower than cable modems. Plus, they work only if you live near a phone-switching station, and the closer you live to the station, the faster your connection. Some people ask a realtor if a house is near good schools. Others ask if it's close to a phone-switching station. If your realtor shrugs, call your phone company and give them the address.

Baud, bps, Kbps, Mbps, and other tidbits

Modem speed is measured in *bps* (bits per second). Some people measure modem speed in baud rate, a term that only engineers really understand.

If you see the term *Kbps*, it's the metric system way of saying, thousands (Kilo) of bits per second or 56K.

With the advent of broadband technologies like the cable modem, a new unit of measure arose: 1 Mbps means roughly 1,000 kilobits, or roughly a million bits per second.

All you need to know is the bigger the number, the faster your computer can access the Internet.

Installing an External Dialup Modem

Dialup modems plug into a port on your computer, making them the easiest type of modem to install. Most plug into your USB port; older models plug into your computer's serial port. (My SupraFax serial port dialup modem from 1994 still works fine.)

To install an external modem, follow these steps:

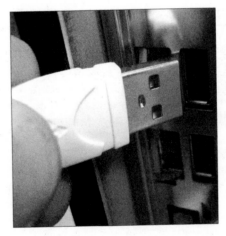 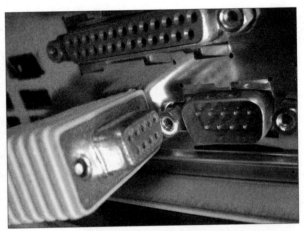

1. Plug either your new modem or its cable into your computer's USB port (left) or serial port (right), depending on its connection. Most modems plug into a USB port. If the plug doesn't push easily into the port, turn the plug upside down and try again. (Only friction holds the USB plug in place.)

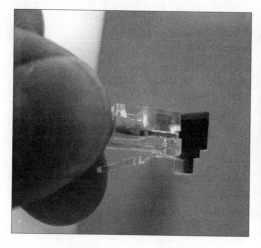 

2. Plug one end of your phone line into your wall's phone jack (left), and the other end into the jack on your modem (right). If your modem has *two* phone jacks, the phone jack labeled "Line" is for your telephone cable, and the one labeled "Phone" is for an optional telephone. No labels on your two jacks? Then just guess at which line plugs into which jack. If the modem or your phone doesn't work, swap the two plugs. (Having them wrong at first doesn't harm anything.)

3. If your modem plugs into a serial port (refer to Step 1, right), plug its power adapter into an outlet. Then turn on the modem's power switch. Modems that plug into a USB port don't need power.

4. As soon as you turn on your newly plugged-in modem, Windows should recognize it and set it up for use. If Windows 7 starts asking for drivers, now's the time to insert the CD that came with your modem and let Windows install the drivers. (I cover driver mishaps in Chapter 17.)

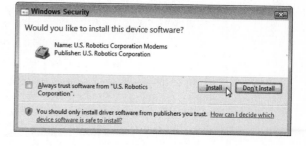

5. When you're through, tell Windows 7 your ISP's dialup phone number, username, and password, a subject I cover in this chapter's "Helping Windows 7 Set Up a Dialup Modem" task.

Installing an Internal Dialup Modem

Stuff You Need to Know

Toolbox:
- One hand
- Screwdriver

Materials:
- Dialup modem on a PCI card

Time Needed:
Less than an hour

Adding an internal modem takes a bit of work. You need to open your computer's case, push the new modem into an empty slot, screw the modem in place, and replace your computer's case. Don't want to bother? Then plug an external modem into a USB port, a far simpler chore described in the preceding task.

But if you're willing to open your computer's case, an internal modem is a wise investment. Internal modems cost less than half the price of external modems, and they're usually better quality. Plus, they never get lost, and you can't step on them, as you can with those tiny USB modems.

To install a modem inside your desktop computer, follow these steps:

1. Turn off your PC, unplug it, and remove your computer's case, as described in this book's Cheat Sheet, downloadable from www.dummies.com/cheatsheet/upgradingandfixingcomputersdiy. If you're adding a new internal modem — not replacing your old one — jump to Step 4. Otherwise, proceed to Step 2.

2. Look inside your computer and find your existing modem living in a plastic slot on your computer's flat, circuit-filled motherboard. See that row of metal slots toward the back of your computer's case? Those metal slots are where you plug in many of your computer's cables. Look to see where you plug in your phone cable — that's the back end of your internal modem card; the bottom of the card rests inside a slot.

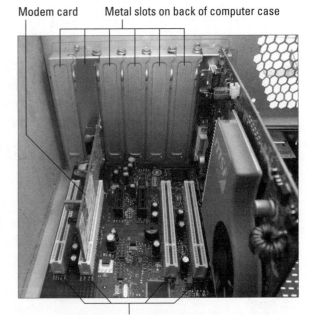

Modem card   Metal slots on back of computer case

Plastic slots on motherboard

3. Remove your old modem card. With a small screwdriver, remove the single screw that holds that card in place. Save that screw, as you need it to secure the new card in place. After you remove the screw, only friction holds the card in its slot. Pull up on the card until it pops out of the slot. If you're adding a new card to an empty slot, remove the screw holding the cover in place and then remove the cover.

4. Push the new card into its slot. Line up the tabs and notches on the card's bottom with the notches in the slot. Push the card slowly into the slot. You may need to rock the card back and forth gently. When the card pops in, you can feel it come to rest. Don't force it!

TIP

If you drop the screw inside your computer, poke it out with a screwdriver or chopstick. If that fails, shake your computer upside down until the screw falls out.

5. Secure the card in the slot with the screw you removed in Step 3. Yep, those delicate electronics are held in place by one screw.

6. Replace the computer's case, plug the computer back in, and turn it on. Windows usually recognizes newly installed cards and sets them up to work correctly. If your modem came with a CD, be sure to insert it when Windows 7 begins clamoring for *drivers* — translation software that helps Windows 7 talk to new parts.

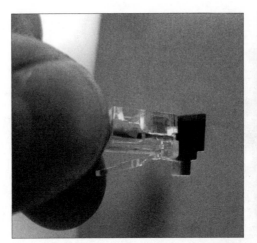 

7. Connect a phone cable from the modem's Line jack to the phone jack in the wall. If you need a place to plug in your telephone, plug it into the modem's second phone jack — the one with the icon of the phone next to it.

Helping Windows 7 Set Up a Dialup Modem

After you've installed your dialup modem, you're not quite through. Whether you've plugged the modem inside your computer, plugged it into a USB port, or you're using a dialup modem already built into your computer, you still need to tell it the magic words that give you a connection.

And for dialup modems, those magic words are your ISP's dialup phone number, your username, and your password. (The username and password are usually the same as the ones you use for your e-mail.)

1. Click Start, choose Control Panel, and choose Connect to the Internet from the Network and Internet category.

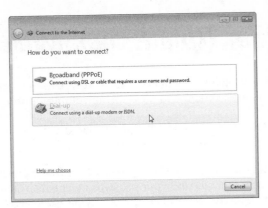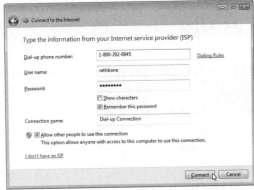

2. When the Connect to the Internet window appears, choose Dialup (left). Then enter your ISP's dialup phone number, your user name, and password (right). The username and password are usually the same as the ones used for your e-mail address. To make the connection available to everybody with an account on your computer, select Allow Other People to Use This Connection.

3. Load your Web browser and marvel at how long a Web page takes to fill the screen. Dialup access is slow, but it's better than nothing.

Do you need to enter a special number to reach an outside line? Then click Dialing Rules, enter your area code and carrier code or outside line prefix, and then click OK. Finally, click OK to save your changes.

Installing a Broadband (Cable or DSL) Modem

Stuff You Need to Know

Toolbox:

✔ One hand

Materials:

✔ A broadband modem compatible with your ISP
✔ A coaxial (cable) or phone (DSL) cable coming out from the wall
✔ A telephone to call your cable company

Time Needed:

Less than an hour

Perhaps your ISP mailed you a new modem, with hints on how to install it. Maybe you're tired of paying your cable company a monthly rental fee for its cable modem, and you want to buy your own. Or perhaps your ISP sent you a notice saying your old modem must be replaced with a newer model. Either way, this task is for you.

If you're installing a cable modem, drop by your ISP's Web site to see when their technical support department is open. *You must talk with your cable company's technical support people before your modem will work.*

If you're installing a cable modem that contains a built-in router, it still installs the same way I describe here. Later, where I describe how to install a router in Chapter 15, you can conveniently ignore the step that says to attach a cable between the modem and the router: Yours is already attached!

1. Visit your ISP's Web site to see what modems it accepts, as not all broadband modems work with every provider. Then buy a modem brand and model that's compatible. You'll find many modems available online at Amazon (www.amazon.com) or NewEgg (www.newegg.com). If your city has offered cable service for a year or so, you may find also cable modems available at computer stores and even home stereo stores.

2. Choose a time to install the modem. If your cable company's open from 8 a.m.–5 p.m. only, for example, install the modem during those hours, as you'll need to call and ask them to authorize your modem. If your company offers 24-hour technical support, replace your modem in the late evenings or weekends so that you don't have to wait on hold so long.

3. Turn off the power to your computer and modem, unplugging the modem's adapter from the wall. Then plug the new modem's adapter into the wall and set the new modem next to your old modem.

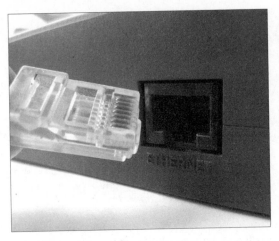

4. Unplug the cables from your old modem and plug them into the same spots on your new modem. You'll find two cables: a network cable (left) and a coaxial cable (right). The jacks fit only one way — the right way. (If you're installing a DSL modem, you'll insert a telephone cable instead of a coaxial cable. Don't put the DSL filter on the line that plugs into your modem!)

5. Turn on your new modem and turn on your computer. Don't panic when your new cable modem doesn't work. It's not supposed to work yet. Every cable modem has a *MAC address* (Media Access Control) — a special code number that enables the cable company to find it over the Internet. You often find your cable modem's MAC address on a sticker placed on its side or bottom. If it's not there, check the modem's box. Can't find it? Then hope your cable company's smart enough to be able to read the number from their end of the connection.

6. Call the cable company's technical support line and give them your new MAC address — a formality not required by DSL providers. The technical support people diligently type your new MAC address into their computers, replacing the old modem's MAC address. If your Internet service provider is really savvy, they'll be able to read your new modem's MAC address automatically, without your reading it to them.

7. Play FreeCell until your new modem starts working. It takes your cable company's network anywhere from a few seconds to several hours to start working. During this time, the new modem's lights will flash, frantically trying to find someone to talk to. When the cable modem finally connects, your browser and e-mail program start working again. Whew!

Chapter 15

Linking Computers with a Network

A few years ago, if you wanted a computer network in your home, you were automatically considered a nerd who built robots in the garage.

Now, networks are for average, everyday folk. Many families today are on their second or third computer, having outgrown the first a few years ago. Throw in a netbook or laptop, and it's not strange to see a computer in every room.

And that's when a *network* comes in handy, to let all the computers talk amongst themselves. Connecting your computers with a network lets them all share a single Internet connection, a printer, or even the stash of music and videos stored on other computers.

Whatever your networking needs may be, this chapter explains how to set up a simple home network between your computers, letting them chat through cables or wirelessly through the air waves.

Choosing the Right Networking Equipment

No matter what type of network you use, you're likely to stumble into some very odd terminology when shopping online or reading packaging on the boxes lining the store shelves. Here are translations for the most common stumbling blocks:

- ✔ **Network adapter:** Most computers already come with a *network adapter:* a gadget that can communicate with other parts of the network. A *wired* network adapter looks like an extra-wide phone jack. *Wireless* network adapters — commonly found on laptops, netbooks, expensive cellphones, and even the latest TV sets — send and receive network signals.

- ✔ **Router:** This little box sends information between your networked computers, letting each computer access both the Internet and your other computers. Most routers today let you plug in at least four computers, as well as send and receive wireless network signals to dozens of other computers. Buy a router that includes the cryptic phrase "802.11n" (a speed rating) on its box.

Routers make fantastic firewalls, as explained in Chapter 16. Because the router sits between your computers and the Internet, the bad guys can't get in nearly as easily.

✔ **Network cables:** Also called Ethernet cables, these wires connect your computer's network adapters to your router. (Wireless adapters skip the wires and just broadcast the signal like miniature radio stations.) Network adapters and the router are the two main parts of any network.

✔ **Local area network (LAN):** A relatively small group of connected computers, modems, and printers. When you create a network, you create a LAN. The Internet, by contrast, is a *wide area network*, also known as a WAN.

✔ **Gateway:** A connection between a smaller network and a larger one. A router, for example, works as a gateway that lets all the computers on your home network connect to the biggest network of all: the Internet.

✔ **Encryption:** A coding method for keeping information private. Each computer on an encrypted network uses an automated password system to scramble and descramble information sent between them. Wireless networks use encryption to weed out eavesdroppers.

✔ **WEP (Wired Equivalent Privacy), WPA (Wi-Fi Protected Access):** These two different security methods use encryption to keep eavesdroppers out of your wireless network. Although Windows 7 supports both types of encryption, choose WPA — if your equipment allows it — as it's *much* more secure than WEP.

✔ **IP (Internet protocol) address:** Each computer on a network has an *IP address* — a unique identifying number. By routing information to and from IP addresses, the network enables everything to communicate.

Buying the Right Parts for Your Network

This task presents your shopping list and offers some help in picking out the items that meet your own particular needs.

1. Buy a wireless 802.11n router, as it's the brain of the network: Every computer must connect with it. Most routers include built-in wireless that will connect *dozens* of other computers farther than a cable stretch away. If your computers sit close to the router, however, skip wireless and just connect the cables to the router's built-in ports. Cables transfer information more quickly and securely than wireless connections, so feel free to run long cable to any of your stationary computers.

2. Buy one Ethernet cable for each computer that won't be using wireless. Ethernet cable comes packaged with a wide variety of names, including 1000Base-T and CAT-5e. But if you're hunting for it at the computer store, just look for the network cable that looks like telephone cable and says "CAT-5e" or "Category 5e" on the label. Buy each cable several feet longer than you think you need, because they'll flow around corners and desktops.

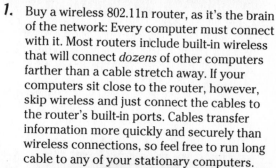

3. Buy network adapters, if necessary. Each computer needs its own network adapter, either wired or wireless. Most computers and laptops already include built-in wired adapters, into which you can plug an Ethernet cable (left); most netbooks and laptops include wireless, as well. If one of your computers lacks a wired or wireless network adapter, they come as both plug-in USB gadgets (right) and internal cards, which cost less and perform just as well or better than their USB counterparts.

Installing Wired or Wireless Network Adapters

Chances are, you won't need to bother with this task. Most computers come with built-in wired or wireless network adapters. If you own one of those few deadbeat computers that lacks a network adapter, you have several options:

- **USB adapters:** The easiest solution, these come in both wired and wireless models that plug into any computer's USB port. If Windows doesn't automatically recognize and install it, run the bundled software, and you're done: Head to the "Setting Up Windows 7 Computers to Connect Wirelessly to a Wireless Network" task.

- **PC Card adapters:** These slim adapters simply slide into a laptop's PC Card slot, that credit-card sized slot in the side of some laptops. Again, Windows usually recognizes the cards, but run the card's bundled software if Windows doesn't take notice.

- **PCI card:** The fastest and cheapest wired adapters come on cards that slide into a slot inside your desktop computer. If you're not afraid of a screwdriver, you can save a few bucks and transfer files more quickly between your computers.

To install a network card — either wired or wireless — into a desktop computer, follow these steps:

1. Turn off your PC, unplug it, and remove your computer's case, as described in this book's Cheat Sheet, downloadable from www.dum mies.com/cheatsheet/upgradingandfixingcomputersdiy.

2. Look inside your computer and find an empty plastic slot on your computer's flat, circuit-filled mother-board. Then find the row of metal slots toward the back of your computer's case. Those metal slots are where you plug in many of your computer's cables. With a small screwdriver, remove the single screw that holds that card in place. Save that screw, as you need it to secure the new card in place.

3. Push the new network adapter card into its slot; its network port will be visible through the metal slot on the back of your computer. Line up the tabs and notches on the card's bottom with the notches in the slot. Push the card slowly into the slot. You may need to rock the card back and forth gently. When the card pops in, you can feel it come to rest. Don't force it!

4. Secure the card in the slot with the screw you removed in Step 2. Yep, those delicate electronics are held in place by one screw.

5. Replace the computer's case, plug the computer back in, and turn it on. Windows usually recognizes newly installed cards and automatically sets them up to work correctly. If your network adapter came with a CD, be sure to insert it if Windows 7 begins clamoring for *drivers* — translation software that helps Windows 7 talk to new parts. (I cover drivers more thoroughly in Chapter 17.)

Connecting Your Router to Your Wired Computers and Modem

Now that all of your computers have network ports, you're ready to begin setting up your router. Some of today's routers include a broadband modem bundled inside, letting you skip one of these steps. (And if you're replacing only a broadband modem, head to Chapter 14's task, "Installing a Broadband (Cable or DSL) Modem.")

Follow these steps to connect both your broadband modem and any cable-connected computers to your router:

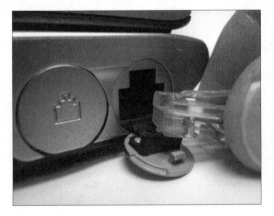

1. Connect the cables between your computer's network adapters (left) and the router (right). The cables all snake around until they plug into a numbered port on the router. (Most routers come with four ports.) You may need to route cables under carpets, around doorways, or through a hole in the floor or ceiling to move between floors.

2. If your router doesn't include a built-in broadband modem, connect a network cable between your broadband modem's Ethernet port (left) and the only port on your router that's labeled WAN (middle). If your router *includes* a broadband modem, screw the modem's coaxial cable into the router/modem's cable port (right).

3. Plug the power cords for your modem and router into the wall outlets, and then turn on your computers and their monitors, if necessary. Windows usually recognizes newly installed equipment and automatically sets up everything to work correctly.

4. Select a location for your network. When Windows 7 wakes up and notices the newly attached network equipment, it asks you for your network's *location:* Home, Work, or Public Network. Choose whether you're working at home or work (safe) or in public (less safe), and Windows 7 automatically adds the proper security level to protect you. If you choose Home as your location, take Windows up on its offer and follow its instructions to let your computers share files. To see the other computers on your network, click the Start menu and choose Network.

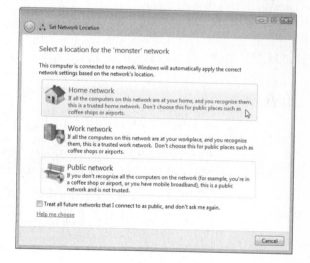

Setting Up a Wireless Router

Stuff You Need to Know

Toolbox:
- Your hands

Materials:
- A router
- A computer connected to the router
- The router's setup software, if provided

Time Needed:
Less than an hour

Wireless connections bring a convenience enjoyed by every cellphone owner. But they're also more complicated to set up than wired connections. You're basically setting up a radio transmitter — your router — that broadcasts to little radios attached to your computers. You need to worry about signal strength, finding the right signal, and even entering passwords to keep outsiders from listening in.

Unfortunately, different brands and models of wireless routers all come with slightly different setup software for controlling the wireless signal, so there's no way I can provide exact instructions for setting up your particular router.

However, the setup software on every wireless router requires you to set up these three basic things:

1. **Choose *Network Name* or *Service Set Identifier (SSID)*.** Enter a short, easy-to-remember name in this spot to identify your particular wireless network. Later, when you tell Windows 7 to connect to your wireless network, you'll select this same name to avoid accidentally connecting to your neighbor's wireless network.

2. **Choose *Infrastructure* instead of the alternative-and-rarely-used mode, *Ad Hoc*.** Ad Hoc lets two computers connect *without* a router, a mode usually reserved for engineers playing games surreptitiously during board meetings.

3. **Choose your security option and password:** This option encrypts your data as it flies through the air. Turn it on using the recommended settings. Some routers include an installation program for changing these settings; other routers contain built-in software that you access with Windows' own Web browser.

4. **As you enter settings for your network name and password, write them on a piece of paper.** You'll need to enter those same settings when setting up your computer's wireless connection, a job tackled in the next task.

Setting Up Windows 7 Computers to Connect to a Wireless Network

After you've set up your wireless router to broadcast your network, described in the preceding task, you must tell Windows 7 how to receive it. You'll follow these same steps, whether connecting to your own wireless network; your neighbor's; or one in a hotel, airport, or coffee shop.

To connect to any wireless network, follow these steps:

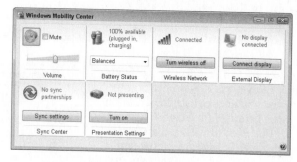

1. Turn on your wireless adapter, if necessary. Many laptops and netbooks turn off their wireless adapters to save power. To turn it on, open the Control Panel from the Start menu, choose Mobile Computer, open the Mobility Center, and click the Turn Wireless On button. Not listed? Unless you find a "Wireless On/Off" switch on your laptop, you'll need to pull out your laptop's manual, unfortunately. (Some laptops and netbooks toggle their wireless by holding down a key labeled Fn and pressing a Function key, such as F2.)

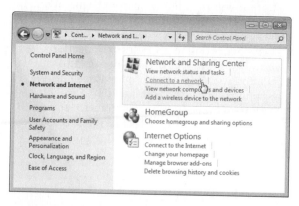

2. Open the Start menu, choose Control Panel, choose Network and Internet, and choose Connect to a Network from the Network and Sharing Center section. (Alternatively, you can click the tiny Network icon in your taskbar's bottom-right corner.) Windows lists the names, also known as SSIDs, of all the wireless networks it finds within range, including wireless networks run by your neighbors. (That's why security is important.)

When Windows 7 says that it can't connect to your wireless network, it offers two choices: Diagnose This Connection or Connect to a Different Network. Both messages almost always mean this: Move Your Computer Closer to the Wireless Router.

3. Connect to the desired network by clicking its name and clicking the Connect button. Choose the SSID name you gave your wireless router when you set it up in the preceding task, for example, or select the name of the wireless network offered by the coffee shop or hotel. Don't see your network's name listed? Then move the laptop or computer closer to the router and try again. The little vertical bars next to each network's name resemble a cellphone's signal strength meter: The more bars you see, the stronger the signal.

4. Choose the type of security, if required, enter your password, and click OK. On your own network, this will be the same password you entered when setting up your router. Networks listed as *Unsecured Network* don't require a password: You can hop aboard and start surfing the Internet for free. Unsecured, however, means they aren't encrypted, which allows snoops to eavesdrop. Unsecured networks work fine for quick Internet access — checking airline arrival times, for example — but aren't safe for anything requiring a password.

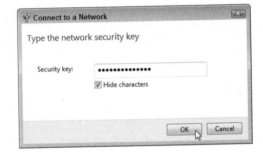

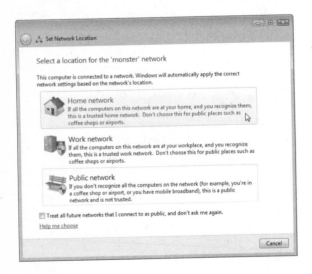

5. Choose whether you're connecting from Home, Work, or a Public Network. Windows 7 asks whether you're connecting from Home, Work, or a Public Network so that it can add the right layer of security. Choose Home or Work only when connecting to a wireless connection within your home or office. Choose Public Location for all others to add extra security. If you choose Home as your location, take it up on its offer and follow its instructions to let your computers share files. To see the other computers on your network, click the Start menu and choose Network.

Unless you specifically tell it not to, Windows 7 remembers the name and password of wireless networks you've successfully connected with before, sparing you the chore of reentering all the information. Your computer will connect automatically whenever you're within range.

Windows XP Home edition and workgroup names

Like anything else in life, networks need names. A network's name is called a *workgroup*, which is quite ignorable information — except, unfortunately, if you're running Windows XP Home on one of your networked computers.

Microsoft gave Windows XP Home edition computers a workgroup name of "MSHOME" but gave the name "WORKGROUP" to Windows XP Professional edition, Windows Vista, and Windows 7 workgroups. The result? Put a Windows 7 computer and a Windows XP Home computer on the same network, and they can't find nor talk with each other: One computer searches in vain for other MSHOME computers, while the other looks for WORKGROUP computers.

The solution is to give them both the *same* workgroup name, a fairly easy task with these four steps. (Not sure which version of Windows XP you own? You'll find out in Step 1.)

1. **On your Windows XP Home computer, click the Start menu, right-click My Computer, and choose Properties.**

The System Properties window appears, revealing techie details including whether your computer runs Windows XP Home or Professional.

2. **Click the Computer Name tab, and click the Change button.**

The Computer Name Changes dialog box appears.

3. **In the bottom box, change the Workgroup name to WORKGROUP.**

That puts your Windows XP Home computer on the same workgroup as all your other computers.

Tip: Be careful in this step to change the computer's *workgroup* name, not its *computer* name, as they're different things.

4. **Click OK to close the open windows and, when asked, click the Restart Now button to restart your computer.**

Repeat these steps for your other networked Windows XP Home computers, making sure that the same name appears in each Workgroup box.

Connecting to and Sharing Files with Older Computers on Your Network

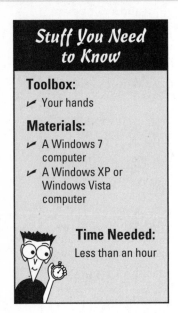

Stuff You Need to Know

Toolbox:
- Your hands

Materials:
- A Windows 7 computer
- A Windows XP or Windows Vista computer

Time Needed:
Less than an hour

Windows 7's Homegroup system works very well for trysts between Windows 7 computers. But what about that lonely Windows XP or Windows Vista computer? Those folks aren't allowed to join a Homegroup, effectively locking them out. When those poor folks try to connect to a Windows 7 computer, they see only a username/password screen, not your files.

Here's how to lighten up Windows 7's security enough to let your Windows XP or Vista computers in on the action:

1. Create a working network on your Windows XP and Windows Vista computers. I describe how to create networks on those versions of Windows in my books, *Windows XP For Dummies* and *Windows Vista For Dummies* (Wiley).

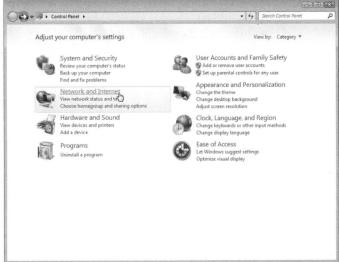

2. On each Windows 7 PC, click the Start button, choose Control Panel (left), and choose Network and Internet (right).

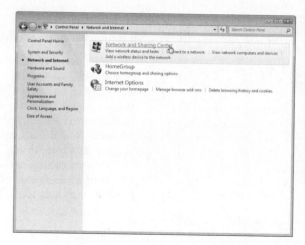

3. Click Network and Sharing Center (left), and then click Change Advanced Sharing Settings from the left pane of the Network and Sharing Center window (right).

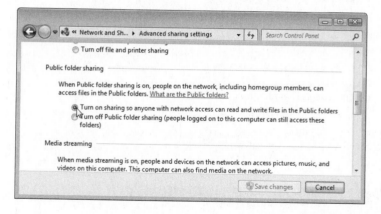

4. When the Advanced Sharing Settings window appears, make sure Public Folder Sharing is turned On. To share files and folders with others, place them into your computer's Public folder. The Public folder lives one click away in every Windows 7 folder: The contents of everybody's Public folders are automatically listed in everybody's libraries.

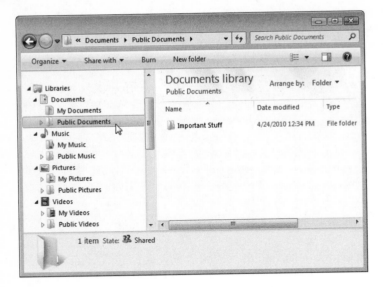

5. To move items to the Public Documents folder, for example — or to see what items are already there — click the little arrow next to the word *Documents* to see two folders: Your documents (the My Documents folder) and Public Documents, which shows you the contents of what everybody on the network has stored in their Public folders.

I explain more about libraries and public folders in *Windows 7 For Dummies* (Wiley).

Connecting to a wireless printer on your network

After you've set up your wireless router, your computers can find any wireless printers you may have on your network. To tell any Windows 7 computer about a wireless printer, follow these steps:

1. **Click the Start button and choose Control Panel.**

2. **Click the Hardware and Sound category, and choose View Devices and Printers.**

3. **Click Add a Printer from the top menu. Then choose Add a Network, Wireless or Bluetooth Printer; click your wireless printer's name; and click Next.**

Repeat these steps on any other computer that needs to print to that particular printer.

Chapter 16

Filtering Out Evil with Firewalls

Tasks in this chapter

✔ Turning on (or off) Windows 7 Firewall

✔ Allowing or stopping a program from poking through Windows 7 Firewall

✔ Manually changing Windows 7 Firewall settings

Even if you're not using a traditional network in your home or office, you're exposed to a network nearly every day. The *Internet* is a vast network connecting computers around the world. And those connections come with dangers.

See, your computer opens a door to the Internet whenever it asks for information. And naturally, because your computer needs to receive information — a Web page, for example — the computer holds that door open.

Unfortunately, some people make a habit of looking for open doors and trying to sneak in when nobody's looking. Why? For some people, the childish thrill of seeing if they can snoop around in Jeff's locker without getting caught is just too tempting to resist.

Others sneak in like burglars, looking for credit card numbers, e-mail addresses, or other private files. Still others are vandals, destroying whatever they get their hands on. The business-minded crooks quietly take over computers, and then sell them to spammers, who surreptitiously crank out junk mail, all unnoticed by the computer's owner.

Simply put, your computer needs somebody to stand guard at the door, opening and closing the door at the right times to filter out the bad folks.

A *firewall* is that security guard, and this chapter explains how to turn on Windows 7's built-in firewall, how to let the right programs through, and how to keep the bad ones out.

Turning On (or Off) Windows 7 Firewall

Stuff You Need to Know

Toolbox:
- Your hands

Materials:
- Any version of Windows 7

Time Needed:
Less than an hour

Every version of Windows 7 includes a built-in firewall. Like Windows Vista, Windows 7 turns on its firewall automatically.

To see for yourself that Windows 7's Firewall is running — and to turn it *on* if it's accidentally turned off — follow these steps:

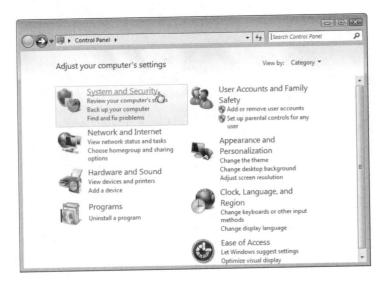

1. Click the Start menu, and choose Control Panel. When the Control Panel appears, click System and Security.

Why cable and DSL modems need firewalls

Cable and DSL modems can be more dangerous than dialup Internet connections, and here's why:

Whenever you connect to the Internet, your Internet service provider (ISP) assigns your computer a number known as an *IP address.* Because a dialup user's computer's IP address changes each time he dials the Internet, a hacker may have more trouble finding and relocating that particular computer. That keeps the computer safer from unauthorized connections. Even if a hacker breaks in once, the computer will have a different address the next time it connects to the Internet, making it more difficult for the hacker to relocate.

Most cable and DSL modems, by contrast, remain constantly connected to the Internet, which means that the computer's IP address doesn't change nearly as often — if ever. After a hacker locates a susceptible computer's address on the Internet, he or she can break into it repeatedly. Firewalls help weed out hackers trying to break into your computer.

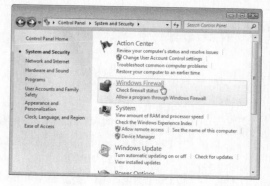 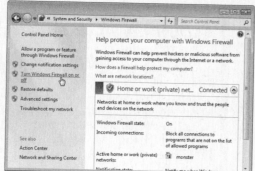

2. From the System and Security window, choose Windows Firewall. Then, from the Windows Firewall window's left pane, choose Turn Windows Firewall On or Off. The Windows Firewall's Customize Settings window appears, showing the firewall's current settings: On or Off.

3. Make sure the firewall is listed as On in both network areas, Public *and* Home or Work. This keeps your computer the safest. The two sets of settings let you customize the firewall's settings differently depending on whether you're connected to a "public" or "home or work" network.

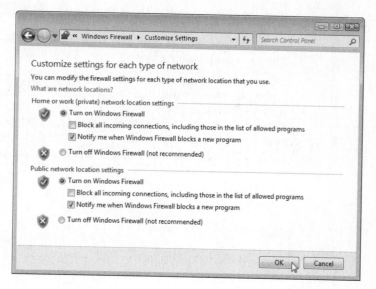

4. If you want to turn off the firewall, click Turn Off Windows Firewall (Not Recommended) in the Home or Work area. (*Always* leave the firewall turned on in Public.) Then click OK to save your settings. Turn off the firewall only as a last resort while troubleshooting a network connection. When you're through troubleshooting, turn the firewall back on, or you'll be unprotected.

If you install a third-party firewall, it will automatically turn off Windows' built-in firewall. (Firewall programs interfere with each other, so you should run only one firewall.)

Turning on Windows XP Firewall

Windows 7 and Windows XP turn on their firewalls in slightly different ways. If you're still using Windows XP, follow these steps to examine your computer's network connections, see which ones are firewalled, and turn on the connections you want protected.

Using America Online to connect to the Internet in Windows XP? Then these instructions won't help at all. America Online uses its own, special dialup connection that doesn't allow members to tinker so easily with their network settings. That includes turning on the firewall.

1. **Choose Control Panel from Windows XP's Start menu, click the Network and Internet Connections icon, and click the Network Connections icon.**

   Windows XP lists all your computer's network connections, including dialup and broadband Internet gateways (a network's Internet connection), and network bridges (a connection between two networks, like FireWire and an Ethernet network).

2. **Right-click the Internet connection you want to protect and choose Properties.**

3. **Click the Advanced tab, and then click the Settings button.**

4. **Click the "On (Recommended)" button in the Internet Connection Firewall section.**

   Clicking in the little box turns on the firewall.

5. **Click the OK button.**

   Depending on whether or not you've left a little dot in Step 4's On button, you've turned the firewall on or off.

Enable Windows XP Firewall on connections to the *Internet* only. (You needn't turn on the firewall for your Bluetooth connection, for example, even though Windows XP lists Bluetooth as a network connection.)

Allowing or Stopping a Program from Poking Through Windows 7 Firewall

Stuff You Need to Know

Toolbox:

- Your hands

Materials:

- Any version of Windows 7

Time Needed:
Less than an hour

Although firewalls offer protection, they can be as annoying as an overzealous airport security scan. In their zest for security, firewalls sometimes stop programs that you *want* to work. If you find one of your newly installed programs being denied Internet access, here's how to handle the situation:

1. Run or install a new program. If the program accepts or makes an unexpected Internet connection, Windows 7 stops the program from connecting, and immediately sends you a Windows Security Alert.

2. If you spot that window and you *haven't* tried to run a program, click the Cancel button: You've effectively stopped what could be a rogue program from connecting with the Internet. But if you're trying to install a program that needs to connect with the Internet, click the Allow Access button, instead. Windows 7 Firewall adds that program to its exceptions list and no longer bugs you about it.

Manually Changing Windows 7 Firewall Settings

Stuff You Need to Know

Toolbox:

✔ Your hands

Materials:

✔ Any version of Windows 7

Time Needed:

Less than an hour

On a rare occasion, you'll need to delve deeper into the firewall's settings. You may need to remove a previously approved program, for example, or add a new program to the "Good Guys" list.

To change the firewall's list of programs, follow these steps:

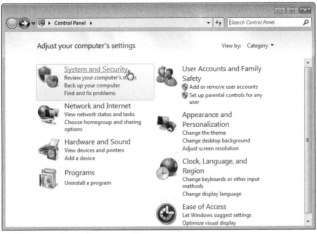

1. Choose Control Panel from the Start menu, and click System and Security.

2. From the Windows Firewall section, choose Allow a Program through Windows Firewall. The Windows Firewall Settings window opens to show every program currently allowed or forbidden to cross the firewall. Programs with a checked box are able to accept incoming connections through the firewall. No checkmark in a program's box? Then that program may connect to the Internet, but not accept incoming connections.

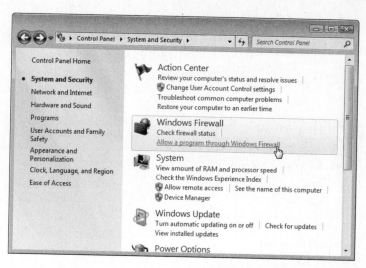

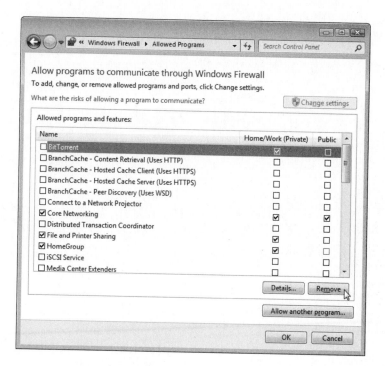

3. To remove a program you've mistakenly approved, click the program's name, click the Remove button, and click Yes. To *add* a program, click the Allow Another Program button and choose your program from the list. Not listed? Then click Browse to browse to the program's name. (Hint: Programs live in your C: drive in the Program Files folder.) Then save your changes by clicking the OK button.

Think you've messed up your firewall settings? In Step 2, click Windows Firewall, and then click Restore Defaults from the left pane. That removes any changes you've made to the firewall, leaving it set up the way it was when first installed. (Clicking Restore Defaults may also keep some programs from working until you add them to the Exceptions list again.)

Part V
Introducing Parts to Windows

The 5th Wave   By Rich Tennant

"Well, the first level of Windows security seems good – I can't get the shrink-wrapping off."

In this part . . .

*T*he physical act of installing a part into your computer is fairly straightforward. Most connectors align themselves, letting you simply slide them together easily.

But what if they won't work, even after you've snugly nestled their connectors together? That's where this part of the book comes in. It walks you through tracking down and installing *drivers,* those little pieces of software that serve as matchmakers between Windows and the newly added part.

Another chapter walks you through installing Windows 7, whether it's on Windows XP, Windows Vista, or an empty hard drive.

This part also explains how to move information from your old computer to your new one. And it offers troubleshooting tips when nothing seems to work like it should. Dig in.

Chapter 17

Hiring the Right Driver for Windows

Sometimes upgrading a computer goes as smoothly as throwing a well-catered party. You install the new part, and Windows instantly recognizes it, announcing its name in a merry pop-up window for everybody to see. Windows embraces the latest arrival, hands it a drink, and immediately introduces it to all parts of your computer.

Other times, well, it's a party disaster. Windows snubs the part when you plug it in, and the computer turns a cold shoulder, as well. Or when you turn your computer back on, your computer responds with an antisocial error message that ruins the fun for everybody.

Installation problems rarely lie with the part itself, but with its *driver* — the software that lets Windows put the part to work. Although Windows 7 comes with thousands of drivers, some of your computer's parts will probably go unrecognized. This chapter shows you how to go about finding and installing competent drivers. If a driver doesn't seem to be doing the job, you discover how to replace it politely, with a minimum of hard feelings on everybody's account.

And if the new driver does an even worse job than the old one, heaven forbid, this chapter reveals the button hidden in Windows 7's Secret Panel: At one click of a button, Windows fires the new driver and puts the older driver back in place until you can find a suitable replacement.

This is a meaty chapter, and troubleshooters will spend a lot of time here.

Choosing a Compatible Driver

Whenever anything goes wrong in Windows, nearby computer gurus often exclaim, "Sounds like a driver problem! You'd better get an update." Of course, it's an easy conversation stopper, freeing the guru from fixing your computer.

But what exactly does that mean? What's a driver? Where do you find an updated one? How do you know which driver works the best?

A *driver* is a piece of software that enables Windows to communicate with a specific computer part — it's an interpreter, if you will. Some drivers use several files to carry out their duties; others use just one. Their names vary widely. But every piece of hardware in your computer needs its own, specific driver, or Windows doesn't know how to communicate with it.

Because outside companies — your printer's manufacturer, for example — write drivers for their own products, tech support people like to pass the buck. If you have a problem with your printer, your printer's tech support people may say you have a *Windows* problem and should contact Microsoft. Microsoft's tech support people, in turn, tell you that you have a *driver* problem, and that you should contact your printer's manufacturer.

Unfortunately, that leaves the job of finding and installing drivers up to you. To equip you in your search for compatible drivers, here are the terms you'll constantly encounter:

✔ **Version:** Well-established manufacturers continually update their drivers and release replacement versions. Sometimes new versions add new features. More often, they fix problems with the old driver. And sometimes, if a version is too new to be tested under a wide variety of conditions, that new version doesn't work as well as the *old* driver.

✔ **Version number:** Manufacturers usually assign the number 1.0 to a driver when it's first released to the public. Whenever they release a new version of the driver, they increase its version number. Version 1.1 is newer than version 1.0, for example. And version 2.5 is even newer.

The driver bearing the *highest* version number is the most current release. It's usually (but not always) the most reliable. Windows' Device Manager, described later in this chapter, lets you view a driver's version number.

✔ **Version history:** The best companies stock their Web sites with a detailed description of every driver's version number, its date of release, and the features that each version repaired or added. By examining a driver's version history, you can easily spot the newest driver and discover whether it repairs the problems that you've been experiencing.

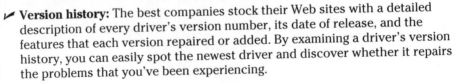

✔ **Device Manager:** Windows collects more information about drivers than your local DMV. Windows *Device Manager*, the archive of driver details, lists the drivers used by every part of your computer. Device Manager serves as the starting point for anything to do with drivers, including their installation, update, or removal.

✔ **Device provider:** Listed in Device Manager, the *device provider* is the company that created the driver. Most manufacturers write their own drivers for their products. They then hand the drivers to Microsoft; Microsoft then bundles those drivers with each new release of Windows. When you install Windows, it can then recognize and begin using a computer's parts.

Many manufacturers balk at creating drivers for their older parts, unfortunately, because the companies are too busy pushing newer products. Not wishing to strand the millions of people still using older computers, Microsoft picks up the stick and writes its *own* drivers. Drivers listing *Microsoft* as the device provider often came bundled with Windows.

Microsoft's drivers are often generic, though. Microsoft writes a driver that recognizes *all* game controllers, for instance, allowing any game controller to move things around on the screen. However, manufacturers often write separate drivers for specific models of a game controller. When you update to the manufacturer's driver, Windows suddenly realizes that your game controller has *seven* programmable buttons, for instance, and finally enables you to use them.

✔ **Driver signing:** Desperate to keep drivers on the straight and narrow path, Microsoft wants to inspect each newly released driver and, if it meets approval, stamp it with the Windows logo. If you install a driver that hasn't been through Microsoft's approval process, Windows flashes an "unsigned driver" warning message.

Despite the warning message's fearful appearance, it usually appears when you're installing parts created by smaller companies. Those small companies don't have enough time or money to wait for Microsoft to approve their drivers. So, install the driver anyway, if allowed. (You're not allowed to install unsigned drivers in the 64-bit version of Windows.) If the new driver doesn't work, you can revert to the old one, as described in this chapter's last task, "Rolling Back to an Earlier Driver."

Paying for drivers is something you needn't worry about. All drivers are *free*. If anybody tries to charge you for one, walk, run, or double-click your way out of there quickly.

Discovering Whether You're Running a 32-Bit or 64-Bit Version of Windows

Stuff You Need to Know

Toolbox:
- Your hands

Materials:
- A computer running Windows 7

Time Needed:
Less than an hour

You may have heard about Windows 7 coming in both a 32-bit version and a 64-bit version. That information doesn't matter much until it comes to *drivers* — the programs that let your computer talk to its physical parts.

If you're running a *32-bit* version of Windows, you need to install *32-bit* drivers. Likewise, the *64-bit* version of Windows requires *64-bit* drivers.

So, how do you know whether you're running the 32-bit or 64-bit version of Windows 7? By following these steps:

1. Click the Start menu, right-click Computer, and choose Properties from the pop-up menu. The View Basic Information about Your Computer window appears.

2. Look for the line beginning with the words "System Type." There, Windows reveals whether you're running a 32-bit or 64-bit version of Windows. That little line lets you know which type of drivers you need to install for your computer.

Automatically Installing a New Driver

Stuff You Need to Know

Toolbox:

✔ Your hands

Materials:

✔ A part that plugs into a USB port

✔ A Windows 7 computer

Time Needed:
Less than an hour

Sometimes installing a driver is an automatic, one-time-only process — especially when you insert a plug-and-play device into a USB or FireWire port. It works like this:

1. Plug in the new part and turn it on, if necessary. For example, plug a digital camera into your computer's USB port, and turn on the camera. Watch as Windows recognizes and greets your new part. Windows tosses up a message saying it notices a new part.

2. Windows rarely takes more than a few seconds to recognize that you've attached a new part. It searches for drivers. If it finds them, Windows sends up a second message, saying the new part is ready to use.

3. If Windows *doesn't* find a driver, though, a less comforting message appears, saying Device Driver Software Was Not Successfully Installed. That's your cue to take matters into your own hands.

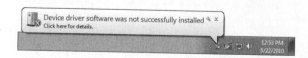

Windows almost always beeps in excitement when you plug something into a USB port. If Windows doesn't beep, unplug the device, wait about 15 seconds, and then plug it back in. Never quickly unplug and plug in a device. Instead, give Windows a chance to recognize whether the part's being plugged in or unplugged.

Running a Driver's Installation Program

Stuff You Need to Know

Toolbox:

✔ Your hands
✔ A computer part that won't install automatically

Materials:

✔ The part's installation software, or a driver's installation software downloaded from the Internet

Time Needed:

Less than an hour

Windows isn't always smart enough to recognize every part you plug into your computer. That's why many computer gadgets come with their own setup software on a CD or DVD. The setup software automatically installs the drivers and programs that help your computer put your new part to work.

Whether you've downloaded an installation program from the Internet or you're running the software that came with a product, you'll follow steps slightly similar to these:

1. Double-click your downloaded driver's installation file, or insert your installation or setup disc into your computer's CD or DVD drive. Windows usually sends up a window automatically asking for permission to run the setup program. Click Yes to let it run the highlighted program, and click Yes to the permission screen that follows.

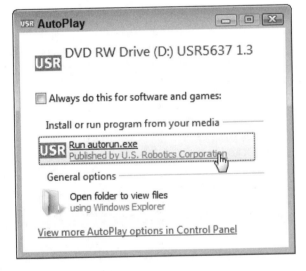

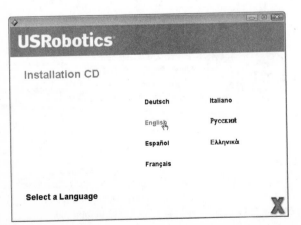

2. Choose your language, if asked, and click Next.

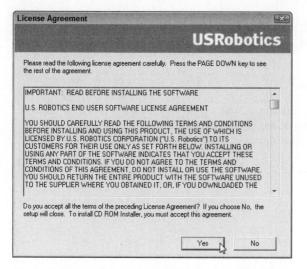

3. Click to approve the licensing agreement, if asked, and the program installs the driver. Windows often ends the setup process by asking you to restart your computer. When the computer wakes up, Windows takes notice of the new part and begins its welcome messages as shown in the preceding task.

If the part still doesn't work after you insert the installation disc, don't start worrying quite yet. The driver is probably on the disc, but the manufacturer didn't write software to install it automatically. In that case, move on to the next task, "Installing Drivers That Refuse to Install." That task walks you through making Windows locate the driver on the disc and install it for you.

Part V: Introducing Parts to Windows

Installing Drivers That Refuse to Install

Stuff You Need to Know

Toolbox:
- Your hands

Materials:
- A part that refuses to install
- The part's driver, either on a bundled disc or downloaded from the Internet

Time Needed:
Less than an hour

If you install a new part and Windows doesn't recognize it, the first thing to try is to fire up the bundled software that came with the part, described in the previous task. Most bundled software discs install the part for you, but a few leave you stranded. When that happens, let Windows' handy Device Manager install the driver by following these steps:

1. Click the Start menu, type **Device Manager** in the Search box, and press Enter. (Or click the words "Device Manager" that appear at the top of the Start menu's search window.) Device Manager rises to the screen.

2. Device Manager lists every part connected to your computer, as well as whether they're working correctly. Device Manager flags any malfunctioning part with special symbols, letting you know something's wrong. The USB Modem entry shown here, for example, wears an icon bearing an exclamation point inside a yellow triangle.

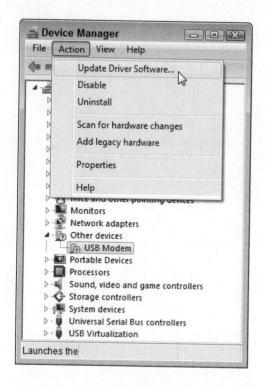

3. Click the item that needs attention, click Action from the Device Manager menu bar, and click Update Driver Software from the drop-down menu. The Update Driver Software window appears, ready to help you resuscitate the problem part.

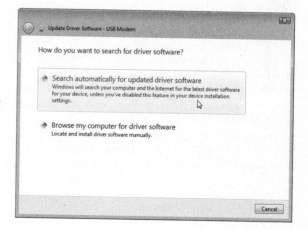

4. Choose Search Automatically for Updated Driver Software. That tells Windows to track down the missing driver in the usual spots. If you're lucky, Windows finds the driver, installs it, and much rejoicing is heard around the office.

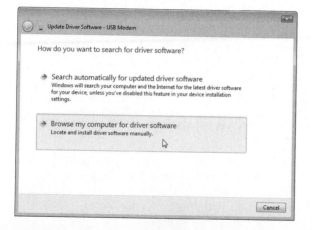

5. If you're not lucky, though, click Close, and repeat Step 3: Click the malfunctioning part, click Action from the Device Manager menu bar, and choose Update Driver Software. The Update Driver Software window appears, once again.

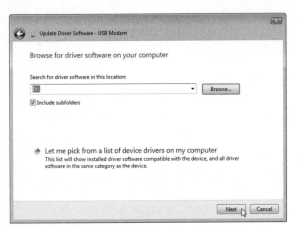

6. *This time*, however, take the manual approach by choosing Browse My Computer for Driver Software. Click the Browse button and navigate to the CD/DVD drive containing the installation software. (Or navigate to the folder where you've placed a downloaded driver.) Then click Next, which tells Windows to search for the driver in your specified location.

7. When Windows finds the driver, click Install to give Windows approval to install it. Finally, after the driver is installed, click Close to give Device Manager a rest. You've both earned it.

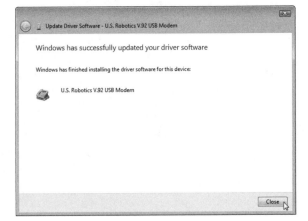

If Windows doesn't find the driver, however, the burden falls on your own shoulders, a chore I cover in the following task.

Finding a New Driver

Stuff You Need to Know

Toolbox:

✔ Your hands

Materials:

✔ A part that won't install, and doesn't include a driver

✔ Windows 7

Time Needed:
Less than an hour

Occasionally, Windows forces *you* into the role of grunt worker, and you have to ferret out a driver for a computer part. Your part might not be working well with the current driver, or you might want a newer driver that fixes problems or adds features.

The most reliable way to find a driver is to search the Internet for the manufacturer's Web site and, hopefully, the part's driver. This task walks you through the basic procedure, although it varies from site to site:

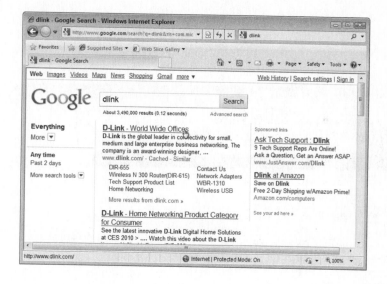

1. Find the manufacturer's name by examining the part's box, packaging, or the part itself. Sometimes the manufacturer's name (and the part's model number) appear in fine print etched on the part's circuits. After you've found the manufacturer's name, head for www.google.com with your Internet browser, type the manufacturer's name into the search box, and click the Google Search button. When you spot the manufacturer's Web site, click its name to visit.

2. Find the Web site's page containing the downloadable driver. Some sites list a menu for *Downloads* or *Drivers* on the opening page. With others, look for *Customer Support* or *Technical Support*. Try clicking a *Site Map,* if you spot one, and search for downloadable drivers from there.

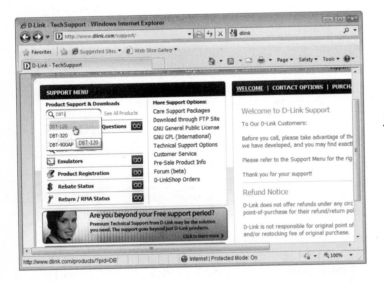

3. Enter your part's name and model number to visit its support page.

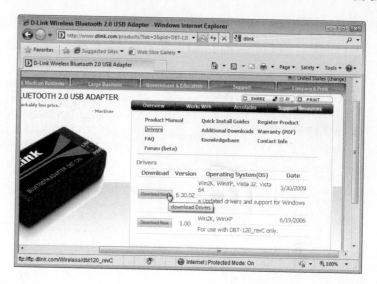

4. Locate the correct driver for your part *and* Windows 7, either 32-bit or 64-bit. No Windows 7 driver available? Download the Windows Vista driver, instead, which will probably work. Don't bother with drivers for earlier Windows versions, though, because they probably won't work.

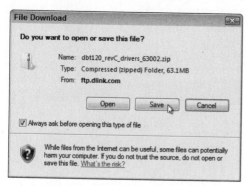

5. Save the driver into a folder on your computer. Windows 7 usually saves downloaded files in your Downloads folder. You can find those downloaded files by clicking the Start menu, clicking your username, and opening the Downloads folder. (To extract the drivers from your newly downloaded file, right-click the file name and choose Extract All.)

6. If the driver came with an installation program, install it by following the steps in the "Running a Driver's Installation Program" task. No installation program? Then install it by following the steps in the task, "Installing Drivers That Refuse to Install."

Updating an Old Driver

Even after installing a brand-new part and installing its bundled driver, sometimes the thing *still* doesn't work right. That's probably because the manufacturer put that driver in the box several months ago, yet technology kept moving. Chances are, a newer and better driver awaits you on the company's Web site.

If your current driver isn't working correctly, or you want to switch to a newer driver with more features, follow these steps:

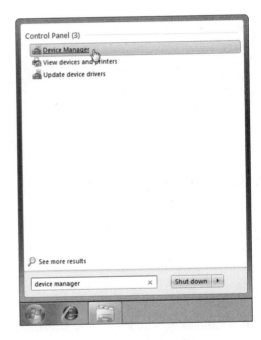

1. Click the Start menu, type **Device Manager** in the Search box, and press Enter. (Or click the words "Device Manager" that appear at the top of the Start menu's search window.) Device Manager rises to the screen.

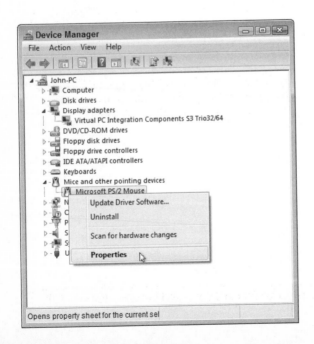

2. Right-click the problem part — the mouse, for example — and choose Properties from the pop-up menu.

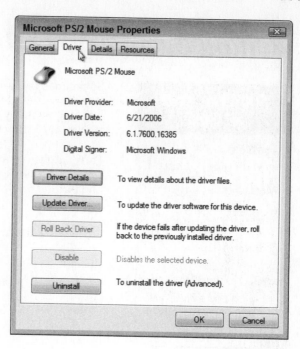

3. When the Properties window appears, click the Driver tab. Then, find the driver version and driver date, both listed on their own lines near the top of the box. Write them down so that you know when you find a newer driver.

4. Find and download an updated driver, as described in the preceding task, "Finding a New Driver." Be sure to remember where you've saved the new, updated driver.

5. After you've downloaded the newer driver, repeat Steps 1-3 to return to the Driver tab. This time, though, click the Update Driver button. From there, the steps are the same as Steps 5-7 in the "Installing Drivers That Refuse to Install" task. (Basically, you browse to the new driver's location, click its name, and click Next for Windows to install it.)

If your new driver makes things even *worse*, feel free to roll back to the original driver using Windows' Roll Back Driver feature, described in the next task.

Rolling Back to an Earlier Driver

Stuff You Need to Know

Toolbox:
- Your hands

Materials:
- A part with a newly installed driver that's worse than the old driver

Time Needed:

Less than an hour

Sometimes the new driver isn't the panacea you'd hoped it would be. Your computer doesn't work any better at all. In fact, sometimes you've not only wasted your time searching for a new driver, but you've made things much, much *worse*.

Fortunately, Windows keeps your previous driver in its back pocket for times like this. Tell Windows to *roll back* — reach into its back pocket and put the original driver back in place. To do just that, follow these steps:

1. Follow the first two steps in the preceding task, "Updating an Old Driver," to fetch Device Manager and examine the Properties box for the item with the bad driver.

2. This time, however, click the Roll Back Driver button.

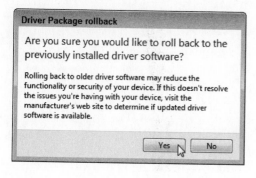

Driver Package rollback

Are you sure you would like to roll back to the previously installed driver software?

Rolling back to older driver software may reduce the functionality or security of your device. If this doesn't resolve the issues you're having with your device, visit the manufacturer's web site to determine if updated driver software is available.

[Yes]   [No]

3. Click Yes at the approval screen. Windows dutifully removes the new driver you just installed and replaces it with the previous driver — the one that worked better. Changed your mind and decided that the new driver really *was* working better? Feel free to install it again. And then roll back again if you change your mind. You can spend hours doing this.

Yes, indeed, you can spend a lot of time with this entire *chapter*. Finding a driver that works perfectly makes it all worthwhile, though. If a device gives you constant trouble, keep checking the manufacturer's Web site for an updated driver.

If you're still having troubles with the latest driver, spend some time on Google. By searching for your Windows version and the part, you can often encounter other people who've described similar problems and, hopefully, solutions as to which driver version works the best. I describe how to find help online in Chapter 21.

Chapter 18

Installing or Upgrading to Windows 7

Walk into nearly any computer store today, and you'll see Windows 7 running on every single computer. Nearly 90 percent of today's computers arrive with Windows 7 already beaming from their monitors. So, who still needs to install Windows 7? Well, you'll be reading this chapter if you fall into any one of these three groups:

- Your computer runs Windows XP or Windows Vista, and you want to move to Windows 7.

- You've replaced or upgraded a hard drive, and need to install or reinstall Windows 7 onto it.

- You're outgrowing Windows 7 Starter edition, which came on your netbook, and you want to upgrade to a more powerful version of Windows.

This chapter walks you through each of those scenarios.

Understanding Windows 7's Hardware Requirements

Windows 7 usually runs well on computers purchased within the past four or five years. Before upgrading your computer, though, make sure that you've run through the following checklist:

- **Compatibility:** Before upgrading or installing Windows 7 onto your computer, download and run Microsoft's Windows 7 Upgrade Advisor, described in this chapter's first task. The program alerts you beforehand if parts of your computer won't run well under Windows 7.

  The program will also tell you that you can't upgrade from Windows XP to Windows 7 very smoothly. Most people have to start from scratch, installing Windows 7, then reinstalling all their programs, and then copying their files back over to the computer. Yes, it's such a hassle that many people consider buying a new computer, instead.

- ✔ **Computer power:** Computers running Windows Vista have plenty of power to handle Windows 7. If you're upgrading from Windows XP, though, you should have at least 1GB of memory, a DVD drive, and at least a Pentium 4 processor. Windows 7 runs admirably well on underpowered computers. It won't be speedy, but it will run.

- ✔ **Security:** Before upgrading to Windows 7, turn off your antivirus software and other security programs. They may innocently try to protect you from Windows 7's upgrade process.

- ✔ **Upgrade path:** Both Windows Vista and Windows 7 come in many different versions, so Table 18-1 explains which versions are eligible for which upgrades.

  After you upgrade, you can pay extra to unlock the features of a fancier version using Windows Anytime Upgrade, a strategic Microsoft marketing move described in this chapter's last task.

- ✔ **Backup:** Back up all of your computer's important data in case something goes wrong. I describe how to back up your hard drive in Chapter 6. If you're switching from Windows XP, be sure to run Windows Easy Transfer program, a task covered in Chapter 20.

Table 18-1	Vista Upgrade Compatibility
This Version of Vista . . .	*. . . May Upgrade to This Version of Windows 7*
Windows Vista Home Basic; Windows Vista Premium	Windows 7 Home Premium
Windows Vista Business	Windows 7 Professional
Windows Vista Ultimate	Windows 7 Ultimate

Choosing between 32-Bit and 64-Bit Windows 7

When you buy a copy of Windows 7, you'll notice two DVDs in the box: a 32-bit version and a 64-bit version. Why are there two copies, and what's the difference?

Windows 7 comes with two copies so you can choose which version to install. If your computer comes with 4GB of memory or more, install the 64-bit version; the 32-bit version can't access that much memory.

But if you have less than 4GB of memory and don't plan to add more, go with the 32-bit version. That version still has more drivers available for it. (The very next task shows how to find out the amount of memory inside your computer.)

Running Windows 7's Upgrade Advisor

Stuff You Need to Know

Toolbox:

- Your hands

Materials:

- A computer running Windows XP, Windows Vista or Windows 7

Time Needed:
Less than an hour

Windows 7's Upgrade Advisor preempts those screams of "Oh no!" when you discover that your software or computer gadget won't run after you upgrade to Windows 7.

To prevent those unwelcome surprises, the program examines your computer, whether it's running Windows XP, Windows Vista, and even Windows 7 itself. The advisor thoroughly probes your computer's parts and software, and then lists any problem children, letting you deal with them before things get nasty.

When run on Windows XP, Windows Upgrade Advisor usually finds software or parts that simply won't survive the transition to Windows 7. (You can run troublemaking software in Windows 7 using a program called "Windows XP Mode," covered in Chapter 19.)

Windows Vista usually fares the Upgrade Advisor's exam much better. And, when run on a computer already running Windows 7, the advisor program handily explains whether or not you should upgrade to a 64-bit version of Windows 7.

Here's how to download and run Windows 7's free Upgrade Advisor to see how your computer will weather the upgrade:

1. Visit Microsoft's Windows 7 Upgrade Advisor Web site (www. microsoft.com/windows/ windows-7/get/upgrade-advisor.aspx) and click the Download the Windows 7 Upgrade Advisor button. In Microsoft's traditional sleight of hand, your click fetches a more complicated Windows 7 Upgrade Advisor page.

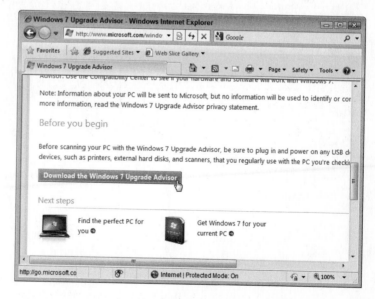

2. On the *second* Windows 7 Upgrade Advisor page, click the Download button. When asked if you wish to Run or Save the file, choose Save, saving the file on your Desktop or in your Downloads folder. When the download completes, install the program by double-clicking the downloaded program's name: Windows7UpgradeAdvisorSetup. Click through the approval screen, if you see one.

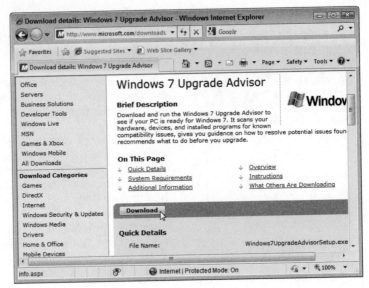

 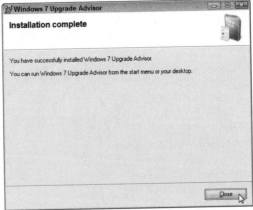

3. Click I Accept the License Terms, and click the Install button. When the program finishes installing, click the Close button.

4. Launch the program by clicking the Start button and choosing Windows 7 Upgrade Advisor. (If not on the Start menu's first page, it's in the All Programs area.) If asked, click Yes to allow the program to make changes to your computer.

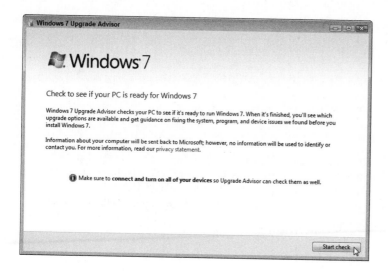

5. When the Windows 7 Upgrade Advisor program appears, plug all of the equipment you want to use with Windows 7 into your computer's USB or FireWire ports. Turn on your printer, or anything else plugged into your computer. Then click the Start Check button. The program begins examining your computer, its software, and all the parts you've plugged into your computer. After a bit of brow furrowing, the program displays its findings.

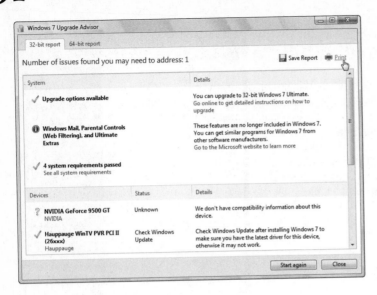

6. Read Windows Advisor's results, which explain which parts need updated drivers (Chapter 17) or must be replaced. Then click both the Save Report and the Print buttons; you can take the printed report to the store while shopping for updated parts and software.

TIP

If you're thinking about upgrading to the 64-bit version of Windows 7, click the 64-bit tab in the upper-left corner to see how your computer will fare. There's no easy upgrade path from 32-bit to 64-bit computing, however. To switch to the 64-bit version of Windows, you need to reformat your hard drive, install the 64-bit version, and then reinstall all your programs. (The process is the same as if you were upgrading from Windows XP or installing Windows 7 onto an empty hard drive. Simply put, it's a lot of work.)

Upgrading from Windows Vista to Windows 7

Before upgrading Windows Vista to Windows 7, be sure to run Windows Upgrade Advisor, described in the previous task. The upgrade is fairly painless, and it will leave all your files and most of your programs alive and breathing.

However, your computer must be running Windows Vista Service Pack 1 or 2 before you can upgrade to Windows 7. Not sure what version of Vista you're running? Click the Start button, type **winver** into the Search box, and press Enter. When the About Windows box appears, the words *Service Pack 1* or *Service Pack 2* should be listed on the box's second line.

No service pack listed? Then grab it through Windows Update: Click the Start menu, choose All Programs, and click Windows Update. Keep downloading *all* the updates marked "Important" until Microsoft slips you a copy of Service Pack 1.

When you're running Windows Vista with at least one of its service packs, follow these steps to upgrade your copy of Windows Vista to Windows 7:

1. Insert the Windows 7 DVD into your DVD drive and click Run Setup, if necessary. You may also need to click one of Vista's permission screens before Windows 7 begins examining your computer. When the installation program finally comes up for air, click Install Now, and Windows 7 begins installing temporary files.

2. Choose Go Online to Get the Latest Updates for Installation (Recommended). This step tells Windows 7 to visit Microsoft's Web site and download the latest updates — drivers, patches, and assorted fixes for your particular computer — that help make your installation run as smoothly as possible. (Your computer must remain connected to the Internet for the downloads, of course.)

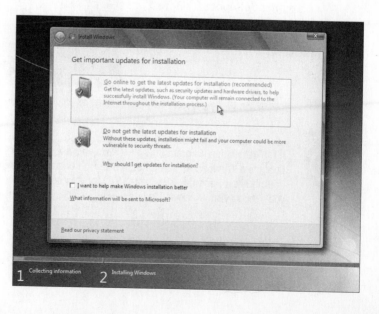

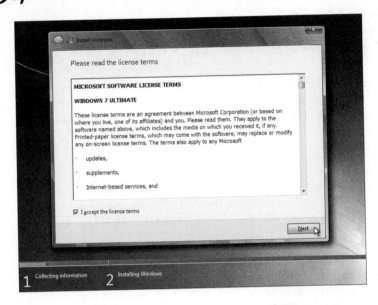

3. Scour Microsoft's 44-page License Agreement, select the I Accept the License Terms check box, and click Next.

4. Choose Upgrade, read the consequences, and click Next. Choosing Upgrade preserves your Windows Vista computer's old files, settings, and programs. If you told Windows 7 to go online in Step 2, Windows 7 explains any compatibility problems it finds with your computer's programs. Read the Compatibility Report, if offered, and then click Next to begin the upgrade, a process that could take several hours.

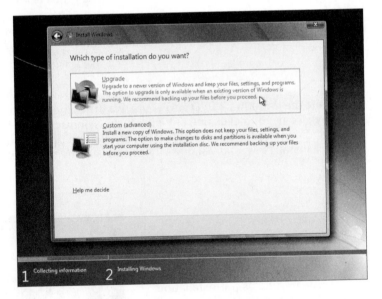

TIP

If the installation program doesn't let you upgrade, any of several things could be wrong: You're trying to upgrade a Windows XP computer, which isn't allowed; you're trying to upgrade a Windows Vista version that doesn't allow upgrades (see Table 18-1), or your copy of Windows Vista doesn't have Service Pack 1, meaning you need to visit Windows Update (www.windowsupdate.com) to download and install Service Pack 1.

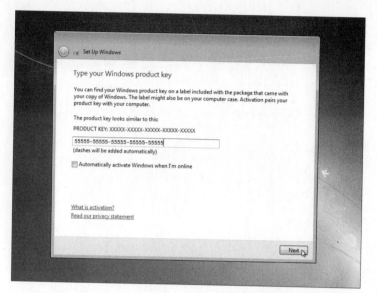

5. Type your product key and click Next. The *product key* usually lives on a little sticker affixed to the CD's packaging. (If you're reinstalling a version of Windows 7 that came pre-installed on your computer, look for the product key printed on a sticker affixed to your computer's case.)

6. Choose Use Recommended Settings. This allows Windows to visit the Internet to update itself with security patches, warn you of suspicious Web sites, check for troubleshooting information, and send technical information to Microsoft to fine-tune Windows' performance.

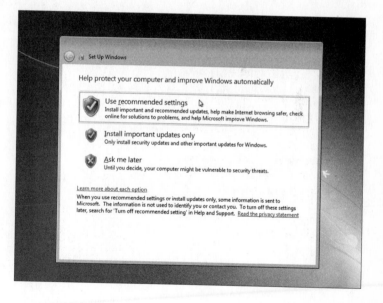

Don't select the Automatically Activate Windows When I'm Online check box. You can do that later when you know Windows 7 works on your computer. (You must enter the product key and activate Windows 7 within 30 days of installation; Windows 7 nags you incessantly as the deadline approaches.) Windows 7's Activation feature takes a snapshot of your computer's parts and links it with Windows 7's serial number, which prevents you from installing that same copy onto another computer.

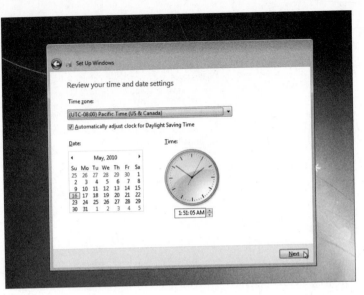

7. Confirm the time and date settings and then click Next. Windows 7 usually guesses these correctly.

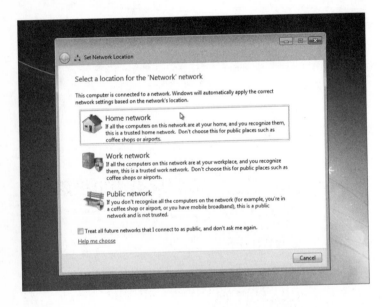

8. If you're connected to a network, choose your computer's location. Windows 7 gives you options: Home, Work, or Public. If you choose Home or Work, Windows 7 eases up on the security a bit, letting the computers on the network see each other. If you're in a public setting, though, choose Public. Windows 7 keeps your computer more secure by not letting other computers share any of its files.

9. After rummaging around inside your computer for a few more minutes, Windows 7 appears on the screen, leaving you at the logon screen. But don't rest yet. After logging on, be sure to run Windows Update to download any security patches and updated drivers issued by Microsoft.

Installing Windows 7 over Windows XP or onto an Empty Hard Drive

Stuff You Need to Know

Toolbox:

✔ Your hands

Materials:

✔ A computer running Windows XP or with an empty hard drive

✔ A Windows 7 retail DVD

Time Needed:

Less than an hour

The steps in this task jump around a bit because you can move from Windows XP to Windows 7 in either of two ways. Your path, oddly enough, depends on whether your hard drive has at least 20GB of free space.

If you have enough free space, follow the steps that *don't* call for reformatting your hard drive. Windows 7 will neatly stash Windows XP, your programs, and your files, into a folder called `Windows.old`. You can't retrieve those stashed files without some expert help, and Windows XP will no longer run. However, those files will remain for an emergency.

If you don't have 20GB of empty hard drive space, though, take the steps that wipe your hard drive clean, giving Windows 7 enough room to settle in.

Finally, if you're installing Windows 7 onto an empty hard drive, insert your Windows 7 DVD into your computer's disc drive, restart your computer, and jump ahead to Step 4.

Got that? Follow these steps to climb into Windows 7:

1. Back up your files and settings by running Windows Easy Transfer on your Windows XP computer, a task covered in Chapter 20. For best results, transfer your files and settings to a portable hard drive that's at least as large as the drive in your Windows XP computer. Then unplug the portable drive and set it aside for copying the files back to Windows 7, also covered in Chapter 20.

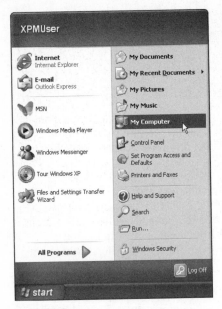

2. Rename your Windows XP drive. This step isn't technically necessary, but it helps you identify the correct drive a few steps later. Open the Start menu and choose My Computer. Right-click your C drive, choose Rename, type **XP**, and press Enter. Finally, hover your mouse pointer over your C drive's icon to see your drive's amount of free space. (The drive in the figure shows 124GB; you need at least 20GB.)

3. *If your drive has less than 20GB of free space,* insert the Windows 7 DVD into your DVD drive and restart your computer. Your computer restarts, but begins loading files directly from the Windows 7 DVD. (You may have to press a key to tell your computer to load from the DVD drive rather than the hard drive.) Then go to Step 4. *If your drive has more than 20GB of free space,* insert the Windows 7 DVD into your DVD drive and choose Install Now. Your computer begins installing temporary files. Then, choose Go Online to Get the Latest Updates for Installation (Recommended). Finally, select the I Accept the License Terms check box, and click Next. Then jump to Step 7.

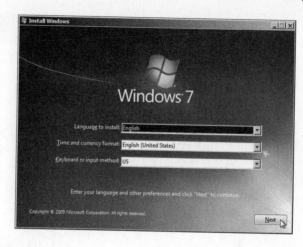

4. Click Next to tell the program to install everything in English, including menu language, keyboard layout, and currency symbols.

5. Click the Install Now button to tell Windows to begin copying the DVD's files to your hard drive.

6. Read the License Agreement, select the I Accept the License Terms check box, and click Next.

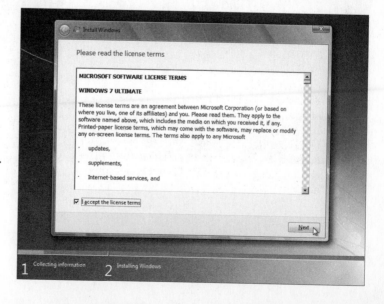

7. Choose Custom (Advanced) instead of the Upgrade option, and the program shows you a window listing your computer's partitions and/or drives. (You can't upgrade from Windows XP, so the Upgrade option doesn't work.)

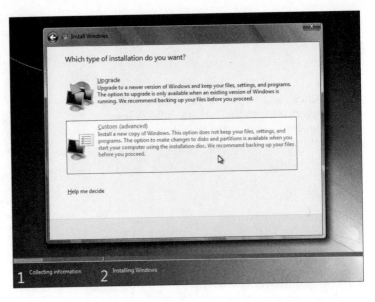

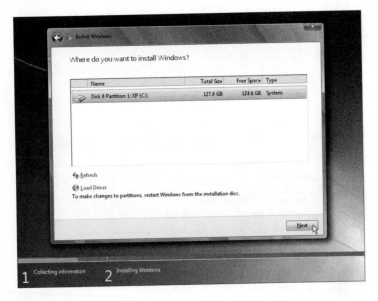

8. If your hard drive *didn't have at least 20GB of free space,* go to Step 9. Otherwise, click your Windows XP drive. (If you see several drives listed, your Windows XP drive will have the letters "XP" listed somewhere in its name.) Your next move depends on your drive's size, which you measured in Step 3. If your hard drive *had at least 20GB of free space,* simply click Next. Windows 7 installs itself over Windows XP, saving your computer's old files in a folder called Windows.old. Now jump to Step 11.

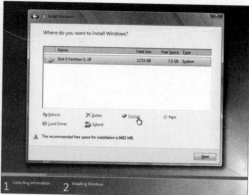

9. Click Drive Options (Advanced) (left). Then click Format (right), and click OK to approve the format process. *Then* click Next. Regardless of which path you choose, the click of the Next button tells Windows 7 to install itself on your old Windows XP drive, a process that consumes about 10 to 30 minutes on most computers.

10. If you reformatted your hard drive in Step 9, Windows now asks you to choose your Country, Time and Currency, and keyboard layout. (Because you reformatted your hard drive, you weren't allowed to do this in Step 4.)

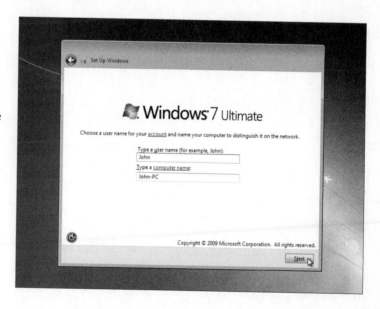

11. Enter your username and a name for your computer, and click Next. Feel free to type in the same username and computer name as you did on your old computer.

Clicking Format completely erases your copy of Windows XP and all of your information on that partition. There's no going back after you finish Step 9, so make *sure* you've backed up your Windows XP files in Step 1.

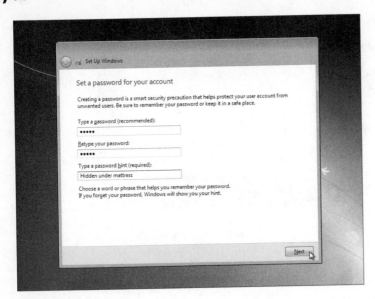

12. Type and retype a password, then type in a password hint, and then click Next. The password hint should be a phrase that reminds you of your password but doesn't give it away. For example, if your password is the name of your elementary school, the password hint could be, "My first elementary school."

13. Jump to Step 5 in the preceding task, "Upgrading from Windows Vista to Windows 7." From here onward, the remaining installation steps are identical to the closing steps in that section.

Upgrading to a Better Version of Windows 7 on a Netbook

Small notebook computers known as *netbooks* usually come with Windows 7 Starter edition — a stripped-down version of Windows 7 lacking the features found in more expensive versions. For example, Windows 7 Starter edition won't let you change the desktop wallpaper, it limits the number of programs you can run simultaneously, and it lacks the fancier graphics found in other Windows versions. There's no Media Center for watching and recording television, either.

If you tire of Windows 7 Starter version's restrictions, you can upgrade to a better version through the built-in Windows Anytime Upgrade program. By entering your credit card number and choosing a better Windows version, your netbook wakes up with the upgraded version of Windows already installed. You don't need to reinstall your programs, nor retrieve your files from a backup: They're all still there.

Follow these steps to upgrade your netbook from Windows 7 Starter to a more powerful version of Windows 7:

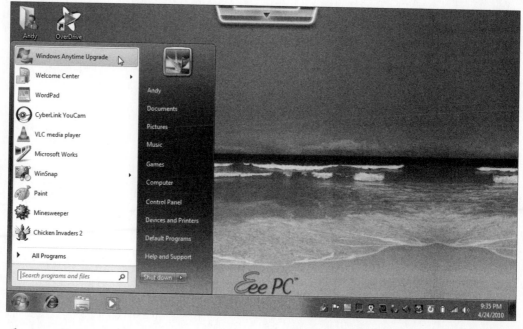

1. Click the Start menu and choose Windows Anytime Upgrade. The Windows Anytime Upgrade window appears, listing your current Windows version in its top-right corner. If you bought an Anytime Upgrade key in a retail store (or online from Amazon), choose Enter an Upgrade Key, type in your key, and jump to Step 6. Otherwise, move to Step 2.

2. Choose the option labeled Go Online to Choose the Edition of Windows 7 That's Best For You. The program's Choose Edition window lists the three versions of Windows you may upgrade to: Windows 7 Home Premium, Professional, or Ultimate.

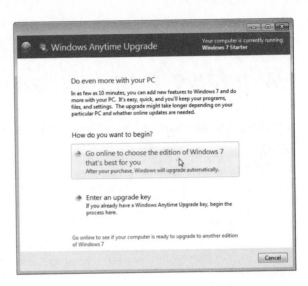

3. In the Choose Edition window, click the Buy button beneath the version you want to buy.

4. In the Billing window, fill out the online form with your billing name, address, and e-mail address. Click the Next button.

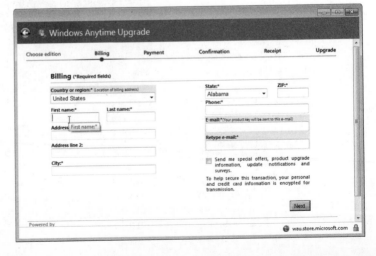

5. In the Payment window, enter your credit card type, number, expiration date, and security code. Then click the Next button. The program charges your credit card, and assigns you a key that lets you upgrade to the newer version.

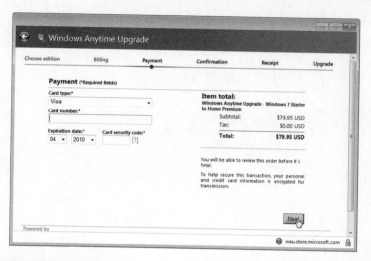

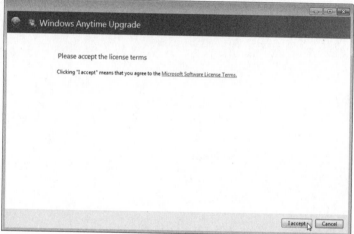

6. In the Confirmation window, click the I Accept button. Because you're basically installing a new version of Windows, you need to agree to Microsoft's zillion-page licensing agreement.

7. Save any work you have in progress, close all your open programs, and click the Upgrade button to begin the upgrade process. After ten minutes to a half hour, depending on your particular computer, Windows 7 returns to the screen wearing the clothes of its new version.

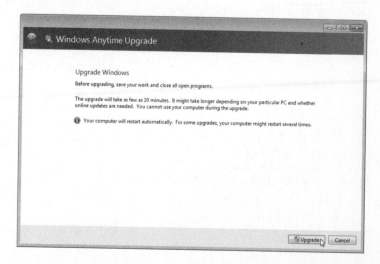

Chapter 19

Troubleshooting and Fixing Windows 7

The easiest way to avoid problems with Windows 7 is to avoid malware: viruses, worms, and other nasty bits that slip inside your computer and make trouble. Now that Microsoft's released a free antivirus program, you have little excuse for letting those buggers in the door.

Chances are, everybody has a few older programs that have trouble adjusting to the new ways of Windows 7. To keep those old programs happy, Windows 7 offers several ways to help them adjust to their new Windows 7 neighborhood.

This chapter's tasks cover it all, from walking you through downloading and installing Microsoft Security Essentials, to keeping your favorite Windows XP programs chugging along happily either in Windows 7 or in Windows XP Mode.

Finally, it walks you through using Windows 7's built-in troubleshooters that work like technicians on call. They examine your computer, look for problems, and offer to walk you through the cure.

Installing and Running Microsoft Security Essentials Antivirus Software

Stuff You Need to Know

Toolbox:
- ✔ Your computer
- ✔ An Internet connection

Materials:
- ✔ A legitimate copy of Windows XP, Vista, or Windows 7

Time Needed:
Less than an hour

Most people hate their antivirus program, and for good reason. First, most antivirus programs demand an annual fee, or they simply stop working.

Even when the programs do work, they often overload your computer with an overblown security "suite," which usually duplicates Windows' built-in firewall and antispyware program (Windows Defender). All that overhead slows down your computer.

To help people who dislike, can't afford, or can't figure out an overly complicated antivirus program, Microsoft released Microsoft Security Essentials, a slim 'n' trim program that checks for incoming viruses, removes spyware, and scans your computer for viruses every week.

Since the program removes spyware, it disables the no-longer-needed Windows Defender when installed on Windows 7 or Windows Vista. When installed on Windows XP, Microsoft Security Essentials uninstalls Windows Defender to avoid redundancy.

Microsoft Security Essentials is fast, unobtrusive, and it works. Plus, it's free to owners of Windows XP, Windows Vista, or Windows 7. (The program doesn't work on older Windows versions.)

To download and install Microsoft's Security Essentials program, follow these steps:

Don't run more than one antivirus program at a time, as they conflict with each other. Be sure to turn off any other antivirus program before running Microsoft Security Essentials. Check with your antivirus program's Web site for instructions on disabling or uninstalling it.

1. Download the program by visiting the Microsoft Security Essentials Web site (`www.microsoft.com/security_essentials`) and clicking the Download Now button. Choose your Windows version, if asked: Windows XP, Windows Vista (32-bit or 64-bit), or Windows 7 (32-bit or 64-bit). To find out your version of Windows, click the Start button, right-click Computer or My Computer, and choose Properties.

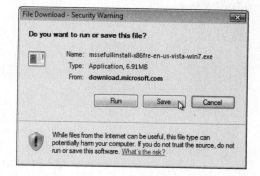

2. Click Save to save the program's installation file to your computer. Download it to a place where you can find it easily, like on your Desktop, or in your Downloads folder.

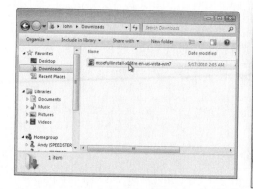 

3. Start the Installation program by double-clicking the downloaded file (left), and then clicking Next (right) when the installation program appears onscreen. (You may need to click an approval screen before clicking Next.)

4. Read the licensing terms, and click the I Accept button to agree to their conditions. Then, if asked, click Validate to make sure your Windows copy is legitimate. Yep, this is the only catch: Microsoft Security Essentials installs only on computers running authentic copies of Windows. Computers purchased with Windows pre-installed will pass this test, as will people who've purchased and installed Windows themselves. But if you're running a bootleg copy of Windows, the install won't work.

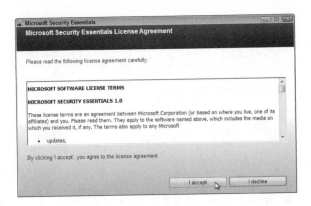

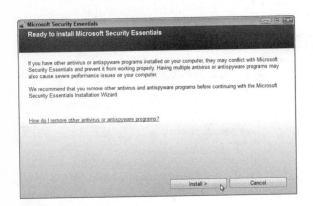

5. When the computer passes the validation test, click Install. The program takes a few minutes to install itself and download the latest virus definitions from the Internet.

6. Click Finish to complete the installation and scan your computer for any existing viruses. The program will scan your computer for viruses during the next few minutes, but you can minimize the program while it works in the background. That's it. The program automatically checks your downloads, your opened programs, and it scans your entire computer every Sunday at 2 a.m. To change the scanning time, click the Settings tab, click Scheduled Scan from the left pane, and choose a different day or time from the drop-down menus on the right. Click the Save Changes button to save your updated scanning schedule.

7. When you're through, click the minimize button and let the program live in your taskbar's notifications area, in the lower right. The program starts automatically when you log in to your user account, and it notifies you if it detects any incoming viruses.

Running Older Programs Well in Windows 7

Stuff You Need to Know

Toolbox:

✔ Your hands

Materials:

✔ An older program that won't run well in Windows 7

Time Needed:

Less than an hour

You don't need to replace *everything* that Windows 7 flags as incompatible. Some of your computer's outdated parts, for example, will spring back to life once you track down and install updated *drivers,* a task I walk you through in Chapter 17. Similarly, some of your older software can run freely once again with the help of Windows 7's Program Compatibility settings.

Windows 7's security systems can confuse an older program accustomed to Windows XP's free reins. Windows 7's Program Compatibility program places a soothing blanket of settings over your confused program, tricking it into thinking it's still running in an earlier Windows version. The program still runs, Windows 7 still keeps things secure, and you still get your work done.

Best yet, Windows 7 remembers which settings the program finds most cozy. Then, whenever you run the program in question, Windows 7 automatically fetches those settings, saving you time. Although Program Compatibility won't help you with computer parts, it works well at resuscitating some older software.

To apply Windows 7's Program Compatibility settings, follow these steps. (They'll differ slightly depending on your particular program.)

1. Try to install the older program. You may be pleasantly surprised to find that it still installs and runs correctly. If it refuses to run, go to Step 2.

TECHNICAL STUFF

Don't want to bother with Windows 7's step-by-step Program Compatibility program? If you know what settings the program requires, enter them yourself by right-clicking the program's name on the Start menu, choosing Properties, and clicking the Compatibility tab. There, you can enter the program's desired version of Windows (Windows 95-Windows Vista), choose its video settings, and let it run with Administrator privileges. (Many support sites list Windows 7 compatibility settings known to work with specific programs.)

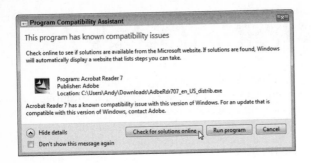

2. If Windows 7 offers a helpful suggestion to make the program run, take it up on its offer. The suggestion might be a link to a newer version of the program, for example, or a way to download a program that can read your program's older Help menus.

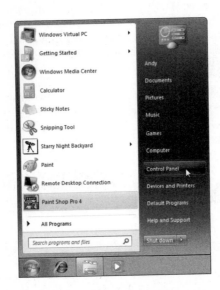

3. If Windows doesn't offer any helpful suggestions, fire up the Program Compatibility window: Choose Start, choose Control Panel, and click the Programs category. The Programs category appears, listing all the Control Panel settings that cover programs.

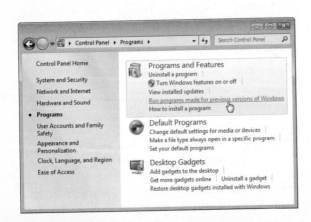

4. In the Programs and Features category, choose Run Program Made for Previous Versions of Windows. When the Program Compatibility window appears, click Next. Windows examines your computer's programs to see if it detects any troublemakers. If it finds one, it offers a suggestion. If it doesn't find one, it lists all of your programs, letting you finger the culprit.

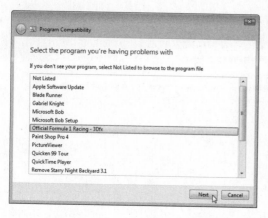 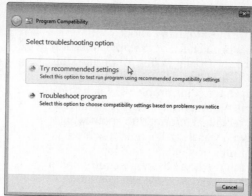

5. Click the name of the program giving you trouble, and click Next; then, choose Try Recommended Settings. That tells Windows to automatically guess at the settings your program needs and apply them temporarily.

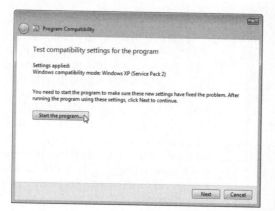 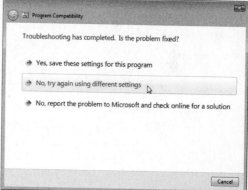

6. Click Start the Program to see if the program works, wait to see if the program runs or not, and then click Next (left). If the program worked, click Yes, Save These Settings for This Program, and breathe a sigh of relief. Didn't work? Click No, Try Again Using Different Settings.

7. Fill out the questionnaire about your program's problems. For example, does it not install or run? Or is it asking for permission to run? Or does it open, but not fit on the screen, or have color problems? Click the applicable button, then click Next. Windows may ask technical information about what the program wants, so it's time to whip out the program's original box and look at the fine print in the box's System Requirements section. You need to know what version of Windows the program expects, for example.

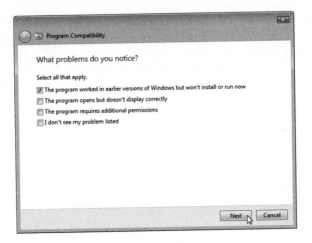

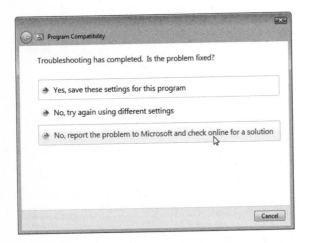

8. If nothing seems to work, and you end up on the screen that says, "Troubleshooting Has Completed. Is the Problem Fixed?" choose No, Report the Problem to Microsoft and Check Online For A Solution. Microsoft might send you a solution, but it will probably pass the buck by saying, "Incompatible Application." At this point, you have two options: Look for help on the Internet from others plagued by the same problem, as I describe in Chapter 21. Or try running the program in Windows XP Mode, which I walk you through in this chapter's next task.

Installing Windows XP Mode to Run Incompatible Windows XP Programs

Many Windows XP programs run fine under Windows 7, but a few oldsters refuse to adjust to the new world of Windows 7. To help your old Windows XP programs keep gasping along, Microsoft released the Windows XP Mode application.

This free downloadable program places a fully licensed copy of Windows XP on your screen inside its own window. That's right: Your Windows XP programs run while sequestered inside their own Windows XP window within Windows 7. The boxed-in Windows XP programs have access to your real computer's files and disk drives, making for a peaceful coexistence with Windows 7.

The downer? Windows XP Mode runs only on Windows 7's Enterprise, Professional, or Ultimate versions. (I describe how to upgrade to a different Windows version with Anytime Upgrade in Chapter 18.)

Once installed, Windows XP Mode differs from a "real" version of Windows XP in several ways:

✔ To install a program from within your Windows XP Mode window, insert the program's CD or DVD into the drive. Double-click your CD or DVD drive's icon to open it, and then double-click the file named setup.exe to begin installing the program. That tells your computer to load the program inside the *Windows XP mode window,* and not within Windows 7.

✔ Windows XP Mode runs Windows XP Service Pack 3, not the first version of Windows XP. That newer version includes the billions of patches Microsoft has released over the last decade. Windows XP Mode installs *much* more quickly than that old Windows XP CD sitting in your desk drawer.

✔ USB plug-in drives — flash drives, portable hard drives, and their cousins — show up in both Windows 7 and Windows XP, making them a handy way to transport files.

✔ You can cut and paste between your Windows XP and your Windows 7 worlds, which is another handy perk.

✔ Once you've installed Windows XP programs in Windows XP Mode, those programs show up on your Windows 7 Start menu, as well. Click the Start button, choose All Programs, click Windows Virtual PC, and you see your Windows XP program listed.

> ✔ Close down Windows XP Mode from its own Start menu. Or click the Ctrl+Alt+Del menu atop the window; then click the Shut Down button.
>
> ✔ Windows XP Mode loads your virtual Windows XP world with 512MB of memory. Surprisingly, this is plenty for most old Windows XP programs. But if you need more memory, close Windows XP Mode and perform a virtual upgrade: Click the Start button, choose All Programs, and click Windows Virtual PC. Windows Virtual PC opens, looking like any other folder. Click the Windows XP Mode entry, click Settings on the menu bar, and start tweaking any of its settings, including its 512MB memory limit.

Windows XP Mode isn't for everybody, and it's not as easy to use as a stand-alone Windows XP computer. But if you simply must keep that cranky Windows XP program running, it's a convenient life-support system, especially for fast, memory-stuffed computers that can afford to share their memory with a Windows XP world.

Follow these steps to install Windows XP Mode on your Windows 7 computer and begin running your holdout Windows XP programs within their own happy Windows XP world:

1. Visit Microsoft's Windows Virtual PC Web site (www.microsoft.com/windows/virtual-pc/download.aspx) and fill out two questions: What language do you want on Windows XP's menus? And are you running a 32- or 64-bit version of Windows 7? Then download each of the three files listed on the Web site: Windows XP Mode, Windows Virtual PC, and Windows XP Mode Update. (You may also need to download and run Microsoft's Windows Activation Update to prove you're running a legitimate version of Windows 7.)

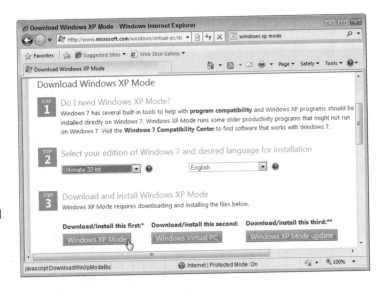

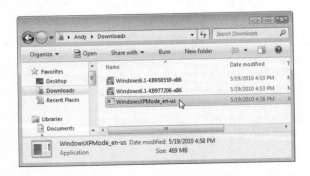

2. First, install the Windows XP Mode program by double-clicking its filename in your Downloads folder and clicking through the approval and Next screens. Second, install the Windows Virtual PC program, also known as KB958559. You need to restart your computer afterward. Finally, run the Windows XP Mode Update, also known as KB977206, and restart your computer, yet again.

 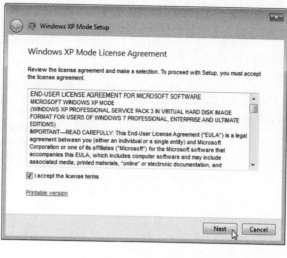

3. Open Windows XP Mode by clicking Start, choosing All Programs, clicking Windows Virtual PC, and choosing Windows XP Mode. Accept the license agreement — after all, Microsoft is giving you a *free* copy of Windows XP — then click Next.

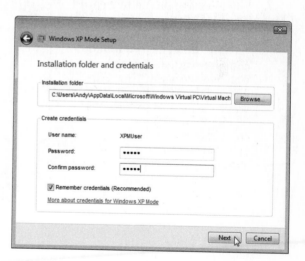

4. In a strange déjà vu, you find yourself installing Windows XP once again, entering a password for your Microsoft-given username of "XPMUser."

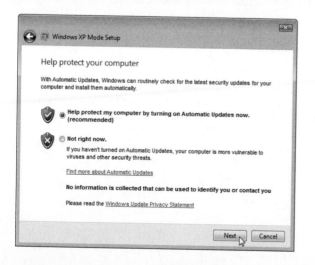

5. Let the program turn on Automatic Updates to keep your virtual XP world updated through Windows Update. Remember, Windows XP isn't nearly as secure as Windows 7.

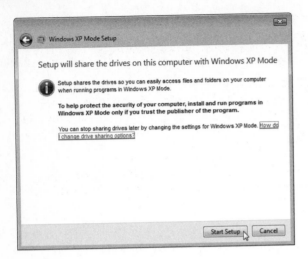

6. Finally, click Start Setup to give your Windows XP window access to the files and folders on your Windows 7 computer. (This is yet another reason to keep your Windows XP world as secure as possible by turning on its Automatic Updates.)

7. Windows 7 begins setting up Windows XP Mode; a few minutes later, you see Windows XP running within its own window, complete with its nostalgic welcome message: "There are unused icons on your desktop." Welcome back to Windows XP!

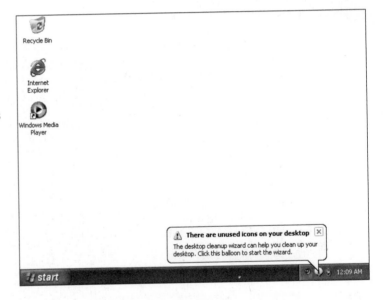

8. Start exploring by opening the Start menu's My Computer program, and you see your computer's disk drives. Then be sure to install Microsoft Security Essentials, described in this chapter's first task, to keep your virtual XP world safe.

Freeing up Disk Space with Disk Cleanup

Stuff You Need to Know

Toolbox:
- Your hands

Materials:
- Windows 7

Time Needed:
Less than an hour

You've probably felt the symptoms. Your computer slows down. You see errors about low "virtual memory" and "insufficient disk space." You want to install a new hard drive (a task described in Chapter 6), but you're trying to put off buying one. How do you identify the things you can safely delete to free up some disk space?

Windows 7's built-in Disk Cleanup tool makes that decision for you by identifying leftover housekeeping and maintenance files, and then offering to delete them for you.

Here's how to employ Disk Cleanup to sweep Windows 7's leftovers into the trash, making more room for your own files:

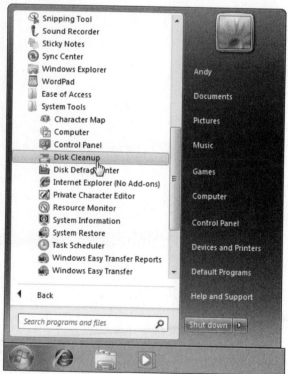

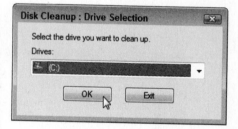

1. Click Start, click All Programs, click Accessories, click System Tools, and then click Disk Cleanup. If your computer has several drives, the program asks which one to clean up. Choose your (C:) drive, as that's where Windows stashes most of its housekeeping files, and click OK.

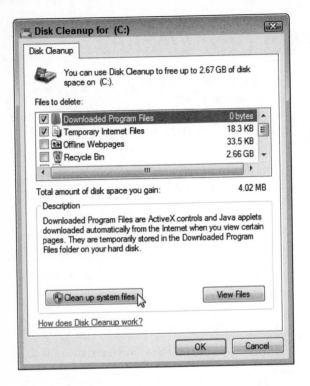

2. Disk Cleanup spins its gears, calculating what to delete, and then lists the candidates. Place a check mark in each category except for Recycle Bin, as you may want to retrieve some of those recently deleted files later. If you're desperate for space, click the Clean Up System Files button, which lets you delete a few extra files.

3. Click OK to start purging the files. After a minute or two, the Disk Cleanup dialog box disappears, leaving your computer with extra storage space.

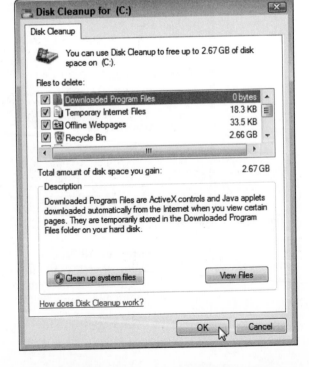

Making a Windows 7 System Repair Disc

Stuff You Need to Know

Toolbox:
✔ Your hands

Materials:
✔ Windows 7
✔ A CD or DVD burner
✔ A blank CD or DVD

Time Needed:
Less than an hour

Today, very few computers come with a Windows 7 DVD. Most of them come with "Recovery" discs that simply erase everything on your computer and return your computer to the same condition as when you purchased it: Windows 7 and a few bundled programs. What's missing are the programs you've installed and all the files you've created with them.

To fix that problem, I describe how to create a system image — a complete copy of your hard drive — as a task in Chapter 6. In order to put that System Image back onto your computer, you need a System Repair disc.

That System Repair disc comes in handy for other reasons, as well. When Windows no longer loads, for example, the System Repair disc can search your hard drive for your Windows installation and often bring it back to life.

Follow these steps to create a System Repair disc:

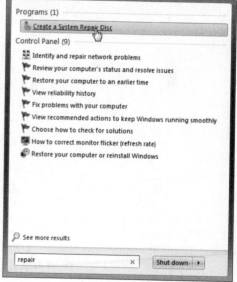

1. Click the Start button, type **repair** into the Search box, and choose Create a System Repair Disc.

2. Choose your CD or DVD drive from the drop-down menu, insert either a CD or DVD, and click Create Disc. Windows begins creating the disc. When it's through, grab a felt-tip pen and write the words **Windows 7 Repair Disc** on the disc's printed side, and then stash it in a safe place. You'll need that disc to restore your computer from the system image you've made in Chapter 6.

Troubleshooting Problems and Boosting Your Computer's Performance

Stuff You Need to Know

Toolbox:
- Your hands

Materials:
- Windows 7

Time Needed:
Less than an hour

You can improve your computer's performance by throwing money at it: Buy a faster graphics card, more memory, and a faster hard drive. But before opening your wallet, fire up Windows 7's built-in Performance tool, one of many tools included in Windows 7's built-in troubleshooting area.

The troubleshooting area is chockfull of shortcuts that point to separate troubleshooting tools spread throughout Windows' many areas. Click any troubleshooter that meets your needs, and follow its path of adjustable settings and troubleshooting tips until you solve your problem.

For example, these steps show how to fire up the Performance troubleshooter. After all, just about everybody wishes their computer performed a little better. Since everybody's computer will have slightly different performance issues, your troubleshooter will probably find slightly different issues to correct.

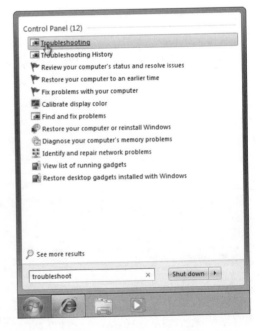

1. Click the Start button, type **troubleshooting** in the Search box, and press Enter. (Or, as soon as you see "Troubleshooting" appear on the list, click the term to start the Troubleshooter.) The Troubleshoot Computer Problems window appears, listing a dozen troubleshooting programs spanning five categories.

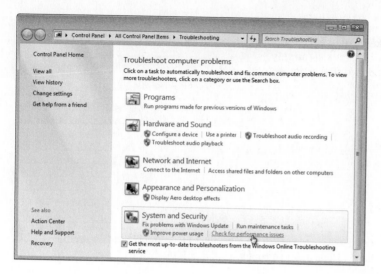

2. Choose the troubleshooter pertaining to your problem. To help speed up your computer, for example, choose Check for Performance Issues, and then click Next at its opening screen.

3. The program analyzes the most common problems that slow down your computer's performance, and lists the first culprit: Programs that automatically run whenever you start Windows. To weed out any unnecessary programs, click Start System Configuration.

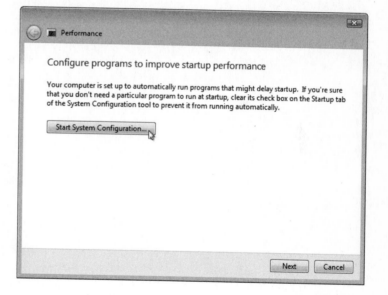

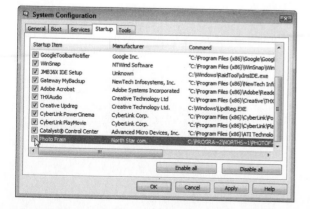

4. The System Configuration window appears, listing all the programs that start automatically whenever you start your computer. And it's a *long* list. How do you know which programs do what? Look them up in Google, of course. For example, one listed as "Photo Fram" displays a slideshow of digital photos whenever I insert a memory card into my Gateway computer's memory card slot. Since I never do that, I unchecked "Photo Fram" and clicked the OK button to disable it.

5. Click the Restart button to apply your changes, and then restart your computer to make sure everything works correctly. (If your computer behaves strangely, repeat the preceding steps but *re-enable* the program you disabled.)

Run Windows 7's Performance checking tool — as well as the other tools in the Troubleshooting area — whenever you could use a helping hand to heal a sick computer.

Chapter 20

Moving from the Old Computer to the New Computer

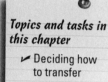
When you bring home an exciting new Windows 7 computer, it lacks the most important thing of all: your *old* computer's files. How do you copy your files from that drab old computer to that exciting new Windows 7 computer? How can you even *find* everything you want to move?

To solve the problem, Microsoft created a virtual moving van named Windows Easy Transfer. The Windows Easy Transfer program sweeps up your old computer's data and program settings: your Web browser's list of favorite Web sites, for example. After packaging them up, the transfer program copies them to your new computer.

There's one big catch: Windows Easy Transfer won't move your *programs*. You need to install those onto your Windows 7 computer by hand. (Start searching for your old discs. . . .)

Windows Vista owners don't need the transfer program, as Windows 7 keeps their files, most programs, and their settings in place during an upgrade. But Windows XP owners should all walk down this chapter's path.

Note: Windows Easy Transfer doesn't work with older Windows versions such as Windows Me or Windows 98.

Choosing How to Transfer Your Files

Windows Easy Transfer packages all your files and program settings into one huge file, leaving you with one huge decision. What's the best way to move that *huge* file over to your new Windows 7 computer? The envelope, please:

- ✔ **Easy Transfer cable:** A natural choice for the budget conscious, this cable resembles a normal USB cable. Plug one end into each computer's USB port, and you're ready to transfer the file. (No, a normal USB cable won't work.) Easy Transfer cables cost less than $30 online and at computer stores.

- ✔ **Portable hard drive:** Costing around $100, a portable hard drive can plug into your computer's USB port to grab or deliver the file. Some portable drives plug into a wall outlet for power; others draw their power right from the USB port. (I describe how to create your own portable hard drive in Chapter 13.)

- ✔ **Flash drive:** These little memory sticks plug into any computer's USB port. They're handy for transferring small batches of files or settings, but they lack enough storage space to hold much else.

- ✔ **Network:** If you've linked your two computers through a network (a chore I cover in Chapter 15), the Easy Transfer program can place the magic transfer file in any folder that's accessible to both computers.

I recommend the portable hard drive. Even if you have to buy one, you can leave the drive plugged into your Windows 7 computer and use it for backups.

Picking and Choosing the Files, Folders, and Accounts to Transfer

When running Windows Easy Transfer, you'll eventually face the window shown in Figure 20-1, along with the program's stern demand: Choose What to Transfer.

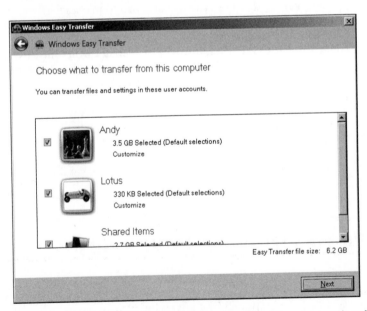

Figure 20-1: Windows Easy Transfer transfers files and program settings from your old computer to your new one.

To transfer *everything* from *all* your old computer's user accounts to accounts on your new computer, simply click the Next button. If your new computer has enough space, the program copies everything for later transfer to your new computer. You can always delete unwanted items later from your new computer, if you want.

But if your new computer doesn't have enough storage space or you don't want everything copied, here's how to choose which items to transfer:

- ✓ **User Accounts:** Want to transfer your own account to your new computer, but leave the other accounts behind on the family's computer? Here's your chance: Windows Easy Transfer puts a check mark next to each user account it will transfer, as shown in Figure 20-1. Click to remove the check mark from the user accounts you *don't* want transferred.

- ✓ **Customize:** Sometimes you don't need it all. To pick and choose what categories of items should be transferred from each account, click the Customize button under each account's name. A window pops up, shown in Figure 20-2, letting you exclude certain categories. Remove the check mark from Desktop, for example, to grab everything but your Desktop's items from your old computer.

- ✓ **Advanced:** The Advanced button, shown at the bottom of the pop-up list in Figure 20-2, works for techies who enjoy micromanaging. By weeding through the tree of folder and filenames, this area lets you pick and choose individual files and folders to copy. It's overkill for most people, but it's an option, nevertheless.

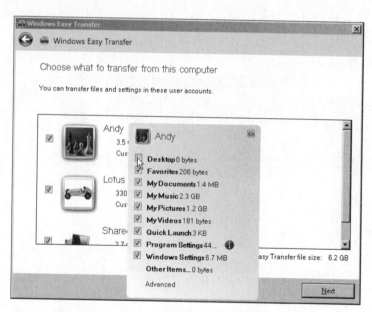

Figure 20-2: Click Customize to whittle down what's transferred from each account.

If you've customized your transfer, click the Save button to return to the Choose What to Transfer window. Then, click Next to continue the transfer process.

Collecting the Files from Your Old Windows XP Computer

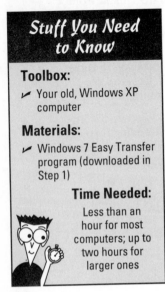
Windows Easy Transfer only copies files and program *settings,* not the programs themselves. So, before copying your files and settings to Windows 7, dig out your old program discs. Hopefully, you've kept them in the box on the shelf. Install those programs on your Windows 7 computer so they're ready to receive their incoming settings.

Then follow these steps on your old computer to run Windows Easy Transfer:

1. Windows Easy Transfer is built into Windows 7, but not Windows XP. To download the program onto your old computer, head to Microsoft's Web site (http://windows.microsoft.com/en-us/windows7/products/features/windows-easy-transfer). (Every Web site mentioned in this book is mentioned on my Web site at www.andyrathbone.com for your point-and-click convenience.) Nearly every Windows XP owner should download the program's 32-bit version.

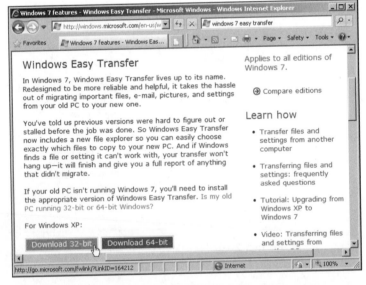

Description: Self-Extracting Cabinet
Company: Microsoft Corporation
File Version: 6.3.15.0
Date Created: 5/20/2010 11:11 PM
Size: 7.25 MB

2. Install the program by double-clicking the downloaded file's name. The file's name should resemble wet7xp__86.exe or something very similar. (At this point, close any other open programs so that their settings can be copied successfully.) Click Next, agree to the 12 pages of licensing terms, and then click Next again to finish installing the program. You'll need to restart your computer.

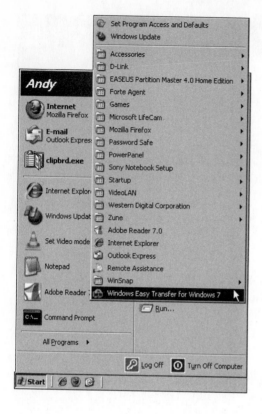

3. Click the Start button, click All Programs, and click Windows Easy Transfer for Windows 7 to launch the program.

4. Click Next at the opening screen.

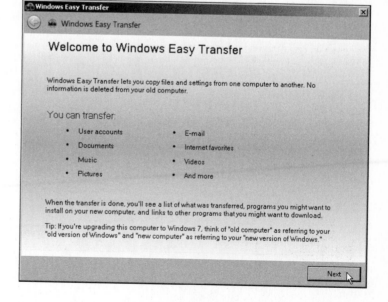

5. Click the method you'd like to use for transferring your files and settings to your Windows 7 computer, as I described at the beginning of this chapter. You can use an Easy Transfer cable, a network storage area, or my favorite option, a portable hard drive.

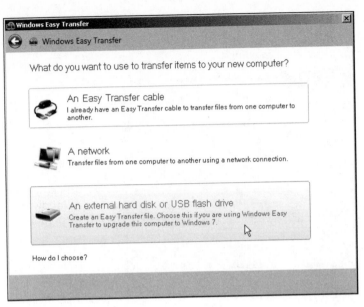

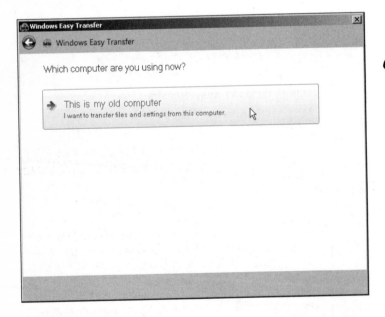

6. Choose This is my Old Computer. If you're transferring through a network, write down the secret code that appears. If you're using an Easy Transfer cable or a network, shuffle over to your new Windows 7 computer and run Windows Easy Transfer. (To find Windows Easy Transfer in Windows 7, click the Start menu, click All Programs, click Accessories, and click System Tools.) Using a portable hard drive to transfer files? Jump to Step 7.

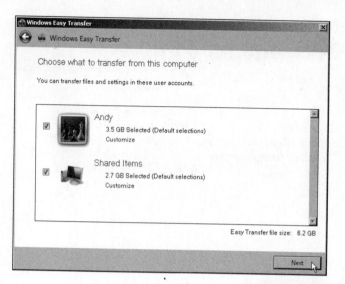

7. To transfer everything possible, just click Next. To fine-tune your selection, perhaps leaving out some folders or user accounts, read this chapter's earlier section, "Picking and Choosing the Files, Folders, and Accounts to Transfer." When you're done choosing, click Next.

8. Enter a password if you're concerned that others might have access to your transfer file, and with it, your private files. Then click Save.

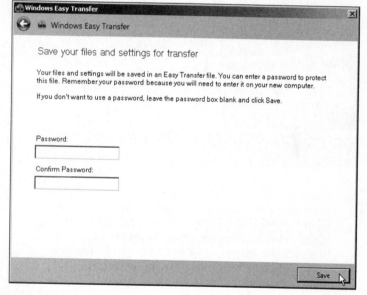

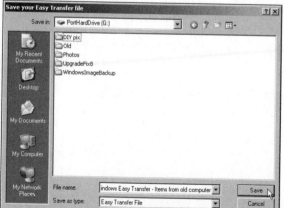

9. Choose the location to save the file, be it a portable hard drive or network location, and then click Save. Then relax — don't work on your old computer — until the program has packaged all the information and stashed it in your chosen spot. When the program's finished, click Next, and then head to the next task, where you retrieve all those files on your Windows 7 computer.

Placing the Files and Settings on Your New Windows 7 Computer

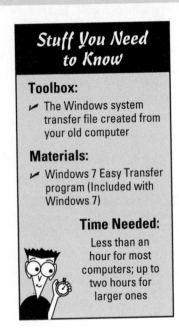

Stuff You Need to Know

Toolbox:

✔ The Windows system transfer file created from your old computer

Materials:

✔ Windows 7 Easy Transfer program (Included with Windows 7)

Time Needed:

Less than an hour for most computers; up to two hours for larger ones

After you've collected the files and settings from your old computer, here's how to unpack them on your new Windows 7 computer. The Windows Easy Transfer program may ask a lot of questions, but most require simple Yes or No answers, followed by a click of the Next button.

Here are the steps:

1. Open Windows Easy Transfer on your new Windows 7 computer by choosing Start and clicking All Programs. Under Accessories, click System Tools, and then click Windows Easy Transfer. When Windows Easy Transfer jumps to the screen, click Next. Groggy from being woken up, Windows Easy Transfer leaves you at a screen saying, What Do You Want to Use to Transfer Items to Your New Computer?

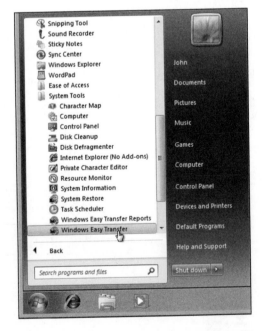

2. Choose the transfer method you chose while in the preceding task — a portable hard drive, an Easy Transfer Cable, or a network.

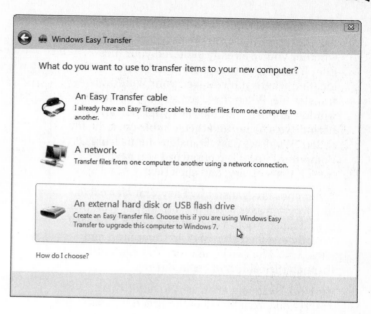

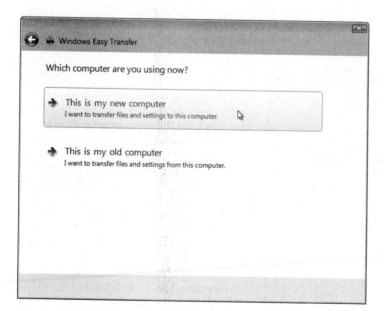

3. Choose This Is My New Computer.

4. If you chose to transfer by portable hard drive, flash drive, or network, the program asks whether you've already gathered your files. Click Yes, plug in your drive, and browse to the location where you've saved your Windows transfer file. When the Open an Easy Transfer window appears, double-click your portable hard drive's name, and then double-click the file called "Windows Easy Transfer – Items from Old Computer." Enter the password you gave it earlier, if necessary, and click Next.

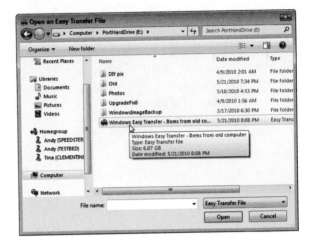

   If you chose to transfer by Easy Transfer cable, the program asks if you need to install Windows Easy Transfer onto your old computer. Choose I Already Installed It on My Old Computer, and click Next. The two computers find each other through the cable and begin talking.

   Network swappers are asked to enter their secret code from Step 6 of the preceding task before being allowed to grab the transfer file.

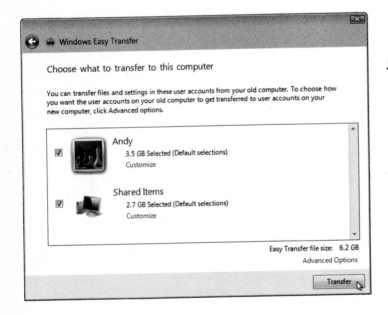

5. Click the Transfer button on your new computer to begin copying the information. After clicking, let the computers work undisturbed. If you've grabbed more information than your new computer can hold, you'll encounter the Choose What to Transfer window from Step 7 in the preceding task. There, you must whittle down the information you want to transfer. (I cover that window and its whittling process in this chapter's earlier section.)

6. The program leaves you with these two options. See What Was Transferred fetches a dry, technical report listing exactly what was transferred. The more useful option, See a List of Programs You Might Want to Install on Your New Computer, tells you the programs you'll need to install before you can open some of your transferred files.

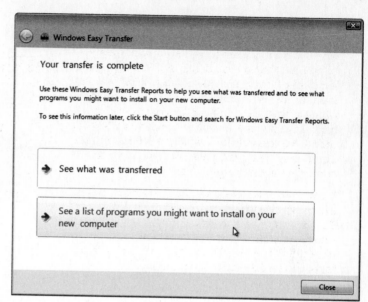

Part VI
The Part of Tens

The 5th Wave   By Rich Tennant

"Why am I modding my PC? I pimped my Xbox, my fish tank, and my Water Pik. This was next."

In this part . . .

Those of you with sharp eyes will notice something scandalous about this part right away: One chapter *doesn't* contain ten items.

But by the time most people get to this part of the book, they're tired of counting numbers, anyway. That's why these lists aren't numbered. They're just a bunch of facts tossed into a basket.

So when you read these chapters, remember that it's quality, not quantity that matters. Besides, would you want to read a tip about 8255 PPI (U20) messages just because one of the chapters in this part needed a tenth tip?

Chapter 21

Ten Ways to Find Help Online

Some problems can't be fixed by reading a book, unfortunately. The most troublesome problems pop up only when a certain version of software tries to run on a specific model of computer containing a specific combination of hardware. Only a small handful of people will ever experience that particular problem in their lifetime.

That little fact doesn't make it any less frustrating when the problem occurs on your computer, though. So, in this chapter, I show how to find that small cluster of other people who have experienced your same problem, stumbled upon a solution, or posted the solution on the Internet.

This chapter explains how to arm yourself with the tools you need to extract those solutions from the gazillions of informational tidbits living throughout the Internet.

Finding Help through Search Engines

Without a doubt, the first stop when you're searching for solutions to computing problems should be Google, the best search engine on the Internet. As I write this, Google's search robots are scouring billions of pages across the Internet, indexing them word by word, and enabling you to search the results for free.

Google lets you locate information several different ways, and I describe the most effective methods in the following sections.

Searching Google for specific information

When I'm troubleshooting a computer problem, I *always* begin my search on Google (www.google.com), as shown in Figure 21-1. Google provides a quick and easy way to find just about any company's Web site, as well as Web sites dealing with particular types of computing problems.

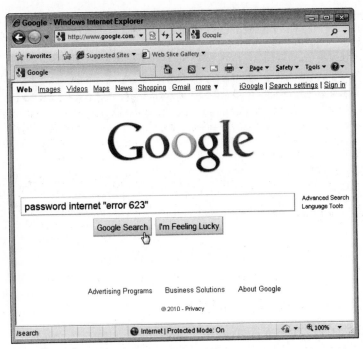

Figure 21-1: Click the Google Search button to see Internet sites containing the words password, internet, and "error 623".

Google lets you search by specific words, exact phrases, or a combination of the two. The key to using Google is in knowing when to search by *words* or *phrases*.

- ✔ **Words:** Search for specific words when you don't care where those words appear on a Web page. For instance, if you're having password problems when you connect to the Internet, you could type this:

  ```
  password problem internet connect
  ```

- ✔ **Phrases:** Search for phrases only when you want to see pages containing two words sitting next to each other, and not mixed in with other words. For example, if your password problem always brings up an error message that says *Error 623,* type this into the search box:

  ```
  password internet "error 623"
  ```

By choosing the right combination of words and phrases in your search, you can make sure that Google knows exactly which pages to bring to your attention.

Now that you know how to properly question Google, here's how to use Google's different buttons and tabs:

- ✔ Google offers two buttons: Google Search, and I'm Feeling Lucky. Clicking the Google Search button tells Google to display a list of Web sites that contain your search words or phrases. Clicking the I'm Feeling Lucky button immediately displays the Web site that most closely matches your search.

- ✔ Use the Google Search button most of the time and visit the Web sites that it lists. By contrast, use the I'm Feeling Lucky button as a time-saver when you're confident that Google knows exactly what page you're looking for. Typing in **Andy Rathbone** and clicking the I'm Feeling Lucky button, for instance, immediately brings up my Web site: www.andyrathbone.com.

- ✔ When you click the Google Search button, Google lists many Web sites containing your words, using a patented ranking method to place the most likely choices at the top of the list. Google offers searches in several other online areas, including Images, Video, Maps, News, Shopping, and Gmail, but it always searches for Web pages unless you click on one of those other areas.

- ✔ Clicking the word Images before clicking the Google Search button tells Google to search for pictures. It's great for finding pictures of obscure CDs or albums. For instance, a Google Images search for *"cities in fog" "jeff greinke"* immediately displays several CD covers of that landmark release. Save the best image as a JPG file named folder.jpg, place it in the folder holding the album's files to see that photo on the folder's icon.

Mastering the art of pinpoint Google searching

Although Pinpoint Google Searching would make a great band name, successful Google searching is also an art in its own right. Google is so good that it often brings thousands of pages to your attention. The trick is to find *only* the pages that solve your problem. Here are my favorite tips:

- ✔ **Search for specific error messages by placing the message in quotes.** Error messages confuse *everybody*. Because messages look the same on every Windows computer, other frustrated people have probably already discussed that error message online. If you're lucky, one of them also posted a solution or workaround.

- ✔ **Make your first search as specific as possible, and then expand your search from there.** For instance, type an error message exactly as you see it and put the message in quotation marks, like this: "Faulting application netdde.exe". If you get too many results, add some context, such as the name of the problematic program, or your version of Windows. Not enough results? Remove the quotes from the phrase, or search for the most confusing words in the error message.

- ✔ **Watch out for misspellings.** Many people misspell when they post messages. Although Google's built-in spell checker kicks in if it can't find any answers to your query, it can't catch everything. Use quotes only on short phrases or specific error messages.

- ✔ **Add your Windows version to your search.** Adding the word *Vista,* for instance, usually limits your search to Windows Vista issues. Similarly, adding the letters *XP* after a search limits your search to Windows XP problems. To search for Windows 7 problems, either include the numeral **7** or type **"Windows 7"** in quotes.

- ✔ **Search for the letters FAQ.** FAQ stands for Frequently Asked Questions. Toss in this acronym along with the name of your problematic subject/product/part.

You just might stumble upon a site that contains a FAQ dealing with your particular problem.

✔ **Sort your results by date.** When Google displays results, it normally sorts them by relevance, with the most likely candidates near the top. To search for recent solutions, sort them by date: Click the words More Search Tools on the results page, and then choose whether to see results from the last 24 hours, three days, week, month, year, or a custom date range. Much of the Internet's computer information is already obsolete, so sorting by date ensures you're finding the newest information.

Think somebody e-mailed you the latest virus? Before opening the suspect e-mail, search Google for the exact words used in the e-mail's subject line. Then sort the results by date to see if people are already talking about it.

✔ **Don't give up too early.** Keep rephrasing your search slightly, adding or subtracting a few words and changing your phrases. Give it five or ten minutes before giving up. Remember, you'll be spending much longer than ten minutes waiting for tech support staff to answer your phone call.

Searching within a specific Web site

Many Web sites aren't organized very well, making it difficult to find your treasured solution. If the Web site isn't turning up the right information, tell Google to limit its search to that specific *site* rather than the entire Internet.

The key is to type the word **site**, a colon, the name of Web site you want to search, followed by the search term.

For example, to search my Web site for the words *system image,* you type this:

```
site:www.andyrathbone.com system image
```

Google immediately fetches any pages on my Web site mentioning those two words.

This trick works *really* well when searching large sites that have amassed a huge amount of information. As always with Google, you can put your search term in quotes to narrow down the results.

Checking the Manufacturer's Support Web Site

Manufacturers spend big bucks for people to staff the technical support lines. Unfortunately, these employees often don't know any more about computers than you do. Instead, the tech support departments work like telemarketing departments. A person listens to your description of the problem, types the symptoms into his PC, and reads back the scripted responses.

Sometimes this tactic helps, but it's expensive, both for your phone bill and for the company. And sometimes your questions still go unanswered. That's why an increasing number of companies pack as much technical support information as possible onto their own Web sites, helping users find answers as easily as possible.

When you visit a manufacturer's Web site, look for hyperlinks like <u>FAQ</u>, <u>Technical Support</u>, or <u>Driver Downloads</u>. The sites mentioned in the following sections offer much more in-depth help.

Microsoft's Support site

Shown in Figure 21-2, Microsoft's Support site (`http://support.microsoft. com`) contains a continually updated, indexed list of more than 250,000 articles created by Microsoft's support staff.

See the words *Solution Centers* in the menu along the top of Figure 21-2? The Solution Centers let you limit your search to any Microsoft product ever released, making it easy to isolate searches for specific products.

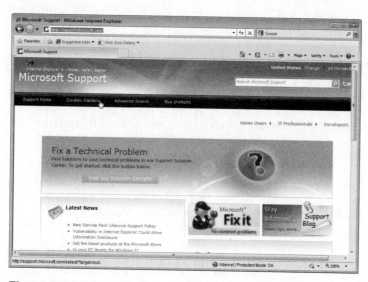

Figure 21-2: Microsoft's Support searches for solutions to problems with particular products, as well as specific error messages.

For example, follow these steps to search for a particular problem with Windows 7:

1. **Visit Microsoft's Support site at `http://support.microsoft.com`.**

2. **Click Solution Centers from the main menu, and in the Quick Product Finder, type the name of your problematic Microsoft program.**

   In this case, you'd type Windows 7. (As you begin to type, a drop-down menu begins filling in the product's name; when you spot the name, click it to automatically fill out the box.)

3. **Narrow down your search by choosing a topic from the left sidebar, and then keep selecting from the suggestions that appear on the right.**

4. **If you still haven't found an answer, try typing a few key words into the Search box at the page's top, next to the word Bing.**

Here are a few tips for further exploring Microsoft's support site:

✔ Microsoft's Support site can be quite versatile. Sometimes it offers to fine-tune your search by asking you questions, or letting you search within its displayed results. Other pages supply a general overview of the problem, and include links to other pages that provide specific solutions for specific problems.

✔ If a techie gives you a "Knowledge Base number" for a solution, you can jump directly there by including it in the hyperlink. To jump to article number 887410, for example, type this into your browser's address bar: `http://support.microsoft.com/kb/887410`. Googling the term **kb88741** will usually fetch the Knowledge Base article, as well.

✔ Although Microsoft's Web site only covers Microsoft products, it also contains information on how Microsoft's products interact with hardware and software from other manufacturers, viruses, and other potential problem causers. And, should Microsoft's support site point the finger at another company, you'll usually find a clickable link to shift your search to the other company's site.

Serial number and service tag Web sites

Some manufacturers stamp a serial number or service tag on the invoice of every computer they sell. (Many place a sticker with the number onto the computer's case.) Then they create a custom-built Web page based around that particular computer: its motherboard chipset, expansion cards, CPU, and other hardware, as well as its bundled software.

Long after you've lost your computer's invoice and manuals, a quick trip to the manufacturer's Web site enables you to view everything that came with your computer, including part models and numbers, specific support information, warranty expiration information, driver downloads, and in some instances, upgrade information.

Dell and Gateway, among other computer makers, offer this service on their Web sites. If you're unlucky enough to have lost everything *and* scraped off your computer's serial number sticker, visit Dell or Gateway's site anyway. Both sites have technology that can peek inside your computer, grab its long-lost serial number, and fetch the customized Web site for you.

Manufacturer's Web sites in other countries

Most manufacturers sell their computers worldwide. And for some reason, some countries offer better support than others.

If a foreign site appears while you're searching, don't be afraid to give it a visit. If it turns up while you're searching in Google, use Google's Translate This Page button, if necessary, and Google offers to translate the site's language into one you can understand.

Community Support Web Sites

For some people, computers aren't just a way to get work done — they're a passion. I've compiled a list of sites to visit for information about their particular niche.

Tom's Hardware Guide

www.tomshardware.com

Although this site aims at a tech-savvy crowd, it's one of the best sites for up-to-date information on computer hardware. You can find the latest performance rankings on CPUs, motherboards, memory chips, video cards, hard drives, and other computer parts. Tom's site is chock-full of reviews, how-to articles, community forums, and techie news.

Even though it's written mainly for techies, Tom keeps the site surprisingly easy to understand. On charts and tables, for example, the site kindly explains things like "Bigger numbers mean better performance."

When you're ready to buy a computer part, especially a graphics card or hard drive, choose Charts from the menu. That fetches the Performance Charts, making it easy for you to choose the right balance between bang and buck.

Wikipedia

www.wikipedia.org

An editable online encyclopedia created by visitors, Wikipedia offers a wealth of information on all subjects, including technology. It doesn't offer help for specific questions, but the site gives you general background on computer parts and technologies, making for more informed shopping.

Since Wikipedia can be edited by anyone who visits, don't take it as an authoritative source. Instead, use it as a branching-off point for finding further information.

Acronym Finder

www.acronymfinder.com

No one understands *everything* about computers, so don't be depressed if you spot YACA (Yet Another Computer Acronym) that you don't understand. Instead, head to the Acronym Finder site, type in the mystifying initials, and see the definition.

Although the site works well for technology-oriented items, it provides definitions for acronyms from many other areas, as well. GL2U.

NewEgg

www.newegg.com

I've mentioned NewEgg several times in this book, as it's a great source for buying computer parts. But it's also a way to find community support once you've bought that item. If a particular part is acting up, head for its purchase page on NewEgg, and click the User Reviews area. There, you'll find posts by people who've already purchased that part.

Many times, you'll find just the right tweaking tips to bring the part back to life, or crank it up to its full performance.

Amazon

www.amazon.com

Like NewEgg, Amazon sells a wide variety of computer parts. It also offers customer reviews. Even if you're buying a product from a competing retailer, drop by Amazon to read the customer reviews. After all, these customers have already held the product in their hands and used it. Their opinions can give one product an edge over another.

Chapter 22

Ten Cheap Fixes to Try First

· ·

Before you spend any money at the shop, try the quick fixes in this chapter. You might get lucky. If you're not so lucky, flip back to Chapter 19 for some more labor-intensive exploratory surgeries.

Plug It In

Sure, it sounds silly. But industry experts get paid big bucks to say that unplugged equipment is the leading cause of "electrical component malfunction." Check your power cord in *two* places: It can creep not only out of the wall outlet but also out of the back of your computer or whatever you've plugged into one of your computer's ports.

If you use a uninterrupted power supply or a surge protector, check *three* places: Check the back of your computer, check that your computer's power cord is plugged firmly into the UPS or surge protector, and check that the UPS or surge protector is plugged into the wall outlet.

Sometimes a yawning leg stretch can inadvertently loosen the cord from the wall. Rearranging a computer on the desk almost always loosens cables that aren't pushed tightly into the back of the computer.

And, uh, the machine *is* turned on, isn't it? (That's the leading cause of printer mal-function, by the way.) Some surge protectors have an on/off switch, so make sure the switch is in the on position.

Turn Off the Part, Wait 30 Seconds, and Turn It On

Before going any further, try closing the troublesome program and restarting it. Doesn't cure the problem? Then log off from Windows, and log on again.

If that doesn't fix it, shut down Windows and your computer, and then turn it back on after about 30 seconds.

Sometimes the computer just gets confused for no apparent reason. If your computer drifts off into oblivion with no return in sight, try tapping the Spacebar a few times. Try pressing Esc or holding down Ctrl while pressing Esc. One of my laptops woke up only when I prodded an arrow key.

Still no return? Then it's time to get ugly. The next few steps may cause you to lose any unsaved work. Sorry!

✔ Press the Ctrl, Alt, and Del keys simultaneously. Sometimes that's enough to wake up Windows and fetch a menu where you can choose Start Task Manager. When Task Manager appears, click its Applications tab and scan its Status column for any program listed as Not Responding. Find one? Right-click the culprit's name in Task Manager and snuff out the troublemaking program with a click of the End Task button.

✔ If the computer still acts like an ice cube, head for the next level of attention grabbing: Press your computer's reset button. No reset button, or no results? Move to the next step.

✔ If the computer's *still* counting marbles on some virtual playground, turn off the computer, hold down its power button for 10-15 seconds to force a shutdown, unplug the darn thing, or in the case of some laptops, remove its battery. (Windows often makes you hold the power button down for ten seconds or so.) Then wait 30 seconds after it's been turned off, giving it a chance to really settle down. Finally, turn the computer back on and see whether it returns in a better mood.

You'd be surprised how much good a little 30-second vacation can accomplish.

Install a New Driver

When you suspect some part is involved — not always an easy call with Windows — your best chance at fixing the problem comes by finding a better driver. Drivers serve as translators between Windows' language and the language spoken by a manufacturer's particular part.

The better the translator, the smoother the conversations. Installing an updated video driver, for example, can fix irregularities in the display you'd been blaming on your monitor. An updated sound driver might rid your music files of odd noises or garbles.

I describe how to track down and install drivers in Chapter 17.

Google the Error Message

When your computer gives you an annoying error message, write it down on a scrap of paper. Then type that error message into the search box on Google (www.google.com). Be sure to type in the *exact* error message, and put it in quotes.

Thousands of frustrated people have seen that same error message. Dozens of them have already posted that error message on the Internet, begging for answers. And if you're lucky, it won't take long before you find the few people who've posted solutions that could be as simple as clicking the right check box.

I describe how to search with Google in Chapter 21.

Find and Remove Malware

Malware programs — programs designed to do harmful things — try to sneak into Windows as you visit Web sites. Some malware hops onto your computer surreptitiously, others piggyback on programs offered by sneaky Web sites.

One type of malware, *spyware,* tracks your Web activity, sending your browsing patterns back to the spyware program's publisher. The publisher then sneaks targeted advertisements onto your computer's screen, either through pop-up ads, banners, or changing your browser's Home page.

Most spyware programs freely admit to being spies — usually on the 43rd page of the 44-page agreement you're supposed to read before installing the supposedly helpful program.

The biggest problem with malware-like spyware comes when you try to pry off the programs: They rarely include a working uninstall program. That's where malware removal programs come in.

The free Microsoft Security Essentials program prevents some malware from installing itself. The program also removes any malware it finds living inside your computer. I describe how to download and install Microsoft Security Essentials in Chapter 19.

Avoid Viruses by Not Opening Unexpected Attachments

This isn't really a quick-fix tip, but it's certainly a way to avoid having to do a lot of fixing when a virus infects your computer. Most viruses can be avoided by following this simple rule: Don't open *any* e-mailed file unless you're expecting to receive it.

That rule works because most viruses spread by e-mailing a copy of themselves to *everybody* in the address book of an infected computer. That means most viruses arrive in e-mail sent by your friends or coworkers.

Before opening any suspicious file, e-mail the sender and ask them if they meant to send you the file. That little bit of effort not only keeps your computer safer, it keeps you from having to clean up problems left over by rogue programs.

Run System Restore

Just like Windows XP and Windows Vista, Windows 7 includes a wonderful tool for setting things right again. Called System Restore, this tool remembers the good times — when your computer worked fine and all the parts got along.

When your computer becomes a problem child, System Restore may be able to send it back to that time when everything worked fine. I explain this miracle worker in Chapter 1.

Check for Overheating

Nobody likes to work when it's too hot, and your computer is no exception. Your computer normally works naked, but after a few months it wears a thick coat of dust.

Your first step is to look at the fan's round grill on the back of the computer. See all the dust specks clinging to the grill, swapping barbecue stories? Remove them with a rag or vacuum cleaner, being careful to keep the worst grunge from falling back inside your computer.

Second, check the vents on the front and sides of your computer case or laptop. Although the fan in the power supply is creating the airflow, the air is actually being sucked in these little holes and crevices. If these vents are clogged with crud, very little air moves across the components to cool them.

Don't just *blow* on the dust, either. The microscopic flecks of spittle in your breath can cause problems with the computer's moisture-sensitive internal components.

If you have cats, dogs, or your computer hasn't been moved for years, buy a cheap can of compressed air from a local computer store, remove your computer's case, and blast the dust off its innards. Dose it with an air blast every few months, paying special attention to crevices and grills. (Unplug it and carry it outside first. Angry dislodged dust particles float everywhere.)

The more parts and peripherals you add to your computer, the hotter it runs. Be sure to keep the vents clean.

Don't tape cards or cheat sheets across the front of your computer's case. That can block your computer's air vents, which are often disguised as ridges across the front of the case. When air can't circulate inside your computer, your computer heats up in a hurry. Also, don't keep your computer pushed up directly against the wall. It needs some breathing room so that its fan can blow out all the hot air from inside the case.

Install a New Power Supply

When computers simply refuse to turn on and do *anything,* and you know that the power cord isn't loose, it's probably because the power supply died.

Power supplies almost always include a built-in fan, so if you don't hear a fan whirl when you turn on your computer, your power supply probably needs replacing.

Chapter 10 provides power-supply replacement instructions.

Run Check Disk

Windows comes with several programs designed to keep it running trouble-free. Every few months — and immediately if Windows starts giving you some vague, unidentifiable trouble — follow these steps to find and run some of the troubleshooters:

1. **Open the Start menu and click Computer.**

   Windows lists your computer's disk drives and other storage areas.

2. **Right-click on your hard drive's icon and choose Properties from the pop-up menu.**

   You want to right-click the Local Disk (C:) drive, as that's the drive where Windows sets up camp.

3. **Click the Tools tab to get to the goodies.**

   The Tools tab reveals three buttons that either check the drive for errors, defragment the drive, or back up the drive.

4. **Click the Check Now button, and then click the Start button.**

5. **When the Check Disk box appears, automate the disk-checking process by checking the two boxes, Automatically Fix File System Errors and Scan for and Attempt Recovery of Bad Sectors.**

   Since you're checking the drive Windows lives on, the program will ask to run the disk check the next time you restart your computer. (That gives the program access to areas it can't reach while Windows is running.)

6. **Repeat the process on your other hard drive icons.**

   If your computer has other hard drives, repeat the process on them, as well. If your computer has a card reader, this trick also works to repair some memory cards, like the ones used in most digital cameras. (It also works on flash drives.) It won't work on CD or DVD drives, however.

 To defragment your hard drive — a way to speed it up by reorganizing its information — repeat the first three steps above, but click the Defragment Now button in Step 4. (Windows 7 normally defragments your hard drive automatically in the background, but this trick lets you start it anytime you wish.)

Appendix

The Rathbone Reference of Fine Ports

● ●

In This Appendix

▶ Identifying the plugs and ports on your computer

▶ Understanding which devices use which plugs and ports

▶ Finding out what ports can be added, expanded, or converted

● ●

Computers come full of holes (ports) where you insert a cable's end (plug). Unlike a fine wine, though, a computer's ports never age well. Instead, they grow obsolete as engineers create newer, more efficient ports to replace them.

Chances are, many of your computer's existing ports will go unused; they're designed for parts you no longer own. And in the years ahead, you may need to upgrade your computer with newer ports so you can plug in the latest gadgets.

Because it's increasingly difficult to keep track of what plugs in where — or what used to go here but now goes there — I've created the Rathbone Reference of Fine Ports.

The reference, spread throughout the following sections, shows diagrams of all the plugs and ports you're likely to encounter on your computer and the gear that plugs into it. Next to the pictures, you see the symbol commonly placed next to a port by computer manufacturers to identify its function.

Feel free to peek at this section whenever you plug something new into your computer during repairs and upgrades.

USB (Universal Serial Bus)

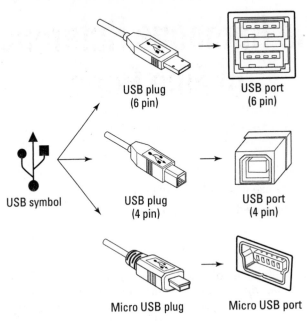

USB symbol

USB plug
(6 pin)

USB port
(6 pin)

USB plug
(4 pin)

USB port
(4 pin)

Micro USB plug

Micro USB port

Found: These ports come on nearly every computer, laptop, netbook, mobile phone, MP3 player, digital camera, and other portable gadgetry. Some monitors and keyboards even offer USB ports for plugging in USB goodies.

The Dirt: USB plugs and ports come in several sizes: The large rectangular ports (sometimes called six-pin) appear on all computers. The large square ports (sometimes called four-pin) appear on printers, and tiny micro-USB ports appear on smaller items like music players, mobile phones, and cameras.

Background: A veteran technology, USB ports now come in three speeds, with USB 3.0 being the fastest of all. Luckily, the ports are all *backwards compatible:* An age-old USB 1 gadget will still work fine if plugged into a USB 3 port. To transfer information at full speed, though, the port's speed must match. For example, you'll only transfer at a USB 3.0 port's blazing speed if you plug in a USB 3.0 gadget.

The Verdict: Windows 7 automatically recognizes almost anything plugged into a USB port, including mice, Webcams, joysticks, printers, hard drives, video capture devices, external CD/DVD burners, and scanners. When in doubt, go with USB.

Standard talk about IEEE

TECHNICAL STUFF

For more than 100 years, the Institute of Electrical and Electronics Engineers (IEEE) has assigned numbers to things. (IEEE is pronounced *eye-triple-e,* by the way, to earn points at geek gatherings.)

For instance, Apple Computers named its speedy information transfer system *FireWire.* Not to be outdone, IEEE named it *IEEE Standard 1394.*

Computer networks, commonly called *Ethernet,* are actually called *IEEE Standard*

802.3. When printers communicate with computers, they use *IEEE Standard 1284.* IEEE's dictionary, where they keep track of all the numbers, is called *IEEE 100.* (Seriously.)

Don't be surprised by all the IEEE numbers that surround ports. For riveting late-night reading, visit the group's Web site at www. ieee.org. Unfortunately, the popular IEEE 100 dictionary is not available online.

FireWire (Also IEEE 1394 or Sony i.LINK)

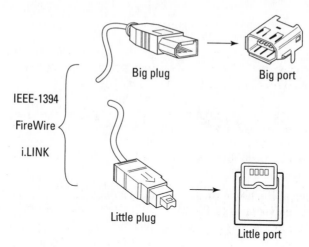

IEEE-1394

FireWire

i.LINK

Big plug

Big port

Little plug

Little port

Found: Found mainly on older, tape-drive digital camcorders and some old audio equipment, these still appear on a few computers, mainly from Apple and Sony. Now that camcorders record directly to hard drives, FireWire's on its way out.

The Dirt: IEEE 1394 officially stands for the Institute of Electrical and Electronics Engineers Standard Number 1394. Apple mercifully dubbed it *FireWire.* And Sony calls it *i.LINK.*

Few computers now include FireWire ports. If you own an older camcorder, you may need to upgrade with a FireWire port on a card, which plugs in the same way as a video card. (I tell you more about that in Chapter 9.)

The Verdict: Don't bother with FireWire unless you're stuck with an old camcorder that needs it.

E-SATA

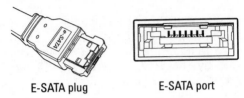

E-SATA plug   E-SATA port

Found: Found on the latest computers, these let you plug in the newest breed of portable hard drives with extra speed and larger capacity.

The Dirt: Hard drives switched to SATA (Serial Advanced Technology Attachment) *inside* your computer several years ago. Now, SATA is reaching for the portable hard drive market by appearing as E-SATA (External-SATA) ports *outside* your computer.

The Verdict: Although not yet a necessity, an E-SATA port or two on that new computer's spec sheet considerably boots its compatibility with future goodies.

HDMI

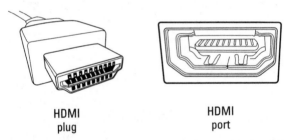

HDMI
plug

HDMI
port

Found: A staple in the home theater realm, HDMI ports commonly appear on high-definition television sets, Blu-ray DVD players, camcorders, video-game machines, computer monitors, and computers.

The Dirt: HDMI (High-Definition Multimedia Interface) carries both video *and* sound, making for one less cable to connect to the TV or a monitor with built-in speakers.

The Verdict: Early suspicions about HDMI's built-in copy protection have waned, and HDMI commonly appears on the video cards on today's computers.

Standard VGA Video Port

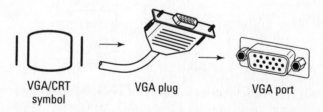

VGA/CRT
symbol

VGA plug

VGA port

Found: These old-school ports still appear on nearly every monitor, computer, laptop, digital projector, and netbook today.

The Dirt: Everybody needs a video port to plug in their monitor, and VGA has been around too long to ignore. It's not digital, so it can't support high resolution, but it works in a pinch.

The Verdict: A lingering technology from the late '80s, VGA ports are a last resort for connecting your computer to a monitor or TV. You won't see the best picture, and your eyes may grow tired, but hey, it works.

Flat-Panel LCD Video Port (DVI)

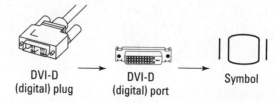

DVI-D
(digital) plug

DVI-D
(digital) port

Symbol

The Dirt: Most monitors and computers now come with either this older port or an HDMI port.

The Verdict: When buying a new monitor or video card, make sure both of them come with the same ports, whether they're DVI or HDMI.

Ethernet (RJ-45)

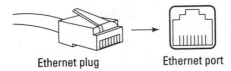

Ethernet plug   Ethernet port

The Dirt: When you accumulate too many household appliances, you hold a garage sale. When you accumulate too many computers, you connect them with a *network* so that they can share resources (like printers, for example) and information. IEEE Standard 802.3, nicknamed *Ethernet,* is the most popular cabling used for small networks, so your computer probably has a built-in Ethernet port (also known as RJ-45 jack).

The Verdict: Ethernet jacks look almost identical to standard telephone jacks, but they're slightly larger. You can't fit an Ethernet jack into a phone jack, but you can accidentally push a phone cord into an Ethernet jack. (The phone won't work, though.) When in doubt, go with an Ethernet cable, as it's more reliable than wireless.

Telephone (RJ-11)

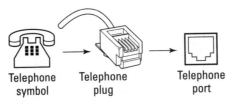

Telephone symbol   Telephone plug   Telephone port

The Dirt: A few computers still come with these, mostly to send and receive faxes through the phone lines.

The Verdict: Examine the two jacks closely. One jack usually says Line; the other says Phone. (The Phone jack often bears a Telephone symbol.) You must run a cord from the Line jack to the telephone jack in the wall. The Phone jack enables you to plug in a telephone handset for convenience sake.

Stereo Sound

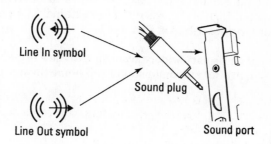

Line In symbol

Line Out symbol

Sound plug

Sound port

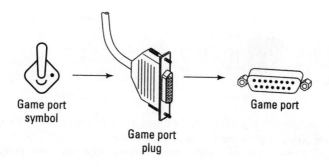

Game port symbol

Game port plug

Game port

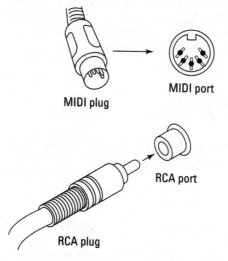

MIDI plug

MIDI port

RCA port

RCA plug

The Dirt: Sound cards come with bunches of jacks, so they get their own special figure, as shown above. Line In is where you plug in stuff you want to record, or have the computer play through its speakers. Line Out is where you plug in your speakers or headphones. (You can also connect that port to your home stereo's Line In port to hear your computer through your stereo.) The joystick or game controller plugs into the game port; most people use inexpensive Y-adapters to fit two joysticks into one port.

Some MIDI adapters plug into the sound card's game port, providing MIDI plugs for musicians to plug into a musical instrument's MIDI ports, such as those on a synthesizer keyboard. Finally, five-speaker sound cards often use an RCA port to power the subwoofer. High-end cards often use external RCA ports for S/PDIF digital audio transfers, described in Chapter 11.

The Verdict: Sound cards vary widely according to their expense. Some offer digital sound options; others offer surround sound and home theater plug-ins. Chapter 11 covers it all.

Coaxial Cable

Coaxial cable   Coaxial port

The Dirt: Found on almost all TV tuners and TV sets, this carries TV channels. The cable usually pokes out of the wall and plugs into your cable box or TV set. The cable usually screws onto its connector by hand, although some simply push on.

The Verdict: You must plug your TV's cable directly from the wall into your computer's TV tuner *without* plugging into a cable box first. If you plug it into the cable box first, you'll be able to record only one channel: The channel your cable box is tuned to. I explain TV tuners in Chapter 11.

RCA (Composite)

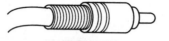

RCA plug   RCA port

The Dirt: These carry either sound or video. To tell which jack carries what, look at its color: Red (right) and white (left) jacks each carry one channel of stereo sound; a yellow jack carries video. Since most computers pipe out sound through a tiny ⅛-inch jack, this jack usually pipes out video on a computer.

The Verdict: Connect a cable from this jack to the same jack on your TV set to bring your computer's screen to your TV set. (To connect the sound to your TV set, run a cable from your sound card's Line Out jack to the red and white RCA connectors on your TV.)

Optical/Toslink

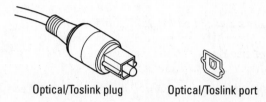

Optical/Toslink plug   Optical/Toslink port

The Dirt: Found on some high-quality sound cards, this carries Dolby AC-3 sound (sometimes called *multichannel, surround sound,* or *5.1)* but no video. Some sound boxes and cards offer an optical jack, others offer a Toslink jack, but they both carry the same thing: High-quality, six-speaker sound.

The Verdict: If your computer has optical but your stereo has Toslink — or vice versa — you can't connect your computer to your home stereo until you buy an adapter, a chore I cover in Chapter 11.

The Legacy Devices

A *legacy* device is simply an older piece of hardware designed for older computers. Legacy devices usually aren't *plug-and-play* compatible, meaning that your computer can't automatically recognize and install them for you when you plug them in.

Although new computers often include these legacy ports, they usually go unused. These connectors are here in case you find a device that still requires one.

PS/2 mouse and keyboard

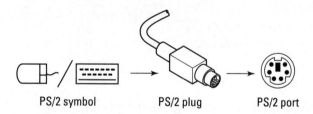

PS/2 symbol   PS/2 plug   PS/2 port

The Dirt: Older keyboards and mice often plug into a slim round goodie called a PS/2 port. Newer models plug into a USB port, instead.

The Verdict: PS/2 keyboards work better for troubleshooting older computers, as they work as soon as your computer boots up — before Windows begins running. Feel free to buy a USB mouse, though.

Serial connectors

Serial symbol   Serial plug   Serial port

The Dirt: Today, serial ports usually remain empty. Modems, their prime users, usually live inside the computer.

The Verdict: Ignore them.

Parallel (printer) connectors

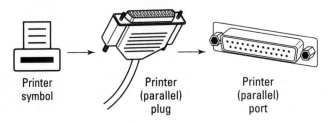

Printer   Printer   Printer
symbol   (parallel)   (parallel)
                 plug   port

The Dirt: Hunkered down next to a computer's serial port sometimes sits a parallel or printer port. (Nerds call it a DB25 port.) It's always been there for connecting to the printer.

The Verdict: Like serial ports, parallel ports have been replaced by USB ports. Some computers sill come with printer ports to accommodate old printers.

Index

• N •

(continued)

● *T* ●

(continued)

Business/Accounting & Bookkeeping

Bookkeeping For Dummies
978-0-7645-9848-7

eBay Business
All-in-One For Dummies,
2nd Edition
978-0-470-38536-4

Job Interviews
For Dummies,
3rd Edition
978-0-470-17748-8

Resumes For Dummies,
5th Edition
978-0-470-08037-5

Stock Investing
For Dummies,
3rd Edition
978-0-470-40114-9

Successful Time
Management
For Dummies
978-0-470-29034-7

Computer Hardware

BlackBerry For Dummies,
3rd Edition
978-0-470-45762-7

Computers For Seniors
For Dummies
978-0-470-24055-7

iPhone For Dummies,
2nd Edition
978-0-470-42342-4

Laptops For Dummies,
3rd Edition
978-0-470-27759-1

Macs For Dummies,
10th Edition
978-0-470-27817-8

Cooking & Entertaining

Cooking Basics
For Dummies,
3rd Edition
978-0-7645-7206-7

Wine For Dummies,
4th Edition
978-0-470-04579-4

Diet & Nutrition

Dieting For Dummies,
2nd Edition
978-0-7645-4149-0

Nutrition For Dummies,
4th Edition
978-0-471-79868-2

Weight Training
For Dummies,
3rd Edition
978-0-471-76845-6

Digital Photography

Digital Photography
For Dummies,
6th Edition
978-0-470-25074-7

Photoshop Elements 7
For Dummies
978-0-470-39700-8

Gardening

Gardening Basics
For Dummies
978-0-470-03749-2

Organic Gardening
For Dummies,
2nd Edition
978-0-470-43067-5

Green/Sustainable

Green Building
& Remodeling
For Dummies
978-0-470-17559-0

Green Cleaning
For Dummies
978-0-470-39106-8

Green IT For Dummies
978-0-470-38688-0

Health

Diabetes For Dummies,
3rd Edition
978-0-470-27086-8

Food Allergies
For Dummies
978-0-470-09584-3

Living Gluten-Free
For Dummies
978-0-471-77383-2

Hobbies/General

Chess For Dummies,
2nd Edition
978-0-7645-8404-6

Drawing For Dummies
978-0-7645-5476-6

Knitting For Dummies,
2nd Edition
978-0-470-28747-7

Organizing For Dummies
978-0-7645-5300-4

SuDoku For Dummies
978-0-470-01892-7

Home Improvement

Energy Efficient Homes
For Dummies
978-0-470-37602-7

Home Theater
For Dummies,
3rd Edition
978-0-470-41189-6

Living the Country Lifestyle
All-in-One For Dummies
978-0-470-43061-3

Solar Power Your Home
For Dummies
978-0-470-17569-9

Internet
Blogging For Dummies,
2nd Edition
978-0-470-23017-6

eBay For Dummies,
6th Edition
978-0-470-49741-8

Facebook For Dummies
978-0-470-26273-3

Google Blogger
For Dummies
978-0-470-40742-4

Web Marketing
For Dummies,
2nd Edition
978-0-470-37181-7

WordPress For Dummies,
2nd Edition
978-0-470-40296-2

Language & Foreign Language
French For Dummies
978-0-7645-5193-2

Italian Phrases
For Dummies
978-0-7645-7203-6

Spanish For Dummies
978-0-7645-5194-9

Spanish For Dummies,
Audio Set
978-0-470-09585-0

Macintosh
Mac OS X Snow Leopard
For Dummies
978-0-470-43543-4

Math & Science
Algebra I For Dummies
978-0-7645-5325-7

Biology For Dummies
978-0-7645-5326-4

Calculus For Dummies
978-0-7645-2498-1

Chemistry For Dummies
978-0-7645-5430-8

Microsoft Office
Excel 2007 For Dummies
978-0-470-03737-9

Office 2007 All-in-One
Desk Reference
For Dummies
978-0-471-78279-7

Music
Guitar For Dummies,
2nd Edition
978-0-7645-9904-0

iPod & iTunes
For Dummies,
6th Edition
978-0-470-39062-7

Piano Exercises
For Dummies
978-0-470-38765-8

Parenting & Education
Parenting For Dummies,
2nd Edition
978-0-7645-5418-6

Type 1 Diabetes
For Dummies
978-0-470-17811-9

Pets
Cats For Dummies,
2nd Edition
978-0-7645-5275-5

Dog Training For Dummies,
2nd Edition
978-0-7645-8418-3

Puppies For Dummies,
2nd Edition
978-0-470-03717-1

Religion & Inspiration
The Bible For Dummies
978-0-7645-5296-0

Catholicism For Dummies
978-0-7645-5391-2

Women in the Bible
For Dummies
978-0-7645-8475-6

Self-Help & Relationship
Anger Management
For Dummies
978-0-470-03715-7

Overcoming Anxiety
For Dummies
978-0-7645-5447-6

Sports
Baseball For Dummies,
3rd Edition
978-0-7645-7537-2

Basketball For Dummies,
2nd Edition
978-0-7645-5248-9

Golf For Dummies,
3rd Edition
978-0-471-76871-5

Web Development
Web Design All-in-One
For Dummies
978-0-470-41796-6

Windows Vista
Windows Vista
For Dummies
978-0-471-75421-3

DUMMIES.COM®

How-to?
How Easy.

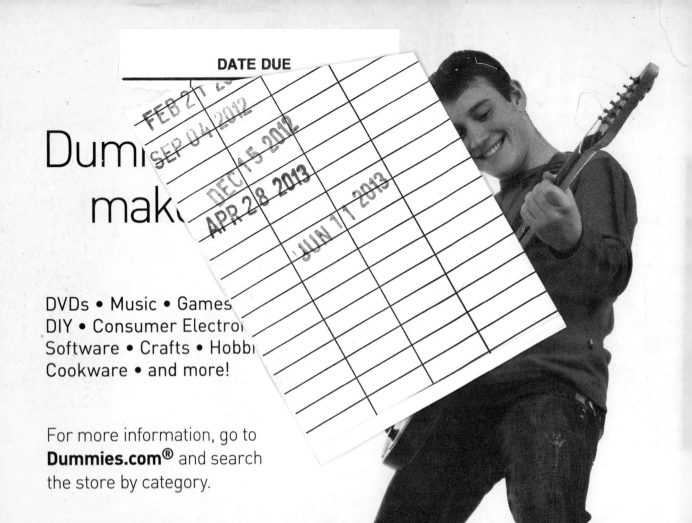